'It is said that there is no greater burden than the untold story. So now that Joe has written the extraordinary, fascinating, intriguing and unique story of his eventful and full life, with such honesty and good humour, and in such detail, I hope he will be completely unburdened – and even liberated – for the rest of his life.'

– Ollie Campbell, Ireland rugby international and British and Irish Lion

'This is a book all can readily identify with: it is a story of family, friends – and the odd foe! It shares a life of compassion, conviction and courage, underpinned by a keen intellect and a generous heart. Joe's narrative is not just a personal story but also a piece of social history. On both grounds, it is worth telling, and worth reading.'

– Alan MacGinty, principal of Blackrock College

'*Clearing the Hurdles* is a gripping account of the writer and his business partner, Tom Brennan, becoming the biggest house builders in the country: pioneers in providing affordable houses at value that will never happen again, selling houses at four times the industrial wage.'

– Ray McLoughlin, Ireland rugby international and British and Irish Lion

'For the past five decades, Joe McGowan has been right at the heart of business, sporting and social circles, both in Ireland and the United Kingdom. His astuteness in business, his brilliance as a horseman and his superb social graces provided him with an entry into every echelon of society. In *Clearing the Hurdles*, Joe McGowan proves to be a very entertaining, charming and honest raconteur as he shares with the reader the ups and downs of his fascinating life, beginning with his upbringing on his parents' farm in County Mayo and moving on to his time as captain of the Irish three-day-eventing team, while in between marrying a beautiful fashion model, becoming the largest housebuilder in Ireland, buying film director John Huston's mansion and winning the Blue Riband of the British National Hunt Season, the Cheltenham Gold Cup.'

– Charles Smyth, country-house and equestrian-estates specialist

'Joe writes as he talks: with honesty. I couldn't put *Clearing the Hurdles* down.'

– Alva Gunne, estate agent

'This book reflects Joe's enthusiasm for life.'

– Pamela Carberry

'In Clearing the Hurdles, Joe McGowan proves to be a very entertaining, charming and honest raconteur, as he shares with the reader the ups and downs of a fascinating life.'

— *Charles Smyth*

'Joe describes the Planning Tribunal, his "Theatre of Ice", in an exceptionally clever and talented way. He courageously got on with his life and competed at the top level in his sport while showing cause in bankruptcy for five years. Truly remarkable!'

— *John Walsh, solicitor*

'An interesting book, beautifully written. Captivating – and more bizarre than a novel.'

— *Alison Oliver, trainer to Princess Anne*

'This book is packed with fascinating stories: from buying film director John Huston's mansion to playing croquet on a small lawn in Coláiste Pádraig, Swinford, under the guidance of the Principal, Father Sean O'Neill. Now, sixty years later, he is the President of the Croquet Association of Ireland.'

— *Stephen O'Connell Miley, solicitor*

'It is a formidable story of two young men in the building and property world, unknown to the general public.'

— *Laurence McCabe, consultant to CBRE, and World President of the International Real Estate Federation in 2000-1*

'*Clearing the Hurdles* is Joe McGowan's extraordinary story. He has lovingly crafted every word of this book with meticulous attention to every detail, from the writing and photography, to the design of the book itself. The end result is the story of someone who has lived life at the pace of a Gold Cup horse in sight of the winning post. His love of words, writing, poetry and music embellish every page, and not only commemorate a life less ordinary but chronicle a remarkable era in the country he helped to build.'

— *Liam Collins, author and Sunday Independent journalist*

'I predicted that Joe, and his exceptional horse Private Deal, would be one of the few riders to complete the cross-country course [the 1989 Burghley Horse Trials] inside the time.'

— *Captain Mark Phillips*

Clearing the Hurdles

Joseph B McGowan

Clearing the Hurdles

J. B. McGowan

First published in 2018 by
Liberties Press
1 Terenure Place | Terenure | Dublin 6W | Ireland
Tel: +353 (0) 86 853 8793
www.libertiespress.com

Distributed in the United States and Canada by
Casemate IPM | 1950 Lawrence Road | Havertown | Pennsylvania
19083 | USA
T: (610) 853 9131 | E: casemate@casematepublishers.com

2 4 6 8 10 9 7 5 3 1
A CIP record for this title is available from the British Library.
Cover design by Roudy Design

Extracts from the work of the following authors are reproduced with
permission: Patrick Kavanagh (page 187), courtesy of the Trustees of the
Estate of Patrick Kavanagh; Rod McKuen (pages 11 and 173), courtesy
of the author; and Paul Durcan (pages 10, 187 and 190), courtesy of the
author. The publishers have made every effort to trace copyright holders;
if any omissions have been made, please contact the publishers.

Printed in the UK

For Anne, Catherine, Joseph and Christine

Contents

Acknowledgements   xi
Author's Note   xiii
Introduction   xv

PART 1 LEARNING FOR LIFE   1

  1. Growing up on an East Mayo Smallholding   3
  2. Corncrakes, Patterns and the Smell o' Turf   9
  3. A Fair Day in Charlestown   15
  4. 'Your Mother Is Still Disappointed You Didn't Become a Schoolteacher' 24

PART 2 A LIFE LESS ORDINARY   29

  5. 'For God's Sake Slow Down, Joe!'   31
  6. Adventures with Sir Henry Cotton   39
  7. A Millionaire Before My Twenty-seventh Birthday   42
  8. Kilnamanagh: The Best Residential Development Ever   52
  9. 'Tallaght to Be a Beautiful City'   56
 10. Bitterness and Resentment: The Ultimate Defeat   70
 11. Disappearing Millions – and a Mareva Injunction   72
 12. Showing Cause in Bankruptcy   75
 13. My Introduction to Building in England   78
 14. How We Almost Sent Dublin County Council Officials to Jail   80

PART 3 A SPORTING LIFE   89

 15. The Galway Blazers Hunt across the Fields of Athenry   91
 16. The Ghost of St Cleran's and Other Country Tales   100
 17. A Mad Hatter's Introduction to the Sport of Kings – and
       Polo in the Park   111
 18. The Cheltenham Gold Cup 1977: A Dream   118
 19. Hartstown: A Horse for the Future   126

20.	No Longer a Gentleman Amateur	131
21.	England Becomes My Second Home	136
22.	'On Your Mark'	142

PART 4 THE PLANNING TRIBUNAL: THE THEATRE OF ICE   147

23.	'Some of the Allegations Are Frivolous'	149
24.	Measure for Measure: The War of the Barristers	153
25.	The Theatre of Ice Meets Its Own Nemesis	164
26.	The Phantom Cup	170

PART 5 LIFE GOES ON   173

27.	Parkinsons	175
28.	Art and Construction: Creating a New Life in Poetry and Song	182
29.	My Favourite Players	189
30.	'My Glory Was I Had Such Friends'	199

Acknowledgements

This book has been a long time in the making: six years, on and off. I wrote this story of my life myself, so I must take responsibility for whatever shortcomings it has. If I had foreseen the labour, and thousands of hours, that would be involved, I'm not sure I would have begun the project at all.

In December 2015, I received a prompt response from John Drennan, the eminent and respected journalist, to my email. The following day, I met John in the Cellar, Merrion Street, with an autobiography in five parts, handwritten. John said: 'This is a good story and should be told; it has it all.' I thank John Drennan for encouraging me to 'get on with it'.

I thank my late father and mother, and my late Uncle John, for providing me with a solid work ethic. My sincere thanks go to my wife, Anne, who has been a constant inspiration, always patient and encouraging, and to our three children, Catherine, Joseph and Christine, for their deep interest in what I was doing.

I remember with gratitude the late Father John McNicholas, my creative English teacher during my five happy years at Coláiste Pádraig, Swinford. Father John taught me everything I know about the English language. This great teacher gave me another gift: a love of poetry, something that has stayed with me down the years.

I thank Mary Shanahan, secretarial organiser. What a task Mary had, trying to decipher my often almost illegible handwriting! I thank my close friends Frank Hayes and Myles McWeeney, who did the proofreading. I thank Tom Brennan, my friend and business partner since 1964, with never a cross word between us.

I owe a special debt to my real-life Guardian Angel. When my confidence waned, sometimes for a month or more, he had the wonderful knack of getting me up and going again, back into the right mood.

A special thanks to Jonathan Powell for his introduction. I thank all my friends who helped me throughout my life, and I sum up my indebtedness and my gratitude in the words of Yeats: 'My glory was I had such friends.'

Joe McGowan
August 2018

Author's Note

Part One, 'Growing up on an East Mayo Smallholding', is intended to give an account of my family and my comfortable and caring upbringing during the 1950s and the early 1960s in East Mayo, where most of the land is borrowed from nature. These were the happy days of primary and secondary school, and hard work on the land, before my Leaving Certificate in 1962.

Part Two, 'A Life Less Ordinary', is a fifty-year history of the efforts of Tom Brennan and myself to achieve success through a determined approach. We started with twelve developed sites in Foxrock in July 1964. Ten years later, we obtained planning permission to build 1,650 houses on 230 acres of land in Tallaght. In doing so, we created a legacy of providing houses for people who thought that owning a house was unachievable. We made possible what many thought impossible: we enabled people with modest incomes to buy homes at affordable prices. The owners were happy to furnish them and make improvements over time. In my story, I relate both the positives and the controversies: the many court battles between Dublin County Council and ourselves, ending with us putting the council into receivership for twenty-four hours.

Part Three is entitled 'A Sporting Life'. It is forty-three years since Davy Lad won his first race at Cheltenham: the Sun Alliance Novice Hurdle. It was a magical time. When I came to Dublin, I fitted easily into the Dublin set: tennis, Old Belvedere on Sunday nights, Lansdowne on Saturday nights and Brittas Bay at weekends. In 1971, I married the 'attractive Anne-Marie Berkeley', so described by Peter O'Sullevan, the golden voice of racing commentators, when she led in four winners at the Cheltenham Festival, including her Gold Cup winner, Davy Lad. Now is the right time to offer a special thanks to his jockey, the late Dessie Hughes, who, after the race, remarked: 'If I'd not known Davy Lad, I'd have given up. I was almost unconscious at the top of the hill, but I knew he was capable of finding something, if I could manage to keep riding him.'

Back in that special time, we entertained Irish society at St Clerans, the house that I bought from John Huston in 1972. Our overseas guests included US Senator Ted Kennedy and his family (on two occasions), US senator John Tunney from California, Sir Hugh Frazier and many others.

I was honoured to have been a Joint-Master of the Galway Blazers and of riding competitively with the likes of Ted Walsh. Of the many horses with which I have been associated, one stands out: Private Deal had personality, and he jumped incredibly difficult solid obstacles with ease. Horse-racing brought me freshness, and the vitality to fight the grim economic recession in the 1980s. Living in England from 1987 to 1993 was a glorious period at a crucial time in my life.

Part Four, 'The Theatre of Ice: The Planning Tribunal', deals with our experience at the Planning Tribunal. Our approach was not as focused as it should have been. We made generous political donations but did not receive any planning favours through the years. I love John O'Donohue's image of the cornfield in his book *Anam Cara*. The image depicts the 'Theatre of Ice' (the Planning Tribunal) for me. 'When the wind catches the corn, it does not stand stiff and direct against the force of the wind; were it to do this, the wind would rip it asunder. No, the corn moves with the wind; it bends low. And when the wind is gone, it bends back and finds its own poise and balance again.'

In the fifth and final part, 'Life Goes On', I express my gratitude for the life I have had, and to the very many people who helped and befriended me along the way. Diagnosed with Parkinsons ten years ago, I have had to make a few adjustments, but life goes on.

Introduction

by Jonathan Powell

In a sustained spell of excellence between 1975 and 1981, merry Mick O'Toole, of the laughing eyes and lightning repartee, trained at least one winner at the Cheltenham Festival each year. The first of them was a resolute mudlark, Davy Lad, who took the Sun Alliance Hurdle in 1975 with eye-catching ease, on atrocious going, that would have tested the endurance of a marauding band of Marines. Two years later, he gained an unexpected but utterly decisive victory in a Gold Cup that will forever be remembered for the tragic death of the former Champion hurdler, Lanzarote.

Mick O'Toole is a man of fun. Though it is not immediately obvious from his rounded, jolly figure these days, he rode in point-to-points and bumper races before switching his interest to greyhound racing. In 1965, he became the first Irishman to train the winner of the greyhound Oaks at Harringay. The lure of horse-racing proved too strong, and for a while he trained both racehorses and greyhounds at Ashtown, just a couple of furlongs from Phoenix Park racecourse.

Nothing was impossible for the ambitious trainer, whose eternally cheerful banter does not entirely conceal the razor-sharp mind lurking behind. If there was a 'stroke' to be pulled, a gamble to be organised or a deal to be done, Micko was yer man. For him, the intrigue and the plotting were almost more important than the result. To this day, when Mick O'Toole wins, everyone celebrates. Even those on the periphery of his company are swept along irresistibly by the sheer force of his personality.

When his stables at Ashtown were overflowing with horses, he bought a larger yard, named Maddenstown, close to the Irish National Stud, with scope for expansion. He is, you will perceive, the very opposite of a cautious man. His routine at the time was to buy batches of horses and not begin to think of selling them on until they were broken, being ridden and displaying a glimpse of potential. It was a system that required an iron nerve, convincing powers of persuasion and a particularly friendly bank manager.

Dessie Hughes, O'Toole's stable jockey and loyal lieutenant for so many years, relates: 'Only when he saw a spark in a horse would he consider finding an owner. If the horses were no good, he would get rid of them, often five or six at a time, in one lot, to a horse-dealer.'

Breeding purists who spend days, even weeks, agonising over the mating arrangements of their brood-mares will be dismayed at the eccentric methods employed by Kathlyn Westropp-Bennett and her husband when they came to choose a stallion for Davy Lad's dam, Chateau.

Though Chateau was a half-sister to Majority Rule, winner of the 1963 King's Stand Stakes over five furlongs at Royal Ascot, Mrs Westropp-Bennett had bought her cheaply from her uncle. She decided to send the mare to be covered at Martin McEnery's stud in Kilkenny, which housed two stallions, Polyfoto and David Jack, at the time. Polyfoto's fee was cheaper, but Liam Westropp-Bennett chose David Jack to mate with Chateau for the perfectly understandable reason that he had a cousin of that very name in England.

Kathlyn chuckles, 'My husband told Martin we would not have Polyfoto even if he offered us a free service!' It proved an uncannily sound decision. David Jack was a high-class stayer on the flat, winner of the Magnet Cup and Ormonde Stakes, and he passed on his bountiful stamina to Davy Lad, who was sent to Goffs by Mrs Westropp-Bennett as a yearling, with a reserve of 2,000 guineas. Imagine her profound disappointment when he was led out unsold. Outside the sales ring Maura Hanley, the breeder of the Irish Grand National winner, Olympia, agreed to pay seven hundred guineas for Davy Lad. 'He had no pedigree whatsoever and was quite small, but he was a good looker and a good walker,' she recalls. 'In the two years we had him at home near Nenagh, he was not a very pleasant person. He had his own ideas about life all right,' she adds.

In the summer of 1973, Mick O'Toole called in briefly at the Goffs sales complex while taking one of his owners, Benny Shcmidt-Bodner, to Dublin Airport. He was particularly keen on the unbroken hardy bay submitted by Maura Hanley, and bought him for five thousand guineas, before completing his journey. 'I assumed I would pass him on to Benny by the time we reached the airport, and had the money already spent in my mind, but I could not persuade him,' he recalls.

So the unnamed three-year-old followed the pattern of so many raw young horses bought by Mick O'Toole and broken in by the tireless Dessie Hughes. Though he kept him for several months, the trainer's patience was amply justified by the promising manner of the horse's work at home. John Mulhern, a high-powered businessman who later became a trainer too, introduced O'Toole to a friend, Joe McGowan, a prosperous property dealer, who bought a three-quarter share in the David Jack colt, now called Davy Lad, for his gorgeous wife, Anne Marie. He was her first racehorse. O'Toole recalls: 'I kept a quarter of him and sold the rest of him for a good bit of money.'

On one of the first occasions when Dessie Hughes schooled Davy Lad over hurdles, the pair turned upside-down, yet the horse exhibited precocious ability on the Curragh gallops from a very early stage. He won two bumper races readily but was beaten, surprisingly and rather fortuitously, when an odds-on favourite in a maiden hurdle at Leopardstown in March 1974, as a four-year-old. This allowed him to start the following season as a novice.

Davy Lad won six hurdle races in 1974–75 but injured his hock badly in midwinter and was confined to his box for six weeks. He recovered in the nick of time for the Sun Alliance Hurdle at the Cheltenham Festival, a meeting Mick O'Toole had been visiting religiously every year since the heady day that he saw Arkle win the Broadway Chase in 1963. He explains: 'The place consumes me. You plan, scheme and dream all year in the hope that you might just have one good enough to bring over for this meeting.'

In boggy ground that some fainthearts considered unraceable, Davy Lad, the 5-2 favourite, sloshed home first by three lengths from the Queen Mother's massive Sunnyboy. Davy Lad returned to Cheltenham a year later, attempting to complete a rare double in the Sun Alliance Chase, but he was already displaying signs of the idleness that would eventually make him an impossibly hard ride. He reacted to the application of a hood by whipping round as the tapes rose, proved unable to recover the lost ground, and finished fifth behind Tied Cottage, who was making the first of many splendid appearances over fences at Cheltenham.

Davy Lad's form as a seven-year-old did not readily advertise his chance as a Gold Cup contender. He ran frequently, won only one minor prize early in the season, and was regularly and easily beaten, though he did seem to improve whenever he encountered extremely testing conditions. The imposing Bannow Rambler, a milk-drinking chestnut trained by Padge Berry on a remote part of the coast in County Wexford, was the shining hope of Ireland. He beat Davy Lad easily in the Thyestes Chase in January, and then narrowly in the Leopardstown Chase a month later. Mick O'Toole's belief in his horse was unshaken. 'Sure, wasn't my lad always going to run at Cheltenham,' he chuckles. 'He had to. I had him backed with £500 at 40-1 to win with Sean Graham before Christmas.'

Now, stories of Mick O'Toole's betting arrangements are legendary, and many of them, no doubt, have improved with the telling. Once, during a hilarious breakfast in his house at Maddenstown, I watched him invest £1,000 each way at 28-1 with a fellow guest, an English bookmaker, on his runner in the Sweeps Hurdle that very afternoon. The horse won. Even an eternal optimist like O'Toole cannot be right every time, and there were many doubters in Ireland in the final month before Davy Lad landed the gamble.

'The horse was hard on himself all his life and the older he became the worse he got,' related Dessie Hughes. 'Every time he ran that Gold Cup season, he would be off the bridle after jumping two fences. He was dead lazy. It was me or him. That was his attitude. If his rider became tired, he would be laughing. But if you could keep going, he would always find a bit more. At home he was a super workhorse with loads of gears. The trouble was finding them in a race.'

Pendil was missing again from the Gold Cup field. He had come back at Kempton, almost as good as ever, in December 1976, and won a three-horse race at the astonishing odds of 10-1. That evening, a telegram arrived from Brigadier Gerard saying, 'Many congratulations. Next to me you are the tops!'

He won twice more and even beat Fort Devon, one of the Gold Cup favourites, in a close finish at Kempton, but then injured his neck and back when a horse from another string in Lambourn cannoned into him as he was being led out by Vince Brooks. He would never again return to Cheltenham.

Once more tragedy enveloped his trainer, Fred Winter, at the Festival, like an undertaker's cloak. Fred chose to run Bula on the opening day in the Two-mile Champion

Chase. The brave and inspiring winner of thirty-four races, he fell heavily at the fifth fence and hit the ground so hard that he broke a bone in his shoulder. Though he was taken gently back to Lambourn, he failed to respond to exhaustive treatment. After three weeks, Fred Winter and his vet, Frank Mahon, decided the kindest course was to put the old horse to sleep. His devoted lad, Vince Brooks, was riding out that morning when the trainer, grim-faced, trotted alongside on his hack and quietly told him that Bula was dead.

Brooks, who later left racing, recalls: 'I was glad his suffering was over, but when I went to work the next day the sight of his empty box was a dreadful thing. He was such a kind, trusting animal, a perfect gentleman in every way.'

With Pendil lame and Bula lingering painfully at home in Lambourn, Winter's hopes for the Gold Cup rested with another Champion hurdler, Lanzarote, a thoroughly solid and dependable citizen, who had taken well to fences despite the misgivings of his owner, Lord Howard de Walden. Lanzarote had begun the season over hurdles and only switched to fences at the end of November, with a creditable and close fourth in the Colonial Cup in South Carolina. Cheltenham, however, is a course that tames lions, and for all his undoubted brilliance Lanzarote came to the Gold Cup dangerously ill-prepared for the supreme test, with only three facile successes in novice company.

Royal Frolic, Brown Lad and Colebridge, the first three home the previous year, were all missing. So too was the mercurial Border Incident, so talented, but injury-prone. Sore shins left him on the sidelines at Cheltenham. Bannow Rambler started a well-supported favourite at 11-4, with Lanzarote next best at 7-2 and the American hope, Fort Devon, trained by Fulke Walway, at 5-1. Traditionally, the Gold Cup start was staged in a chute below and slightly behind the grandstand. It was a highly unsatisfactory position which had become an anachronism, since those watching at home on television had a much better view than the vast majority of racegoers on the course. In 1977, Captain Charles Toller, who ran Cheltenham briefly in the 1970s, took the eminently sensible decision to move the start area to a point on the course that was visible from the stands. In the process, the distance of the race was reduced by seventy-six yards to exactly three miles and two furlongs.

Tied Cottage, successful over the course a year earlier as a novice, set off at a spanking gallop from the new start. Tommy Carberry, his jockey, remembers: 'He went too fast for his own good. The trouble was if you organised him he'd just get thicker and thicker. I tried a couple of times to talk the horse out of it but he would be away again round another bend, down a hill, seeing another fence.'

Zarib was an early casualty at the fifth fence, where Davy Lad, sulking at the rear, gave every indication of his increasingly unwilling behaviour. The more Dessie Hughes pushed, shoved and cajoled his mount, the less response he seemed to achieve.

The pace set by Tied Cottage claimed a notable and tragic victim. Lanzarote was lying fourth as he approached the ninth fence at the top of the hill, where horses seem to jump out into space as the ground slopes away on the landing side. Inexperience round Cheltenham at such a strong speed now proved Lanzarote's undoing. He failed to rise quite high enough, clipped the top of the fence, stumbled along for several strides, then slithered to the ground, his near hind-leg broken. Bannow Rambler, racing directly behind Lanzarote, was brought down in the mêlée. His jockey, Michael Furlong, swiftly remounted and gave chase for another circuit but the task was an impossible one and he, finally, pulled Bannow Rambler up two fences from home.

John Francome waited disconsolately until the racecourse vet arrived to put Lanzarote out of his misery. He recalls: 'It was a sad day for everyone connected with the horse. When push came to shove over the fences, he used to jump very low. He had been hurdling so long he could not round himself properly when jumping. All he did was bend his front legs.'

With the first two favourites gone, Tied Cottage sailed on at full steam ahead. Fort Devon fell, when a close third, at the seventeenth, and as Tied Cottage began to tire, the unconsidered Summerville jumped past him four fences from home. On his day, Summerville was a high-class chaser, an exciting, athletic jumper with immense experience; but often his wayward nature clouded his very real ability. For a few heady moments it seemed that this would be his day. Ridden by Jeff King in place of his regular partner, Andy Turnell, who was injured, Summerville charged downhill with victory beckoning.

Tommy Carberry confirms: 'Summerville came past me running away. I could not believe it.' Far, far behind, Dessie Hughes was close to exhaustion as he continued his battle of attrition with the indolent Davy Lad. 'With a circuit left, I was last and going nowhere. At the fifth-last I was still trailing them, with the next horse six lengths in front of me. If I had not known Davy Lad, I would have given up. I was almost unconscious by then but I knew he was capable of finding something if I could manage to keep riding him.'

Only when Davy Lad started to freewheel downhill towards the third last fence did he begin to respond to the very physical message his jockey had been attempting to transmit for the previous two and half miles through his legs, arms, reins and, it must be said, whip. He was fully fifteen lengths behind Summerville as he soared over that fence, but then, improbably, he was closing rapidly on the two horses still ahead of him.

Jeff King, arguably the finest jockey never to be champion, now experienced the anguish of seeing certain victory snatched from his grasp as Summerville broke down suddenly on his near foreleg shortly after jumping the second-last fence. 'No ifs or buts. He would have won doing handsprings. He was as lame as if he had broken a leg, but I could not pull up, as we were still in front,' Jeff King assured me years later. One moment, Summerville was winning comfortably. The next, the entire complexion of the race changed in a frantic flurry of activity on the run to the final fence.

No sooner had the weary Tied Cottage rejoined poor Summerville than Davy Lad appeared from nowhere, rushed between them, threw an extravagant leap at the last fence and landed a length in front. Victory was his by six lengths from Tied Cottage. Above all, it was a triumph for his jockey's supreme fitness and sustained perseverance. Twenty lengths further back, Summerville, almost hobbling by then, just held third place from his stable companion, April Seventh. The stewards held an inquiry into possible interference by the winner but, though Davy Lad had veered towards the stands-rail, he had been well clear of Tied Cottage at the time.

You could not wish for a more suitable winner of the Gold Cup on St Patrick's Day, but Joe McGowan was not even present to witness the extraordinary triumph of his wife's young chaser. He had a pressing engagement in the saddle elsewhere. Joe had become a wildly enthusiastic amateur after learning to ride at the age of twenty-five, and had flown back to Ireland after the first two days of the Festival to partner a warm favourite in a bumper race at Limerick on Thursday.

Davy Lad followed the depressing pattern of so many young winners of the Cheltenham Gold Cup. He broke down quite badly after running lifelessly on several occasions the following season. He was given a long rest after his tendons were injected, in an unusual attempt at a cure, but there was never any question of his racing again. So Davy Lad retired at the early age of eight to a pleasantly undemanding life at the McGowan's Dollanstown Stud near Maynooth, and later moved with them to their new home at the Hollywood Rath Stud close to Fairyhouse. When Davy Lad was afflicted with arthritis at the relatively young age of fourteen in 1984, the McGowans accepted the advice of their vet, Paddy Kelly, that he should be put down. The horse was buried at the bottom of the garden beside their much-loved labrador, Sheba.

Joe McGowan developed into such a proficient horseman that he won a bronze medal for the Irish team at the 1989 European Three-day Eventing championship at Burghley. He also enjoyed the luck of two more Festival winners, Parkhill and Hartstown, trained, of course, by the irrepressible Mick O'Toole. 'Davy Lad was always a character, so tough, but he became an old scoundrel,' reflects Mick O'Toole. It is a statement offered with obvious affection.

This is taken from Golden Days, *a poignant account of the heroic horses and brave men who have won steeplechasing's most coveted crown – the Cheltenham Gold Cup – over the past three decades.*

Part 1
Learning for Life

Chapter One

Growing up on an East Mayo Smallholding

I was born in August 1943; my brother Pa, two years later. Gerry, the youngest, was born in 1950. We were brought up, in my mother's words, 'to be well behaved and courteous', on a smallholding in Tawnyinah, between Kilkelly and Charlestown, County Mayo. Our holding had a few fertile fields along by the road, sloping gently down to the flat bogland, with hay meadows bordering Harrington's land. My grandfather, Patrick McGowan, married Catherine Flannery, a widow. Catherine's first husband died at a young age, shortly after the birth of their son, John. She had to return to the home of her own family. Those were the days before the Succession Act, which would guarantee the inheritance rights of spouses and children. Catherine's parents continued to rear her child when she married my grandfather.

My father was born in 1912 and, with his two brothers, two sisters and parents, lived in a small two-storey house. It had a galvanised roof, with the gable end parallel to the road. Uncle Pat learnt the carpentry trade, Uncle Tom was a plasterer, and my father could turn his hand to anything. They were kept busy extending and repairing houses and building the occasional new house. So, construction is in my blood.

In 1937, they built a two-storey family house on a quarter of an acre of land, owned by our neighbour Pak McGowan. The new house, on high ground, faced the road and overlooked the yard; the old house was to the right and the sheds for cows and calves were to the left. They built stone steps outside to provide access to the top floor of the old house, now referred to as the workshop, or granary. The ground floor housed the pony, cart and trap. At the rear, they erected a two-bay hay-shed with a lean-to for the turf. The new house had an open fire in the kitchen-cum-living area. One of my early childhood memories is that the parlour had a lovely mantelpiece, made by

3

Uncle Pat. The bedroom fires were only lit when one of us had a bad cold. An outside tank collected rainwater from the house roof; we had another tank to collect water from the hay-shed and outbuildings, for the livestock. We drew spring water from the spring well in Maggie Doherty's field. She was a generous neighbour and gave me pocket-money for helping her with the vegetables and repairing hedges to prevent her cattle from trespassing.

My Aunts Molly and Bea spent two spells in America before returning home to marry locally. Aunt Molly married a hard-working farmer in Curry, County Sligo; Molly died at a young age from breast cancer, leaving her husband, James (Brodie) Feeley, son, Tommy, and daughter, Mary. Mary, on leaving secondary school, went to work in New York, met Mike Gilligan, her husband; she visits her old home every summer with her family. Aunt Bea had a happy marriage to Dominic Gannon from Lurga, the next townland, where Johnnie Gannon, my first cousin, lives; his sister May is married to John Fallon and they live in Dublin with their children; their brothers Jimmy, Pat and Joe are deceased. When all building activity came to a standstill with the Second World War, Uncle Tom moved to Dublin and worked as a plasterer for the remainder of his life. Uncle Pat moved to Essex in England, and married a fantastic woman, Anne Kirby, from Midfield, near Swinford, County Mayo. Uncle Pat died at the very young age of thirty-five, leaving his widow and three children financially comfortable. Kevin, their son, qualified as a chartered surveyor and dabbles a little in property investments. His two sisters, Kathy and Eileen, also had third-level educations and have successful marriages.

My mother, Kate Dolan, was born in the parish of Kilmovee, County Mayo, in 1914. Both her parents had emigrated to America, where they met and were married. They both worked long hours. My grandfather must have saved, as they were considered to be well off when they returned to live in the home-place at Aughadeffin. He made improvements and alterations to the existing cottage. The approach was attractive, with a vegetable garden and fruit trees to the left, and a few barns at the back. He influenced the neighbouring families to plant young ash, birch and hazel trees.

My mother had one sister, Aunt Mary, who left for New Jersey at a young age, met her husband, and brought up a successful family. Her eldest brother, Uncle Mike, also emigrated to America, where he married and reared his family. Her next brother, Uncle Tom, a bachelor, spent most of his working life in Peterborough. His work revolved around potato-picking and other farm-work in Lincolnshire, before he got full-time employment in a large estate at Market Deeping, north of Peterborough, a few miles away from Stamford. Much later, my family and I lived for six years, from 1987 to 1993, in this beautiful part of England. It brought us huge excitement and opened up new connections.

My mother's third brother, Uncle John, was to have a huge influence on my life, from the early years of secondary school. He provided me with a solid grounding in the construction industry and, later, with finance to get me started in business. He was a house-builder in the Terenure, Templegoue, Churchtown and Dundrum areas. He had very high standards and a profound sense of personal honour, keeping his word, once he had pledged it. My mother's fourth brother, Uncle Jim, a stonemason and carpenter, was generous and charming. He married Rita O'Connor from Lisacul, and brought up two sons and two daughters, with whom we keep in touch.

Her youngest brother, Uncle Paddy, remained in the home-place and never married. He was handsome, with a chiselled appearance, and was undoubtedly an Irish hillbilly. He loved fishing, shooting, and snaring foxes and badgers. He had one of the best shots in that part of the county, with his single-barrel shotgun. He could think and talk about little else other than shooting and snaring. Like our uncle, my brother Gerry also has a particular liking for shooting woodcock. My mother told me that Uncle Paddy was in great demand with the girls and would have been considered 'a good catch.'

His indoor life was taken up with his clocks. He once told me that the clock was the most advanced mechanical device for centuries, and that the American clocks were dismissed as inferior to the European ones until recent years. In the early eighteenth century, domestic clocks were expensive: they were spring-driven, and were only produced in very small numbers, as the making of the coil-spring was difficult. He obviously got this love and passion for clocks from his father, who brought home two clocks from America. His pride and joy was an eight-day rosewood-veneered column clock that was made in about 1870; it hung on the kitchen wall opposite the open fireplace. It is a coil-spring with a beautiful design case, thirty-three inches high. This clock now belongs to his niece and is in perfect working condition.

Uncle Paddy only accepted gifts as a token for repairing neighbours' clocks, but they sometimes had to wait for two to three years. Very often, they just left old clocks with him to use for spare parts if he couldn't repair them. He always had three chiming clocks in the kitchen. If one of those clocks failed to chime in harmony with the others, it was banished to the lower room until he got it absolutely correct. Some clock parts he made himself; he often got help from the locksmith, who worked and lived in Ballaghaderreen.

My grandfather Dolan had a mind far ahead of his time. My mother told me that he used to receive a little money from shares that he invested in while living and working in America. My mother brought a dowry of £400 to the marriage to my father – a large sum in those days. This was a great help, as he had spent most of his own money building the new house. My parents never borrowed money, nor did any of their neighbours. They lived within their means – unlike today, when everyone wants everything yesterday. That wise woman, Madam McDermott from Coolavin, Monasteraden, had an old-fashioned saying:

Use it up,
Wear it out;
If you can't afford it, do without.

I was three and a half years old when I made my first trip out of Mayo, to the Eye and Ear Hospital in Dublin, for surgery. It is my first clear childhood memory. I was playing with neighbouring children with sticks and jam jars around the hay-barn and the turf-shed when a piece of broken glass entered my left eye. My parents were consoled by our neighbours and Aunt Bea, who lived only a mile away, in Lurga. As one can imagine, there was a certain amount of panic and crying. My father told the doctor that I should be sent directly to Dublin. According to a regulation at the time, in order to avail of free medical care, I had to be taken first to Castlebar Hospital, from where I would, more than likely, be sent immediately to Dublin.

However, my mother, ignoring this regulation, took me to Dublin on the bus the next morning. On arrival at the hospital, to my three-and-a-half-year-old eyes, the polished corridors appeared like roads. Two days later, my mother returned to Mayo, leaving me in the excellent care of the hospital staff. Uncle John and Uncle Tom McGowan were both living in Dublin, and they took turns visiting me in the hospital. They didn't miss a day. After one month, with two operations done, my left eye was saved. The impressively named surgeon, Mr T. C. J. O'Connell, told my Uncle John that it was fortunate that my father had sent me straight to the Eye and Ear Hospital, as any delay could have resulted in the loss of my eyesight.

On returning home, I remember the neighbourhood trying to cope with the worst blizzard ever, in 1947. My father later told me that, because I was not brought to Castlebar Hospital first, the authorities requested that he pay the entire hospital bill. He cycled to Swinford to seek the opinion and advice of Henry Kenny TD, Enda's father. This was a successful visit: most of the hospital bill was paid by the Health Authority.

Tavneena National School

The National School at Tavneena (spelt 'Tawnyinah' in the Ordnance Survey maps) was one hundred yards from our house. Mr and Mrs Henry (Gerry and Bridget), our teachers, lived up the road in the next holding, in a two-storey house surrounded by trees. I have wonderful, happy memories of my primary-school days. There were just four pupils in my class: Margaret Haran, Frances Henry, Malachy Tiernan and myself. Our teachers prepared us well for secondary school – and, indeed, for life. We had junior classes, taught by Mrs Henry, in one room, and Mr Henry took senior classes in the other room. Both rooms had fireplaces.

Malachy Tiernan was my best pal; we always remained in touch, until he died six years ago. Malachy was a gifted musician. He played the saxophone and guitar and had a good voice. He and his brother, Seán, on trumpet, had a band that was in demand on Sunday nights and Holy Days. Malachy farmed the home-place. His son, David, captained Charlestown to win the Senior County Championship in 2002 – something they hadn't won for ninety years. Seán emigrated to England but visits the home-place often.

Our two-room school had no running water, and the toilets were outside. We were also one of the last areas to get rural electrification. Up to 1956, we grew up with candles and oil-lamps before the electricity arrived. At that time, my father got a month's work helping to secure the poles for the electricity cables. It was rugged work, all done with a pick, crowbar, spade and shovel, for there were no diggers then. The night the lights were officially switched on, we gathered around Our Lady's Shrine, opposite Maggie Doherty's, where the Rosary was recited every evening during the month of

May. However, the school was still heated by turf provided by the parents. In a fine example of community spirit, the parents of the children continued to supply turf for the two school fires for many years.

With the arrival of electric light, my mother really got going on her knitting. My father and the neighbours enjoyed their card game of twenty-five twice a week during the winter months, without straining their eyes. Life had changed. But we still had a candle lighting at every window on Christmas Eve and Christmas night. The electric light was a godsend to my father, who was an avid reader, as was our neighbour, Pak McGowan, with whom he used to exchange books and newspapers. One of them would buy the *Sunday Independent*, the other the *Western People*, and then swap in the middle of the week.

Once, and sometimes twice, a week, our Master gave us mental arithmetic tests. We had to remain behind after school until we got the answers correct. My mother would say to me: 'Pádraig Halligan was out before you today.' Pádraig – a sharp brain – was a year ahead of me. At about half past three, the Master would explain to us the twist to the question, often the difference between simple and compound interest. It was a great preparation, and shaped us for life. I have never used a calculator, and have no need to do so. On Sundays, we were all dressed up in our best. I would cycle three miles to Charlestown with my mother for the nine o'clock Mass, known as the 'first Mass'. Later, I became an altar-boy. Another altar-boy was John Gallagher, now a successful barrister in Dublin. As a junior barrister, he often acted for Dublin County Council against our companies in the High Court and, later, as a Senior Counsel at the Planning and Payments 'Theatre of Ice'.

My father looked after the livestock before going to the last Mass at noon, with my brother Pa on the back of his bicycle. On the rare occasions that he visited a pub, he would wobble home on his bicycle after one whiskey and one bottle of stout. My own tolerance for alcohol is the same: after a few glasses of wine or Guinness, I get into a muttering state and nobody can understand a word that I am saying.

When I was growing up, there was an element of friction in our household. My paternal grandmother lived with us; I suppose, because she was my father's mother, she felt she had a special claim on the domestic territory. For the sake of peace, my mother involved herself working outside, milking the cows, helping on the land, saving the hay, helping gather the turf, and looking after the hens. Back in the 1940s and 1950s, the egg business was a significant part of the economy of a rural home. The former Fine Gael leader, James Dillon, even famously promised to 'flood Britain with eggs', and we did our bit to help him. My father even added a spacious hen-house to the end of the cow-shed, with a piece of land outside well fenced to keep out the fox, which had a taste for hens – and eggs. The egg trade kept my mother busy, and very happy. Sadly, the domestic relationship did not improve when my grandmother said she could no longer negotiate the narrow winding stairs, and took over the best room in the house, the parlour, for the remainder of her long life. My grandmother could easily have moved into the small, but very comfortable, room off the kitchen. But she said that room had only 'a pokey window', as she described it, and that was the end of that.

We started to sow vegetables in the sheltered garden in March or April, depending on the weather. At the same time, our neighbour, Jim Halligan, ploughed a small potato field for us, into ridges rather than drills. His horse was well trained and left the furrows running clean and straight. We planted three splits across the ridge and covered them with farmyard manure. Within weeks, my father ploughed the furrows with the mule: a cross between a male donkey and a female horse. Mules in the pre-industrial age of farming – for that was the world we lived in – were prized for their durability and intelligence. 'Speedy' was our mule's name: leggy, intelligent and fast. We had to be careful with the second covering, so as not to damage the potato stalks. I got blisters every year from this work. Later, my father sprayed the potato stalks to protect them from blight. He had great respect for the advice he received from the travelling Agricultural Adviser. He used to say: 'These men are educated and presentable.'

Chapter Two

Corncrakes, Patterns and the Smell o' Turf

We had Turbary rights over a section of bogland beside our neighbours: this was the right to cut and save turf. Turbary rights were purchased by the Land Commission and distributed to households. The turf rights to each section were attached to the deeds of your dwelling. Even though we were only a mile from home, when working in the bog we lit a fire to make tea to have with our bread. You couldn't beat tea in the bog: it had a wonderful smoky flavour. I used to get dizzy lying on my back on the warm bog, looking for the skylark singing overhead in the clear, blue summer sky. In those days of my youth, I loved the sound of the cuckoo, the arrival of the swallows, the sight of the corncrake in the meadow. That was how we divided time back then: by seasons rather than hours.

Turf was the only heating fuel available in rural Ireland. It was cut by hand, using a slane, then spread out, and when dry enough, was footed and gathered. We brought the turf home to the shed with Speedy. Very few neighbours had sheds for their turf, so they stacked it with great pride adjacent to their homes. Barely a sod was lost, no matter how rainy a winter it was. The bog, with its centuries of secrets, always fascinated me; I held to the view of Patrick Kavanagh, who regarded the bog as a museum which contains the history of the landscape, and of all those who walked – and worked – our fields millennia before us.

I am lucky to have two of Samuel S. McCurry's books of poetry and essays, published by Hodges Figgis and Co. Ltd in 1912. One verse of his poem, 'The Smell o' the Turf', is a good description of my favourite scent:

How poor is the palace, that royalty rears,
How poor is the treasure of princes and peers;
Give me, when the wind in the orchard is shrill,
And the voice of the thrush, in the gloaming is still,
The fragrant aroma the cottage endears – The smell o' the turf.

Much has changed since that halcyon time. For example, the corncrake was then a familiar sight in the countryside. This shy, solitary bird is a summer visitor from Africa. The male gives a loud call during the breeding season; it is repeated during the day and continues through the night until dawn. Breeding is from May to August. They nest on the ground, mainly in hay-fields, until the young chicks are ready to fly, after thirty days. When I was a child, the corncrakes were in abundance in every second meadow, but their numbers have declined dramatically during the last fifty years, and the species is threatened with global extinction. They now arrive in small numbers to North Donegal and parts of Mayo and Connaught. This decline is due to extensive farming, where early mowing and silage-making have driven the corncrakes from their old habitats. Now, landowners are encouraged through incentives and farming grants not to introduce machinery in areas where the old-fashioned hay-making still takes place. Hopefully, conservation will slowly allow that call from childhood days to return from the ghostly memories of old men to the living world of our children.

My parents worked hard on the land. My father drained and reclaimed all of the fields under a Land Reclamation Grant Scheme. He also built a really good track through the land, hauling stones and gravel in a cart from the local Harrington quarry. In my childhood, meadow-fields were not to be cut until August, because the hay-crop was not ready until then. Nobody cut all their hay at the same time, even when machinery replaced the scythe: it would be too risky, as the whole crop could be ruined if there was a spell of bad weather. I remember the priests praying for hay-making weather at the Masses. These are the opening lines of Paul Durcan's poem 'The Hay-Carrier':

Have you ever saved hay in Mayo in the rain?
Have you ever made hay in Mayo in the sun?

My parents were happy when the big turf-shed and hay-shed were filled. Every year, my father was fortunate to get three or four months' work repairing the roads, buildings and bridges. The money he earned was essential to the family budget. In time, the Land Commission gave him two and a half acres of good land half a mile from his own holding. At a time when carving an acre out of rock and bog could take a decade, this was a major boon. Land was life – and a future in your own homeland. This extra land was in Lurga, beside Tom and Olive Doherty's. Tom, known as 'Tom the Shop', had a travelling shop in a small van which stopped at our house every Tuesday and Friday. The egg-money played a big part in the rural economy. My mother kept about forty hens, and every egg was money.

Like all commodities, the egg trade fluctuated with supply and demand. Hens usually laid in nests provided for them, but especially in the loft in the cow-shed. Not all eggs were sold. Sometimes a 'clocker' (a hatching hen), the potential mother of young chickens, was installed in a clean, roomy box, and thirteen eggs (my mother's lucky number) would be put underneath her. She hatched over them for three weeks, until the young chicks arrived.

Mentioning Tom Doherty's travelling shop brings Patsy Dermody to mind. Patsy was Tom's niece. She used to spend a month each summer with Tom and Olive. I always made excuses to visit the shop when I knew she was there. She had an attractive smile, with a smirk. Years later, a verse from Rod McKuen's 'Coming of Age' reminds me of that time.

THIRTEEN
Today she smiled at me,
A queer sort of look,
Of a crooked smile,
That made me all red,
Outside and inside.
I didn't much like it,
But I didn't half wish,
Tomorrow, she'd do it again.

My mother, always progressive, asked Tom the Shop to spread artificial manure on the two and a half acres that my father had recently received from the Land Commission. When my father saw the results, he began to use it in the following years on our own good meadows. He also bought an extra cow, bringing the total herd to six. There were three milking cows, and three more would be due to calve at intervals between Christmas and May. By the standards of our locality, it was quite a herd.

My mother continued making butter in the churn until my brother Gerry changed to single-suckling farming. Once a week, she pounded the handle up and down in the churn until the cream was magically transformed into butter. If neighbours called during this process, which usually took twenty to thirty minutes, they were expected to take their turn pounding the cream up and down in the churn. If they didn't take part, it was considered bad luck; this might result in a poor yield of butter.

When I was twelve, Master Henry suggested that I could help the Rush Family – two elderly brothers and a sister – with their crops. They lived a secluded life on the lower road, a fifteen-minute walk from our house. They were considered eccentric in the area, but they were very good to me: they paid me ten shillings for working after school, and one pound for a full day on Saturday. James, Pat and Annie Rush's greatest joy was to watch the starlings gather in their small plantation; once they had all assembled, the whole throng took flight in unison. Their movements through the air were orderly and breathtaking. Years later, my wife, Anne, and I were staying with the Marshall-Andrews at their home in Oxfordshire. A few miles from their home is a large area of marshy land. It is a haven for wildlife. There, most evenings through the winter months, starlings put on an incredible display of aeronautical skills. First, they gather in small numbers. As the afternoon light fades, they gather in much larger flocks. Having fed, they take to the air in unimaginable numbers. Then the flighted squadrons all join for aerobatics and merge into one orchestral group. We watched them for two evenings and never saw a collision. This event happens most nights throughout the winter. The acrobatics were as fascinating as any theatrical performance.

I have been reading a good deal about starlings lately. Starlings have diverse and complex vocalisations, and have been known to embed sounds from their surroundings into their own calls, including car alarms and human speech patterns. The birds can recognise each other by their calls and are currently the subject of research into the evolution of human language.

One of the most exciting events in our house back then was receiving a parcel of clothes before Christmas every year, from Aunt Mary in America, including shirts and ties. They were almost new, and that was more than good enough for us, in those thrifty times. Uncle Mike's wife, Eileen, sent a similar parcel in the summertime, also from America. They sent dollars to my mother once a year, but always addressed them to her old home in Aughadeffin, Kilmovee. Wisely, she kept a deposit account in Ballaghaderreen, for a rainy day.

I would cycle with her to Ballaghaderreen for the sales after Christmas every year, at Duffs and Flannerys. Duffs was owned by the Fine Gael Dillon family, and was considered one of the best stores in the west of Ireland. As a child, I was fascinated by the speed with which the money travelled to the cashier on a mechanism underneath the ceiling. Later I discovered, with my Uncle Tom McGowan, that Clerys in Dublin had a similar system. At that time, I used to be embarrassed by my mother's haggling for more discount, but I soon got over that. I learned so much from her which prepared me for life.

Thanks to the parcels we got from America, I didn't have to go to Ballaghaderreen with my mother to purchase new clothes for my First Holy Communion and Confirmation. First Holy Communion was an important occasion. We had to learn the Hail Mary, the Our Father, the Creed and the Mysteries of the Rosary. Preparing for my Confirmation was a different matter. Our teacher told us that if we were unable to answer any of the questions that Bishop Fergus asked us, we would have to wait until the following year to be confirmed. For Confirmation we had to remember the answers to over one hundred questions, such as: What is a Sacrament? Name the Seven Gifts of the Holy Spirit. Are you sure of going to Heaven when you are Confirmed? Is there only One God? How many Persons are there in God? Was St Joseph the father of Jesus? Who was the real father? How is Original Sin taken away? What happens if you die in a state of mortal sin?

After all that, you had to recite the Ten Commandments of God. Malachy Tiernan, my pal, and I were sick with worry. I found out later that nobody ever failed.

The Pattern and Other Religious Festivities

Pattern Day was a big occasion in my youth. Our Pattern Day at Tample took place on the Feast Day of St Attracta, at her shrine, at the beginning of August. St Attracta was the patron-saint of hospitality and charity. The sports began after midday Mass at the shrine and went on all day in the big, level three-acre field which belonged to John Doherty – no relation to Tom the Shop. The Pattern drew large crowds every year. There were running and field events, which were keenly contested, horse and donkey races, and the more light-hearted egg-and-spoon race, the three-legged race and the slow-bicycle race. I won the under-fourteen middle-distance race one year. The last and most competitive event of the day, the tug-o'-war, was really cutthroat stuff: it was taken very seriously, with much puffing and grunting.

My mother used to take us to the Pattern Day at Urlar, her home-place, beside the lake, every year. It was more relaxed than our pattern at Tample, but very enjoyable, because Grandmother Dolan and my mother's cousins and friends gave us money for treats. The traditional belief was that if Urlar Pattern was wet, it would be a fine day for the Tample Pattern, and vice versa.

August was a most interesting month. On the Sunday after the twelfth, the beginning of the grouse season, Mr Moffet, the vet, and Paddy McGirl arrived to the lower bog with their dogs at their heels. They would start at Maggie Doherty's, then go onto our land and sweep across Glann over to the Easkey bog. We could hear the gunshots if they were lucky enough to raise a grouse. Unlike the wilier snipe, these wild birds lacked the wit to bob low and keep quiet amongst the heather. Instead, they would flutter upwards with a cackle. If the guns were alert enough, they would bring down at least one bird.

One of my most distinct memories from that time was a visit to Foxford Woollen Mills with my mother. In the morning, we cycled to Charlestown, where she had arranged to meet Maisie O'Doherty and Aunt Molly. We hired a hackney car for the remainder of the journey. My mother had to send four woollen blankets to her sister in New Jersey. Foxford, still a very small country town, had created employment for almost two hundred people – mostly single women, who were expected to leave their jobs when they got married. Wool-making in Foxford had a long history, even prior to my arrival into the world. Mother Arsenius of the Sisters of Charity opened the Providence Woollen Mill in 1892 as part of an ambitious rural-development programme. Funding came from the Congested Districts Board. John Charles Smith, a Protestant and a Freemason, who owned a mill in Ulster, provided the technical advice, including harnessing the power of the River Moy to drive the looms. Later on, steam-power was used. It was unusual at that time for a generous Protestant to provide so much advice and assistance to a Catholic nun and her Order. Had it occurred more often, our history might have been very different.

I remember the building being bright and well ventilated, with large windows. In winter it was warmed by the heat generated by the machinery. The Mills operated a six-day week, with the women working up to ten hours a day, but the children never more than six hours. Sadly, it ran into financial difficulties in the 1980s. Nonetheless, it built a whole town as a monument to Mother Arsenius's foresight and determination. Today, the Foxford Woollen Mills Centre presents a history of the mill and life in the town through an exciting and interesting tour. They also have a lovely shop, which has recently been refurbished, and a café with home-cooked produce.

The Stations

When I was young, 'the Stations' was a big occasion for any family. This meant that all ceilings, doors and windows had to be washed down and painted or whitewashed. Two priests would arrive in the morning. The women would be already in the house, while the men waited outside, chatting amongst themselves. Both priests commenced hearing Confessions immediately; one went to a bedroom, whilst the other remained in the kitchen. Confessions over, one priest proceeded to celebrate Mass. Malachy Tiernan, Pádraic Halligan and I were altar-boys. The other priest visited the sick people in the Station area to hear their Confessions and give them Holy Communion. After breakfast, the priest chatted with the people. As night approached, all the young people from the neighbourhood came for the dance, which, over the years, had become part of the festivity associated with the Stations. My mother, with her deep religious beliefs, felt compelled to attend Holy Mass at least once a year at the Knock Shrine, the scene of the apparition in 1879. She believed that this journey would bring us good luck. I still visit Knock to say my prayers, in particular the prayer to my guardian angel – the first prayer I ever learned.

> Angel of God, my Guardian dear,
> To whom God's love commits me here;
> Ever this day, be at my side,
> To light and guard,
> To rule and guide.

Parish Missions were a universal feature of the Irish Catholic church life until the mid-1960s. Every three years, there was a Mission in our Parish, Charlestown, which lasted two weeks. There was one week for the women, and one for the men. The Redemptorists were considered the toughest preachers because they put the fear of God into people with their fire-and-brimstone sermons. Some of these screaming sermons were taken up increasingly with matters of sexuality, including immodest fashion in women's dress. The preachers were against what they considered immodest fashion in women's dress, such as women wearing slacks. They also opposed English Sunday newspapers and the making of *poitín*.

Nearly every morning of the week of the Mission, my mother would attend seven o'clock Mass, followed by a short sermon. By contrast, sermons in the evening lasted almost an hour. My father had no time for the Missions at all, and he wasn't the only one, for while Ireland was a Catholic country, not everyone conformed unquestioningly. Mayo, after all, was the spiritual home of the Land League and other somewhat different pursuits, such as *poitín*-making. The popularity of the Missions was not enhanced in certain areas where the Redemptorists tried to discourage the ballrooms taking over from house dances. It certainly didn't happen in Tooreen with Monsignor Horan, who would have put them in their place. He was a priest who had firm views on the respective roles of Christ and Caesar!

Chapter Three

A Fair Day in Charlestown

The Fair Day in Charlestown was a very important event, for both the people of the town and the people of the countryside. On the Fair Day, we were up early to clean and prepare the cattle. We walked them with neighbours, to arrive in the fair green, opposite the church, before dawn. My job was tiring: running ahead, to stop the cattle from turning into side-roads and boreens.

Like most of the neighbours, my father was superstitious. He insisted that we always brought the cattle to the same part of the fair green, known as our 'lucky spot'. It was not always lucky, though. Sometimes we had to walk the cattle home unsold, and wait for the next fair day. This was a sad journey. I could see the disappointment on my father's face as he walked silently behind the cattle. And even sadder was the look on my mother's face when we returned.

There were two types of cattle-buyers: the agent dressed in a long beige coat, buying for the rich farmers in Westmeath and Meath, and the jobbers. The jobbers would often meet the farmers before they reached the fair-green, hoping to get a bargain before the farmers had an opportunity to see how the market was going. Pak McGowan, our neighbour, used to say: 'You need to be smart to deal with those boyos.' Pak preferred to wait until he reached the green and got a feeling for the prices on offer. As the cattle were sold, they were herded off by the drovers to the railway station, where they were kept in pens and later put on carriages.

In Ballaghaderreen, on fair days, there were added attractions, such as stalls selling footwear, plants and household goods. Chape (Cheap) Jack was always there with his big stall selling secondhand clothese. There was the three-card-trick man, the trick-of-the-loop man and the fortune-teller. There were men with caps and hats at all angles.

They slapped hands and bargained, buying and selling all day long. On a good day, my father would join others for a whiskey and a bottle of stout.

My Uncle Jim told me a story of two eccentric bachelor brothers who had a big farm – at least by local standards in Castlerea. To prepare themselves for the dealing, bargaining and haggling, they used to hold a rehearsal session, a kind of a mock fair on the day before the big fair days in October and February. One brother gathered the cattle into the yard. He would put a scrawny bullock in with three good ones – which added to the haggling and bargaining. The pretend agent (the other brother), in his long beige coat, would begin bidding for the cattle. This could go on for half an hour before the agent would walk away, pretending to lose interest, only to return ten minutes later with a notepad in his hand, as a stand-in for the chequebook, with an improved offer. If this was accepted, the deal was accepted with a spit and slap of the hands. Uncle Jim went to watch this drama a few times.

A New Town

Charlestown was named after Charles Strickland, who was the land agent for Lord Charles Henry Dillon's estate. The Dillons built a mansion at Loughglynn, having been granted lands in County Roscommon and surrounding areas for their loyalty to England. Strickland wanted to establish a rival town on the Mayo side of the Sligo border because tenants of the estate were treated unfairly in Bellaghy when they went to sell their crops at the marketplace. In order to encourage home-building, he advertised that the first person to complete a house in the town would receive a land offering of several acres, rent-free, forever. News of this offer brought settlers from the neighbouring towns of Swinford, Kilkelly, Kilmovee, Ballyhaunis and Ballaghaderreen. A Mr Mulligan won the prize. Strickland directed that all new buildings should stand two storeys high, to create a uniform appearance, and that the public houses should have private as well as public entryways. He designed roads that were wide and provided access to both the front and rear of each premises. These roads – Barrack Street, Church Street and Main Street – converged in a spacious square in the centre of the town. By 1856, the new town had close to sixty houses and was named Charlestown, in appreciation of Mr Charles Strickland. There were thirty to forty public houses, but these establishments were usually involved in other businesses as well, such as hardware and grocery. The town became better connected to neighbouring counties when the Charlestown railway station opened in 1895. Following the installation of the water and sewerage services in 1911, the first industry came to Charlestown: P. J. Henry's Water Mineral Factory and three bakeries were established about that time. St James's Catholic Church in Charlestown was consecrated in November 1858.

Monica Duffs

I have to mention Monica Duffs here, for my mother, God rest her, would be upset if I didn't write a paragraph about the Dillon family. The Dillons of Ballaghaderreen were not the same family as that of Viscount Dillon, the landlords. Luke Dillon moved his family to Ballaghaderreen from his farm in Lissine when he could not pay the rent. He built the original Dillon House on Market Square. Luke died in 1814. Thomas Dillon, second son of Luke, set up a small grocery in Ballaghaderreen town centre, and expanded it to the adjoining house. He left the business to his widowed sister, Mrs Monica Duff, who later registered it as 'Monica Duffs and Co. Ltd'. Monica left the business to her widowed daughter, Mrs Ann Deane. It became one of the biggest commercial concerns in the west of Ireland.

The most famous members of the family were John Blake Dillon and his son, John Dillon, and grandson, James Matthew Dillon. They were Irish activists and politicians who advocated Irish nationalism and aided tenant farmers in their area. John Dillon was deputy leader of the Irish Parliamentary Party in the House of Commons during the 1916 Rising. He saw the Rising as being detrimental to the prospect of Home Rule, for which he and John Redmond had worked so hard. However, he was also a proud nationalist who, after the stupidity of the 1916 executions, warned the British that, 'when it came to maintaining a union between Ireland and Great Britain, you are washing out our whole life-work in a sea of blood.' He also said, 'I am proud of their [the Volunteers'] courage, and, if you were not so dense and so stupid, as some of you English people are, you could have these men fighting for you, and they are worth having.' After the executions, he angrily warned: 'It is not murderers who are being executed; it is insurgents who have fought a clean fight, a brave fight, however misguided, and it would be a damned good thing for you if your soldiers were able to put up as good a fight as these men in Dublin – three thousand men against twenty thousand with machine-guns and artillery.'

The most high-profile Dillon family member from my time was James Dillon, the former Fine Gael leader. He was a mercurial figure and a fiery orator, but often he appeared to be a man who would have been better suited to the Victorian age. He was certainly unable for the Fianna Fáil of Lemass, though he ran them close a couple of times.

The Forge

In our somewhat simpler world, the Forge was a focal-point in our area. Joe O'Doherty, the blacksmith, wore an apron as he pared hooves and measured for shoes. On the platform was a charcoal fire, the heat of which was controlled by the bellows. Joe would use one hand to hold the red-hot iron with the tongs, while using the hammer with the other hand to shape the glowing iron into a horseshoe or some other creation. I used to watch with fascination when the sparks flew from the anvil – what Seamus Heaney, in his poem 'The Forge', described as 'the unpredictable fantail of sparks'. Across the years, I can still hear the hissing sound of the red-hot shoe being dipped into the water trough.

Our blacksmith was multi-talented: as well as making shoes for horses, he made steel plates for ploughs and gates for farm and domestic use. Joe had carpentry skills too: he made horse carts and donkey carts. He was a creative artist: he made shovels, spades and slanes for cutting turf. Making the five-foot wheels for horse-drawn carts demanded skill and was time-consuming. He would arrange and bend six 'felloes' in the shape of a circle. Then around this wooden wheel he would fit an iron rim, which was heated in his great furnace and shaped with extraordinary skill. Like every blacksmith, Joe kept a huge barrel of water. This water was used to cool the iron once it had been shaped into whatever creation he was working on. There was a belief that if you had warts on your hands, the cure was to dip your hands in the blacksmith's barrel of water, and in three days' time the warts would have disappeared. They would probably have disappeared of their own accord, but the locals swore by the power of the blacksmith's barrel of water. As Longfellow put it in 'The Village Blacksmith':

> Week in, week out, from morn till night,
> You can hear his bellows blow;
> You can hear him swing his heavy sledge,
> With measured beat and slow,
> Like a sexton ringing the village bell,
> When the evening sun is low.

> And children coming home from school
> Look in at the open door;
> They love to see the flaming forge,
> And hear the bellows roar,
> And catch the burning sparks that fly
> Like chaff from a threshing-floor.

The Wren Boys

There was great excitement for us at Christmas when young men and women came home from England or America. Pádraic Halligan, Malachy Tiernan and I, from the age of six until we reached fourteen years, dressed up as Wren Boys on St Stephen's Day. We went out dressed in old clothes with masks made of white towels with black paint, and holes cut out for the nose and eyes. We started at about 11 AM, calling on houses in Tawnyinah and Lurga. When someone answered the knock, Malachy would start on the whistle. We continued calling on houses all day. Sometimes we would be invited in. I had a bag to collect the usual sixpence or a shilling. If the family had visitors, it could be two or three shillings. Brigid Doherty's brother, Mike, a big contractor in England, would give us at least ten shillings. None of the other Wren Boys called to Jim, Pat and Annie Rush, because they had big barking dogs. They would be delighted, though, when we'd call. They'd invite us in, and while Malachy played the whistle, they'd give us biscuits and red lemonade. When we were leaving, Annie would put a one-pound note into the money bag, and ask us not to tell anyone. On a good St Stephen's Day, we would collect as much as would buy a new Raleigh bicycle. At the end of the day, we'd split the takings three ways.

Pathé News

Our dreams were also sparked by a developing knowledge of a world beyond snipe, grouse and the smell o' turf. Growing up in Mayo in the 1950s, our main connection with the outside world was Pathé News in our local cinema. Pathé News covered news and sport from around the world, including the highlights of the world boxing title fights. I remember Floyd Patterson, my father's favourite, even when Cassius Clay came on the scene. Other good boxers I recall were Archie Moore, Ingemar Johansson and Rocky Marciano, undefeated heavyweight champion from 1952 to 1956. Don Cockrell was the English champion. My father used to take my brother Pa and myself to our local cinema from an early age, while my mother preferred her knitting. Pa and I enjoyed Hopalong Cassidy, Roy Rogers and his horse, Trigger, Laurel and Hardy, and the funny antics of the Marx Brothers.

I was eleven years old when *Shane*, the greatest-ever cowboy film, came to the cinema in Charlestown. It is a good story about a greedy and ruthless cattle baron in Wyoming. He hired gunfighters to provoke the settlers into selling their legally owned land, paying them little or nothing for it. Shane (Alan Ladd) arrived at the right moment to help the settlers; at the end it came down to a gunfight where Shane drew faster and killed Jack Palance, the gunfighter. Shane also shot the cattle baron behind him. I remember the last scene: Shane getting on his horse with blood coming down his shoulder, and riding out of town, and the settler's son, Joey, shouting: 'Shane, come back.' The scenery and photography were exceptionally beautiful. I can't remember *Casablanca* coming to the cinema in Charlestown – a film I always enjoy.

Coláiste Phádraig

I started my secondary schooling at Coláiste Phádraig boys' school, Swinford in 1957. My mother came with me on my first day. It was a big event in my life. Coláiste Phádraig took pupils from surrounding areas, including Killasser, Foxford, Bohola, Kiltimagh and Charlestown. Our teachers were from the Diocese of Achonry: Father O'Neill, President, Father Leonard, Father Cawley, Father Towey, Father Finan, Father John McNicholas, our excellent English teacher, and Mr Mangan, who taught Irish and history. I found the first term difficult, especially cycling the round journey of twenty miles each day, sometimes in severe weather conditions. This did not allow me much time for sport; anyway, I just wasn't good enough to get on the school football team – too skinny.

Apart from Gaelic football, we had a small croquet lawn, on which Father O'Neill taught us the rules of the game, and sometimes played it with us. We must have made for a curious sight at a time when croquet was seen as being a somewhat aristocratic preserve. There wasn't even much hurling or rugby or cricket in East Mayo at the time, let alone croquet. Still, we enjoyed ourselves on the manicured small lawn of Swinford. By Christmas I had settled and made good friends; I got on well with most of the class and was happy.

I joined the Fife and Drum Band with Tom Giblin, who played the big drum, and Seán Harrington, on one of the small drums. I was in the front row on the left, concentrating on formation and figure-marching. My fife-playing was limited to just a few tunes. At training, occasionally, Father Towey would say: 'Now, McGOWAN!', then a big laugh from the rest of the band before I started 'The Dawning of the Day'. I did not make any mistake in leading the figure-marching. I enjoyed the outings with the band to St Nathy's, St Muiredach's, the Fleadh Cheoil and the occasional football match.

It was arranged that I could work for four weeks during the summer holidays in Bord na Móna's bog at Rooskey, footing turf. This turf was cut and spread by machine, allowed to dry and marked out in squares. It was a long day: I was collected in the town at seven o'clock every morning and didn't get home until nine in the evening. I managed to stack a square and a half each day; the adults did two squares a day. We got fourteen shillings a square. It was hard work; my back ached and my hands and fingers were sore and blistered.

Every August, Uncle John used to come from Dublin to spend a week with his brother, Paddy. My mother suggested that I could work with him in Dublin during the summer. Over the next four summers, I worked on his sites in Dublin and helped with the paperwork. He had a fantastic working foreman, Jim Ward, originally from County Sligo. He also had good subcontractors. The Carroll family did carpentry and joinery. Mr Carroll even made the stairs for each house, on site. Michael Lindsay, the bricklayer from Dublin, was a real character. The McCarthy family were painting contractors, and they were good boxers. Mr Carroll and his two sons, John and Patsy, were fanatical supporters of the Kilkenny hurlers. In fact, both Patsy and John played hurling to a high standard and trained twice a week.

We worked hard, from eight in the morning up to seven in the evening, and until 4 PM on Saturdays. Patsy Carroll and I enjoyed water-fights during Uncle John's absence. Jim Ward and his wife, Eileen, a wonderful cook, lived in a blissfully comfortable cottage in Churchtown, where I enjoyed Sunday lunch with them on many occasions. Each year, Jim Ward brought me to the Royal Dublin Society Horse Show. The ponies and horses would be impeccably turned out. As we watched the showjumping in the afternoon, my eyes were opened to a different world. You cannot, no matter how lovely it is as a memory, be a child running to school across bogs and turf-smoke forever. A world beyond nineteen acres in Mayo was beckoning, and I was ready and eager.

First, though, there was the small matter of finishing my education – in school, anyway. At least I had company on those long journeys to school. The year of my Intermediate Certificate, my brother Pa started first year in secondary school. He certainly did not enjoy the ten-mile cycle to Swinford, and at one point threatened to leave school. To resolve the problem, my mother persuaded my father to buy a scooter – a Vespa, I remember. My father was adamant that the scooter was for school only. He didn't want us to be different from other children in the neighbourhood. The scooter definitely eased the journey to school. I was the driver, and Pa was a cranky pillion passenger. One frosty morning when the scooter swerved, he fell off, hurt his ankle and told our parents that I had been going too fast: he refused to travel to school whenever the roads were icy. Pa was lucky: he had a great memory, only studied just before his exams, and could afford to take the odd day off school. In contrast, I had to study long hours due to my poor concentration. Father O'Neill and my mother were naturally disappointed when I did not perform very well in the Intermediate Certificate examination. They insisted that I concentrate on the Leaving Certificate and stop daydreaming. As I look back now, I have to admit that I did have a tendency to daydream. Indeed, I never really stopped.

The Leaving Certificate

Back in the cold, real world, before I could join the living world of work and opportunity, there was one other problem. At the start of my Leaving Certificate year, Seán Harrington and I were really struggling with Irish. Back then, you had to pass Irish to secure your Leaving Certificate in order to go on to university, and neither of us had an earthly hope of doing so. Our mothers arranged for us to take private lessons from Mr Mangan, our Irish teacher. He was a wonderful character and had a great way with people. The previous year, he had also taught us Irish history. We only got halfway through the course because he talked so much about the damage that the British had inflicted on us through the centuries. He would have you ready to go to war against the British Empire. Uncle Tom Dolan had a more balanced view: he had no difficulty working in England. He told me that it was the Irish foremen and the Irish subcontractors who took advantage of their own and, in some instances, did not treat them with the respect they deserved. To be honest, as I would find out subsequently, the balance of truth lay with Uncle Tom. Practice can often be a better teacher than theory.

Mr Mangan prepared Seán and myself well for the oral Irish, which had been introduced the previous year. He made sure I could explain everything about the land and livestock in good Irish. Seán had decided that he would study in Dalgan Park for the priesthood, which he did after the Leaving Certificate. In preparation for the oral, he learned to say in good Irish why he wanted to be a priest. We could not believe our luck when the examiner asked us to discuss the very topics we had prepared. Later in life, we realised that this was not a coincidence. We also passed the written examination. Mr Mangan coached us to introduce certain paragraphs, describing weather, scenery and members of our families, which we could apply to any composition. At that time, you could not gain admission to university without at least passing Irish. We have always remained grateful to Mr Mangan for his enthusiasm. Seán got two honours and I got one – which was enough for me to get into Trinity College later as a mature student. Pa achieved a much better result in his Intermediate exam.

The quality of teaching at Coláiste Phádraig was excellent. The purpose of regular testing, according to Father O'Neill, was not to try to fail us, but to determine what we had been able to absorb. Only in this way would our teachers be able to determine if we needed special assistance or if we had any difficulty in understanding a particular subject. What we called arithmetic and 'sums' in the primary school became maths in the secondary school. We had a balance between open-ended practical problem-solving and the more traditional pencil-and-paper practice of important skills and techniques. I am very much aware that our maths in the 1960s was less demanding than the maths of today, but that did not appear to be the case to us, in the age of the blackboard, duster, chalk and pencil.

Recalling my secondary-school days, I remember with special affection and gratitude my English teacher, Father John McNicholas. He taught poetry with feeling and inspiration. It is because of him that I love the English language and literature so much. I attribute my deep interest in poetry to the inspirational teaching of Father John. At this stage of my life, with more leisure time at my disposal, reading poetry affords me hours of enjoyment; more about that later. Father John also gave us a good grounding in grammar and punctuation.

Coláiste Phádraig had a strict regime, but we were allowed to go to the pictures and dances during our final year. I have a clear, almost perfect memory of that year: the music and the rock'n'roll. Most of us didn't bother with alcohol; we just drank minerals. Tooreen, four miles from Ballyhaunis, had a church, a shop beside the garage, and a ballroom with modern facilities. Father Horan, the parish priest, booked all the best showbands, except Brendan Bowyer and the Royal Showband, who played twice a year in the Eclipse Ballroom in Ballyhaunis. I don't know who was responsible for the rumour that the devil appeared in Tooreen hall in the form of a tall dark man with horns, but the crowds continued to flock to Tooreen from the five counties of Connaught. In fact, if anything, rumours of the presence of the horned one improved the takings. The proceeds from the dances contributed to improvements and new facilities for Tooreen. I used to get a lift to the dance at Tooreen with Bridget Doherty, a neighbour, who was going out with Paddy Duffy, a farmer and cattle-dealer. A few years later, they married and brought up a hard-working family.

I remember going to hear the Royal Showband, the Monarchs of Cloudland, Dreamland and the rest of the gossamer and glitz of that world, playing in Ballyhaunis. It is amazing how clear some things can be five decades on. I danced all night, especially with Rosaleen Noone from Ballaghaderreen and Bernadette Dunne from Kiltimagh. They were brilliant rock'n'roll dancers – and unaware of the impact they made. For the first ladies' choice, the band played lively numbers; the second ladies' choice usually ended with a waltz. It was one way of knowing who liked to dance with you. We had great fun.

My socialising during summer holidays in Dublin was mainly in Croke Park, watching counties like Galway and Down play the best Gaelic football ever. We saw players like Mattie McDonagh, Frankie Stockwell, Seán O'Neill, the McCartan brothers and my friend Joe Glynn's brother, George. Uncle John never stopped talking about the terrible twins, Seán Purcell and Frankie Stockwell, who played for Galway. Alec McAdam, who worked with Uncle John, was a Bohemian supporter and occasionally took me to Dalymount Park. On Sunday nights, I had a choice of the State Cinema or the Bohemian Cinema in Phibsboro. I was not allowed near O'Connell Street.

Both my mother and Uncle John were reasonably pleased with my Leaving Certificate results, though they were not good enough to get me into St Patrick's teacher-training college in Dublin. Uncle John resolved the situation to my mother's satisfaction, and, indeed, to mine, by agreeing to keep me in Dublin full-time to learn the building trade in his business. He assured my mother that he would make me attend evening classes in Bolton Street. My mother, who dreaded emigration, was very pleased with Uncle John's plan for me. Her fear was understandable. For her, the concerns of John Healy were deeply felt. She lived through the world described by Healy in both *Nineteen Acres* and *Death of an Irish Town*. His description of the social and commercial effects that emigration had on life in Charlestown in the 1950s and 1960s is evocative and timeless: 'John yes-boy Durcans is closed. No one knocks on Theresa Cassidy's counter no more . . . Jo Gran Gallaghers is no more. Jake Donoghue is closed . . . and Tom McCarthy's place. And James Parson's place.' Healy refers to the morning train passing through Charlestown to Dublin as the 'Emigrant train': 'Week after week in the 1940s they went like droves of cattle.' The train would pull into Charlestown to a crowded platform and carry away our young and not so young. More than likely, I would have been on that train if it were not for the intervention of my Uncle John.

Monsignor Horan: A Visionary

I thought my mother was 'losing it' when she told me that Monsignor Horan was planning to build an international airport half a mile, as the crow flies, from our house. The posh intellectuals of Dublin dismissed the dream as being a case of building a white elephant on a 'foggy, boggy' mountain. But business skills honed in dance halls can be used anywhere. Monsignor Horan collected donations in the UK and the USA, especially from people with Mayo connections. He also persuaded the government to provide some grants.

Interestingly, as I write about Knock Airport, I have just read an interview with Joe Gilmore, CEO of the airport. Mr Gilmore, while recognising the challenges facing the airport, still paints a positive picture of its present state, and expresses confidence in its future. An airport which in its early years handled just eight thousand passengers per annum, will in 2017 handle seven hundred and fifty thousand. That is extraordinary growth. The State may subsidise the airport but it gets value for its money. In the interview Mr Gilmore says: 'Over the course of the thirty-year life of this airport, there's been approximately £30 to £35 million of funding put in by the State. Over the same period, the region has put in the same amount of money because we collect £10 from each passenger. So, if you look for a private-public partnership, you've got it here. If you look for value for money, this airport has thrown off £140 million in tourism revenue to the region, two hundred jobs, one million bed nights and six thousand downstream jobs every year.'

He added: 'Typically we run a very small, tight overhead, and we need to run it that way, that's evident in the fact that over 70 percent of Knock's staff are cross-trained: the person that potentially checks you in could be the person that puts your bag on the aircraft . . . and they could also be a fully trained fireman.'

As a Mayo man I celebrate the drive and vision of Monsignor Horan. I also want to mention with admiration Charlie Haughey, who supported the airport. The critics scoffed at the idea of an airport and said it couldn't happen. Well, it has happened. I can't recall any of those critics and pseudo-experts having the decency to apologise for what they said before.

Chapter Four

'Your Mother Is Still Disappointed You Didn't Become a Schoolteacher'

Even when you leave home, you never really leave. Invisible ties and connections mean you are never fully gone from the parish. In my case, this was certainly true. We may not have been living in the age of digital, but my mother, who wrote letters almost every Sunday of her life to America and England, was almost as efficient as today's e-mail. After I moved to Dublin, I looked forward to my mother's weekly letter, describing the ups and downs of a smallholding, and the joy of the seasons. In the autumn of 1968, almost a decade after I had gone, a very sad and disturbing letter arrived, stating: 'Your father is having difficulties with his breathing because of the asthma and is losing interest in the land.' This time, he was serious about selling the house and the land, and buying a house in the town. The particular house he had in mind had a shed and a parcel of land at the back. He had talked about such a move before, and now his mind was made up. My mother, however, was completely against leaving her farming life and moving into town. She asked me to visit the following weekend, if possible. Dan Miley, my mentor, realised that this was a delicate family matter that required sensitive handling. Dan telephoned my father's solicitor, Roderick O'Connor, to let him know that I was anxious to keep the place in the family and that I was in a position to pay for it.

The following Saturday afternoon, I had tea and scones in the kitchen with my mother before joining my father in the granary, as his workshop was called. It was always tidy, with a permanent long bench, the timbers stacked neatly, the hand-saws, hammers, wood chisels, tape measure and squares, all in their correct place. We sat and talked for hours. The wind was blowing outside and the rain was lashing down. It was a black, threatening evening. My father said he had money to fall back on, and that he did not have to sell the home-place. I refrained from telling him that this idea of moving was selfish. While he could muddle around in the shed and read his books, what would my mother do without the land and her poultry? When I asked him the value of the home-place and land, he asked me if I would be happy to allow Tom the Shop to fix the value. Altogether, Tom was a safe and fair choice.

It was still raining when we went to Tom Doherty. On our way, my father said to me: 'Your mother is still disappointed that you didn't become a schoolteacher.' He also reminded me that in 1951 he took Pa and myself to the official opening of the new Father O'Hara Gaelic football pitch in Charlestown, for a challenge match between Mayo and Sligo. I cannot remember who won.

With the help of Tom the Shop, we settled on a value of £3,000. Later, my parents and I joined Tom and his wife, Olive, in their kitchen for tea and cake by the open turf fire. Ireland was changing. They talked about some good things that were happening: the young people, who had gone to find work in England and America, were coming home to visit every year or so, not like the old days, when a visit home was a rare event for people who had to emigrate. My father remarked: 'All ours want is Dublin, but Gerry is showing an interest in the cattle.'

On Sunday, the weather changed to a glowing, warm day. My parents, two brothers, Pa and Gerry, and I got first Mass. There was great excitement at breakfast: I assured my father that this transaction would not bring me unnecessary pressure – that none of the agreed purchase price would be borrowed. My mother thanked us both. My father gave me one of his sovereigns, which Anne still has. My mother said, 'Why can't you stay the night and head for Dublin early in the morning. There is a dance in Walsh's [Charlestown] tonight, and that lovely, tall girl, Maria Caffrey, might be home from Dublin for the weekend.' Typically, she added, 'Those Dublin girls wouldn't know how to boil an egg.' Maria was not at the dance, but I did enjoy dancing with the girls that I had grown up with, and also chatting with Malachy Tiernan and Pádraic Halligan.

Back in Dublin, Dan Miley advised that the home-place should be transferred to my mother's name, in case it ever happened in the future that I might have difficulties with personal guarantees. My father was upset, a year later, when he was told that I had put the home-place in my mother's name, and he said to me, 'I always knew you were one of them.' He meant that I was like my mother's people, the Dolans. I should have told him in the beginning why I was putting the place in my mother's name.

My father was living in the family home that he had helped build, and that I had now transferred to my mother. Naturally, this was hurting him. Instead of moving to the town, he bought a caravan to occupy during the turf-saving at Egool. He went further: he began to live there for a good part of the year. My mother was in an awful state: she was extremely embarrassed at the idea of her husband living in a caravan. She was hugely relieved when one day he announced that he had made an offer on Tom Pat Jack McDonald's old cottage, together with twelve acres of reasonable land. This offer was £400 short of the asking price. My mother, however, knew that my father was too stubborn to increase his first offer, so the very next day she got my brother Gerry, to drive her to Ballaghaderreen to withdraw the £400 from the post office. Then she went and dealt discreetly with the McDonald brothers, giving them the £400 and getting them to promise not to breathe a word about the transaction to my father.

Moving to his new cottage gave my father a new lease of life. Most days, Gerry brought him to the 'granary' at the old house, where my mother made sure he ate a good dinner. My father made every piece of furniture, table, chairs, and dresser for the kitchen in his new cottage. My mother made the curtains from the flour-bags she got from Tom the Shop. Visitors to his cottage had to walk the long narrow approach from the road to the cottage, as there was no room to turn a car. My father refused to interfere with the stone walls surrounding his cottage, some covered with briars and capped with sphagnum moss. The cottage was tidy and comfortable, in a backward area: just the place for a man and his dog.

Young people today would find it almost impossible to manage life without the internet and mobile telephones. Back in my young days, though, the mystery of the land, the changing seasons, the corncrake, the starlings, the separation of the year between shooting and angling: all those pastimes were our internet. Indeed, growing up in the 1950s and 1960s, we did not have even a landline telephone, for it was an expensive and slow process to get one installed. Some people claimed, rightly or wrongly, that you needed influence – or 'pull', as they called it – to speed up your application for a telephone. Naturally, my parents were delighted when my brother Gerry somehow managed to get a telephone installed in the old house.

Increasingly these days, I think about my youth in Mayo in the 1950s. I remember the bog near Glann, the Forge, the Patterns at Urlar and Tample, the days at school in Swinford, the dances at Tooreen, Christmas-time, and the rock'n'roll music. They were all part of a simple but happy time that is embedded in my storehouse of memory.

Age may always chase youth, but I acknowledge and appreciate the improvements that have occurred in Irish life since the 1950s. This process began when Seán Lemass, the greatest of our leaders, became Taoiseach in 1959. He laid the foundations for Ireland's economic success. Locally, Monsignor Horan's Knock International Airport, three miles from Charlestown, has been the miracle responsible for the modern west of Ireland, as I mentioned in the last chapter. Knock International has daily flights to London airports, Manchester, Liverpool, Birmingham, Bristol, East Midlands and Edinburgh in the United Kingdom, our biggest trading partner. During the summer, there are daily flights to the major European cities, and 750,000 passengers used the airport in 2016. We have moved on a long way from the other side of the Ireland I grew up in, when the emigrant train from Mayo decimated whole families and communities. Our emigrants today are educated and are able to command good jobs abroad. Isolated farmhouses or cottages that come up for sale in the west are being snapped up for weekend retreats for families, whose principal home is in England or Dublin. However often I go back, County Mayo never loses its magic, never fails to reveal something fresh.

Returning to the world I grew up in, for me the historic poem 'Kilkelly' emphasises the nature of that pre-internet, pre-texting, pre-Facebook, pre-telephone society. It was a world where, in terms of communication, the letter was king. In the poem, Peter Jones, whose grandfather left the small village of Kilkelly in County Mayo, found a bundle of old letters sent to him by his father in Ireland. The letters tell of family news, births, deaths, sales of land, and bad harvests. They remind the son that he is loved, missed and remembered by his family in Ireland. The final letter informs him that his father, whom he had not seen for thirty years, has died: the link with home is broken.

Peter Jones used these letters to make his poem:

KILKELLY
Kilkelly, Ireland, 1860, my dear and loving son John
Your good friend schoolmaster Pat McNamara's so good
as to write these words down.
Your brothers have all got to find work in England,
the house is so empty and sad.
The crop of potatoes is sorely infected,
a third to a half of them bad.
And your sister Brigid and Patrick O'Donnell
are going to be married in June.
Mother says not to work on the railroad
and be sure to come on home soon.

Kilkelly, Ireland, 1870, my dear and loving son John
Hello to your Missus and to your four children,
may they grow healthy and strong.
Michael has got in a wee bit of trouble,
I suppose that he never will learn.
Because of the dampness there's no turf to speak of
and now we have nothing to burn.
And Brigid is happy you named a child for her
although she's got six of her own.
You say you found work, but you don't say
what kind or when you will be coming home.

Kilkelly, Ireland, 1880, dear Michael and John, my sons
I'm sorry to give you the very sad news
that your dear old mother has gone.
We buried her down at the church in Kilkelly,
your brothers and Brigid were there.
You don't have to worry, she died very quickly,
remember her in your prayers.
And it's so good to hear that Michael's returning,
with money he's sure to buy land
For the crop has been poor and the people
are selling at any price that they can.

Kilkelly, Ireland, 1890, my dear and loving son John
I suppose that I must be close on eighty,
it's thirty years since you have gone.

Because of all of the money you send me,
I'm still living out on my own.
Michael has built himself a fine house
and Brigid's daughters have grown.
Thank you for sending your family picture,
they're lovely young women and men.
You say that you might even come for a visit,
what joy to see you again.

Kilkelly, Ireland, 1892, my dear brother John
I'm sorry I didn't write sooner to tell you, but father passed on.
He was living with Brigid, she says he was cheerful
and healthy right down to the end.
Ah, you should have seen him play with
the grandchildren of Pat McNamara, your friend.
And we buried him alongside of mother,
down at the Kilkelly churchyard.

He was a strong and feisty old man,
considering his life was so hard.
And it's funny the way he kept talking about you,
he called for you in the end.
Oh, why don't you think about coming to visit.
We'd all love to see you again.

It was a simple and much-loved world. However, by 1962 it was time for me to leave.

Part 2
A Life Less Ordinary

Chapter Five

'For God's Sake Slow Down, Joe!'

Seán Lemass became Taoiseach in 1959, and remained in office for seven years. People close to me, and many others, were delighted to see the end of de Valera. Lemass was a pragmatic leader. He abandoned the narrow protectionist, self-sufficiency policy in favour of a vision of Ireland as an integral part of a wider economic and political unit. It was time for Ireland to leave the edge of Europe, cease being the Robinson Crusoe of the continent, and grow. Lemass is remembered for bringing in new ideas to develop Irish industry and for starting new contacts between the Republic of Ireland and the North of Ireland. Lemass was fortunate to have the greatest economic visionary this country has ever had, the County Down-born Dr T. K. Whitaker, as Secretary of the Department of Finance.

This was the perfect time for Tom Brennan and others like him, especially those with liquid assets, to return to Ireland. Brian Denis from Davy stockbrokers explained to Tom that the Department of Finance had introduced a massive incentive by giving a 50 percent bonus on money returning to this country, provided you could prove that this money was being invested in Ireland. Like many others, Tom had raised his stake in the high-rise buildings of America. At twenty-one, he joined his brother Mike in Chicago, the second-largest city in the United States. Tom was followed two years later by his younger brother, Bill. Their uncle Mike had been living in Chicago for over twenty-five years, and had a great influence on their lives. Tom Brennan's brother, Mike, had a good job with an engineering company, and very quickly developed useful contacts in the construction industry. Tom gained employment with a company associated with his uncle's building company. At that time, military service was a requirement

31

in the United States. He opted for six months in the army, with a further five years in the Reserves, instead of two full years in the army.

In June 1964, I was introduced to Tom Brennan and his sisters, Margaret and Ann, at the Arcadia Ballroom in Bray. The town began as a fishing village, then became a retreat for Dublin's middle class and a major holiday resort. Every June, they had, and still have, a thriving festival. Tom and I found a quiet spot near the mineral bar to chat – mainly about building houses. We arranged to meet up again the following evening at the Kilimanjaro restaurant on Baggot Street. Tom was intent on getting involved in house-building in the Dublin area. He would only return to the United States as a last resort. Tom was surprised at my knowledge of and connections in house-building, given my young age. I was not yet twenty-one, and Tom was twenty-six. We arranged that Tom would come to our site in Rathfarnham the next morning to meet my Uncle John. The two of them spent all day looking at houses under construction and meeting builders. I was busy getting a pair of semi-detached houses ready for the roofer, Tom Grace. Tom Brennan's honesty and positive attitude created a favourable impression on Uncle John.

That evening, as we sat in the Yellow House, a striking gem of a pub constructed in yellow brick over three floors in Rathfarnham, Uncle John gave us a resumé of his career as a builder. Having worked as a bricklayer and saved his money, he started building in 1955. He took a building licence on six sites in Terenure. He completed the first pair of houses, roofed the next two, fitted the windows and doors, and didn't touch the third pair. With mortgages drying up, there was no point in remaining in Dublin: John and his friend Pat Gallagher were lucky to find contract work for bricklayers in Reading, England.

On his return from England, there was more confidence in the economy; he completed the six houses in Terenure and moved to developed sites in Rathfarnham. In 1959, he bought his first car, a Ford Prefect, and in 1962 he bought a yellow Volkswagen Beetle, which he gave me in 1963. I don't think he liked the colour. Mick Lindsay, a very good and fast bricklayer, and a real character, joined us in the Yellow House pub that first evening. 'Do you know, Tom,' he said, 'this young fellow, Joe, was put in charge of twelve houses when he was eighteen years old?' That was true. I remember Jimmy Forbes and myself digging by hand the foundations for those twelve houses.

Tom asked Uncle John in June 1964 if he would have any objection if I went into partnership with him. Uncle John had no objection. In fact, he could not have been more supportive. He took Tom and myself to meet Mr O'Carroll, the manager of the Munster and Leinster Bank in Rathfarnham. We opened a bank account for Brennan and McGowan Partnership and a personal account for Tom Brennan. Tom lodged £5,000 to his own account within a week, and we put £2,000 each into the partnership account. Tom would lend money to the partnership as required. The next four weeks were divided between working on the site in Rathfarnham and trying to locate fully developed sites to start building. John Hand, a representative from Roadstone, told us that the roads and services were nearing completion on 150 sites off Kill Lane in Foxrock. Tom arranged to meet Ian Carmichael, Phil Fitzsimons and Pádraic Hassett, the site agents. Pádraic Hassett persuaded us that they were good value, despite the fact that they overlooked Deansgrange cemetery, in the distance. We agreed to buy the first six sites, and exactly one week later another six, when Tom received a cheque from the sale of shares in America. Phil Fitzsimons introduced us to Dan Miley of Miley and Miley Solicitors, and Dan agreed to act as our solicitor. Uncle John visited our sites every Sunday to inspect progress. He told us that there was a strong culture of expecting success from people born in County Mayo; he was challenging us to succeed. It was the beginning of a lasting partnership which has stretched over fifty years, and still continues.

We paid £800 for each developed site: £400 on exchange of contract and the remaining £400 on completing the sale within two years. There were no financial contributions or onerous conditions; in fact, the ESB and Dublin Gas contributed to our advertising costs. We were building spacious four-bedroomed semi-detached houses, 1,400 square feet, each with a garage to the side. We introduced warm-air heating without radiators, and I think we were the first to fit Arco kitchens, manufactured in Waterford. We were the only one of eight builders to open a fully furnished showhouse in the development. Hassett and Fitzsimons agreed the sale of two houses, and in the first week there were lots of enquiries, followed by two more sales within a month.

Tom and I were taken aback, and extremely disappointed, when Mr O'Carroll, the bank manager at Munster and Leinster Bank, refused to provide finance to speed up our building programme. We were young, and anxious to forge ahead. I still have the image of Mr O'Carroll pointing his walking stick at me and saying: 'For God's sake, slow down, Joe, build two houses at a time.'

At the same time, in 1965, we had the first bank strike in Ireland; it lasted six months. The closing of the banks had a serious effect on businesses such as those in building, which requires a degree of cashflow.

Dan Miley played tennis with Lindsay Wellner, the manager of the Bank of Nova Scotia, which had just opened a branch in Suffolk Street, Dublin. Dan prepared a good report, detailing the building costs, the dates of completion and anticipated profits. Dan told Mr Wellner that there was a strong demand for these houses in a very good location. Mr Wellner met Tom and myself on site the following Sunday. He was impressed with what he saw and arranged that we call to the bank on Tuesday to finalise the documentation. Dan Miley gave an undertaking to the Bank of Nova Scotia that he would lodge the total proceeds from each sale to the bank, excluding the final £400 site cost. Tom Brennan and I gave our personal guarantees that we would honour this commitment. We now had an overdraft facility of £18,000, to be drawn down as work progressed. From that moment onwards, personal guarantees were second nature to us. We built and completed the sales on the remaining ten houses in nine months, leaving the other builders on the development gasping for breath. After Kill Lane, we moved to build on developed sites in Killiney.

In the age of the million-euro ordinary family home, it is interesting to see the breakdown of the cost of building a four-bed semi-detached house with garage to the side, in 1965.

Expenditure and Income

Developed site	£800
Total build costs	£2,850
Agents Fees	£100
Solicitors Fees	£120
Interest	£150
Total	£4,020
Average sale price of a house	£4,900

We had just started building on our site in Foxrock when Colin Holohan called and introduced himself as an estate agent. Colin Holohan completed his Leaving Certificate in Blackrock College in 1957. He got his first job with the estate agent Barryman and Co. on Brompton Road, Knightsbridge, London, directly opposite Harrods. He was seventeen years of age at that time. Mr Laurence Drummond, Colin's boss, was impressed with his dedication and work ethic, and brought him to meetings with clients, from which he gained great experience. After a year, Colin returned to Dublin to work with Albert Estate Agents in Sandycove, and a few years later, another Blackrock College boy, Ken MacDonald, joined the company. Colin and Ken were lucky to be under the guidance of Mr Frank Meldon, chartered surveyor, until Colin took over Armstrong Smith, an old auctioneering firm; Ken joined up with Ronnie Hooke to become one of the leading agents in Dublin.

I dropped in two or three times a month to the Albert Estate Agency in Sandycove for coffee with Colin Holohan, Ken MacDonald and Frank Meldon, who were later to play a huge role in my life. Ken was an excellent team player. He introduced me to the game of tennis: we played at Herbert Park on Tuesday evenings, and sometimes on Sunday morning. Pádraic Hassett, Phil Fitzsimons and Dan Miley invited Tom golfing, but only on Sundays to begin with. We were to have many adventures on the golf course, but that is matter for a subsequent chapter.

In 1965, Colin Holohan introduced us to Dr Dick Belton, whose family was developing eight hundred sites off Rochestown Avenue in Killiney. John McKone and his brothers, Nick and Eddie, were building one hundred dormer bungalows. We could only afford to purchase eighteen fully developed sites. Tom's brother, Bill, who had just returned from Chicago, took another six sites nearby. Sales were slower because we were in the middle of a large development. Our office was a little wooden hut, which was moved from site to site, until we started work on Greenhills Road in 1972. This kept our overheads to a minimum. A representative from the builders' providers took orders once, and sometimes twice, a week, for delivery two days later.

Our third move was to Rathfarnham, in 1966, building twenty houses on fully developed sites again. A problem arose here: for the first time, we experienced the 'mortgage' problem – namely, that they were nearly impossible to get. Dan Miley came to the rescue with an introduction to an estate agent and mortgage broker, Brian Carr, whose uncle, Mr Edmond Farrell, was managing director of the Irish Permanent Building Society. The Irish Permanent provided a certain number of mortgages to our house purchasers every year. We had a steady cashflow and good profits, because sales came faster and better in Rathfarnham. Always quick to learn, we realised that to achieve continuity we needed a sufficient supply of land where we could do all the infrastructure ourselves, building the roads and services, and then the houses. We were even more aware that, then as now, a supply of affordable houses was required in Dublin. In fact, they are always needed – which makes the current housing debacle so inexplicable, except as a calamitous failure of foresight and common sense.

Meanwhile, back in the Dublin of the swinging 1960s, things were happening fast. We purchased land on Terenure Road West, known as the Laurels, which had planning permission for fifty three-bedroomed townhouses. We bought the site through the land agent Peter White, and appointed his company, Gilbert Leon and White, as sole selling agents. Jim Hodgins, Civil Engineering Company, contracted to provide the roads and services. Strange as it may seem, these were the first townhouses in Dublin. There was a constant stream of visitors when the showhouse opened. These houses were tailored to meet the needs of purchasers and were excellent value. Buying a house at that time was for nesting, not for investing.

Colin Holohan and Ken MacDonald, both with rural backgrounds, had energy and drive, and dressed impeccably. They went looking for building land, not waiting for instructions to arrive by post. They got on particularly well with landowners and farmers. One example of this occurred in 1968, when Ken MacDonald introduced us to Mrs Mai Morgan and her family at their home in Castleknock, just outside the gates of the Phoenix Park. The Morgans were turkey-farmers. After a few meetings, we agreed to exchange contracts on ten acres, adjacent to their house and the farm-buildings, which, however, they wished to retain. Jack Collins prepared detailed drawings and submitted a planning application to Dublin County Council for forty-eight large detached houses on Mrs Morgan's ten acres.

Dublin County Council granted full planning permission, but with a condition that we had to get permission from the Board of Works to allow the surface water from our development into their stream on the opposite side of the road, inside the park wall. We could not get the finance to buy the land without this permission. Mrs Morgan extended the completion date on our contract by six months. Happily, the Board of Works granted us permission with just two weeks to spare on the extension to our contract. It was an important lesson never to leave anything to the last minute: not, alas, that we took full heed of it.

Tom Brennan had a great group of friends in Chicago – most of them originally from Connaught. Pat O'Toole was one of them: like Tom Brennan, he too returned from America with money. Peter White's colleague, Tony Leon, negotiated the purchase of three acres of land for us, on Greenmount Road, off Terenure Road East, which had planning permission for flats. Tom and I formed a new company called Greenmount Properties, in which Pat O'Toole had an equal share. To allow the company to grow, we agreed that only Pat would draw a salary. Jack Keenan, architect, applied for a new planning permission for us to build thirty townhouses and thirty two-bedroomed apartments. Peter White was confident that these properties would be snapped up, and he was right. There were few purpose-built flat developments at that time, with the exception of St Anne's in Donnybrook, built by John Byrne and designed by Desmond Fitzgerald and Brian O'Halloran. Saint Anne's was, and still is, one of the most sought-after apartment developments in Dublin.

Jim Hodgins did the development work; that is, roads and services, on the ten acres, now called 'Parkview', in Castleknock. We opened a smart and spacious, well-designed showhouse, with the kitchen supplied by Michael Boland and Arco. They were expensive houses to build, and in the beginning sales were slow because the starting price was considered high, at £12,000 each, and purchasers were still finding it difficult to obtain mortgages. It was hard work making internal changes for fussy purchasers. It was a buyer's market. That discouraged our involvement in the upper middle or top end of the market. It was another lesson learned.

Pine Valley, Rathfarnham

Jimmy Lyons, a close friend of Tom Brennan, moved to Dublin from Chicago a few years before Tom returned. Jimmy bought a house in Park Avenue, Sandymount, and occupied one of its flats before buying a second house next door. Tom suggested to Jimmy Lyons, on their way to play golf at Edmondstown, that he should inquire whether any land in the area could be purchased for building. Jimmy discovered a parcel of land – sixty acres – that was ideal for building, with road frontage to Grange Road and Ballinteer Avenue. It was owned by Larry Lenihan and his wife, Dr Lenihan. We formed a company, Grange Developments Limited, to purchase this land. The company comprised five equal shareholders: Mike Brennan, Bill Brennan, Jimmy Lyons, Tom and myself. Within eighteen months, Jack Collins, architect, obtained full planning permission for 365 houses, with no onerous conditions. This was a huge leap forward from building twenty houses a year. Happily, Mike Brennan, managing director, always achieved his targets and nothing was wasted. Without any doubt, this was the best-run company with which I have been associated.

We devised a number of features to keep costs under control. For example, we had to avoid having projecting windows and other architectural features. Suspended floors were used downstairs. Prefabricated roof trusses were not available at that time. The timber was ordered in correct lengths to avoid waste. The carpenters then cut the rafters and purlins in the compound on site, before erecting the traditional timber-cut roof. Tom Grace Junior and his father, Tom Senior, together with their team, were reliable tilers and did not require supervision. They never took shortcuts. Again, the layout to the drainage system needed to be as simple as possible. This work, and all the different stages, was supervised by engineers from Dublin County Council by appointment and, sometimes, by surprise visits, which kept everybody on their toes.

The county council would only allow low-density development, so there was plenty of space, which made health and safety easy to control. Some of the gardens with corner houses were as big as the small fields in East Mayo. In fact, quite a number of purchasers, especially those from the country, grew their own vegetables.

This development, known as Pine Valley, was hugely successful. They were large four-bedroomed semi-detached houses selling from £8,750 each. A small group of twenty very large detached houses at the Lamb Doyle's end of the site sold for £20,000 each. There is a great demand for these houses today, which have panoramic views over the city. They sell for around €1,000,000 each.

Grange Developments Limited appointed P. J. Burke Sales Limited as the sole selling agent to Pine Valley, in 1968. Jimmy Lyons introduced Tom and myself to Paddy Burke TD, who came from the same part of County Mayo as Jimmy. Mr Paddy Burke, a Fianna Fail TD for twenty-nine years, was warm, welcoming and comfortable at all levels. Paddy didn't seek promotion; he was happy as a TD. He used to say: 'If everyone was a Bishop, there would be no priests.' Ray Burke, his son, continued to run the family auctioneering business. He became a TD in 1973, succeeding his father, who retired.

Ray Burke was hard-working, a lot more ambitious than Paddy, and a great admirer of C. J. Haughey. Ray wanted not alone to get elected on the first count but with as big a majority as possible, so that his surplus and transfers would elect his running mate. Sadly, this did not always work out, for similar reasons to the famous failure of a little known Fine Gael TD, Percy Dockrell, who lost his seat in the 1977 Fianna Fáil landslide. Percy, who was always elected courtesy of the surplus achieved by his running mate, Liam Cosgrave, the former Fine Gael Taoiseach, on being asked why he lost, replied: 'Liam didn't get enough votes.'

Ray certainly spent a lot of time getting two Fianna Fáil TDs elected in his three-seat constituency. During that time, Brennan and McGowan made financial donations to Ray Burke for his own expensive electioneering, and for Fianna Fáil. Ray's passion for and dedication to the party was appreciated within Fianna Fáil, where he was promoted, first by Jack Lynch and then by Charlie Haughey, to Minister for the Environment, then to Justice, from there to Minister for Communications, and finally, by Bertie Ahern, as Minister for Foreign Affairs.

A Time to Buy and a Time to Sell

Hugh Owens, our accountant, introduced Tom and myself to Alan Power in 1967. Alan was looking for an Irish partner to develop land he had contracted to purchase near Kilternan, County Dublin. Tom and myself could only afford to take a 20 percent share. Alan Power exchanged contracts to purchase Saint Bridget's, Kilternan, County Dublin, together with one hundred and thirteen acres of land, for £45,000. This included the priest's house, located just before the Scalp, a mile from Kilternan, on the Enniskerry Road. It had excellent road frontage, with a magnificent stone wall, in good condition, fronting the main road. One of the chief features was an impressive entrance, with a long winding avenue to the main house, which was Georgian in style. The house had deep sash windows and tall chimney stacks. The Sisters of Charity had inherited the property from an only child who joined the Order. They had added two wings to the original house. The Enniskerry wing had a chapel that also acted as a theatre. There were fifty-six rooms altogether, not counting the larders and sculleries, but only two bathrooms in each wing, and two in the original house. The house was in a commanding position, with magnificent views of the sea, and, of course, of the Scalp.

Alan Power was born and brought up in London; he was thirty-seven when we met. He had qualified as a mechanical engineer. Although he had disappointed his father, a stockbroker, by choosing to pursue a career in photography, his father granted him a small monthly allowance to pursue his ambition. He enjoyed this bohemian lifestyle until his late twenties, when an uncle on his mother's side of the family died, leaving him a sizeable inheritance. In 1960, he began a successful building and property company. He always adopted a careful approach, and never over-extended himself. Alan Power was looking for an Irish partner to do a joint venture. Tom and I, as I have already said, could only afford to take a 20 percent share in this venture.

Half of the land at St Bridget's was hilly, and the rest was rich in limestone, and with some magnificent trees. It also had a three-acre lake between the house and the main road. They certainly knew where best to locate a house, two hundred years ago.

The back of the house had become a dense jungle of laurels, briars and snow berries. A yew hedge, unclipped for two or three decades, had grown into a dark row of trees, at the end of which were the graves of the original family's dogs. One weekend, Peter Lang with his JCB, his brother, Noel, on the tractor and trailer, Willie O'Connor, Tom O'Doherty, Tom Brennan and myself, started clearing the fields at the back of the house with a vengeance. It was a tremendous clearance: great chunks of material pulled out of the woodland. Peter made sure that the important things escaped the clear-out. Because the yew tree is sacred, it was considered unlucky to cut down or damage it.

As the building could not be insured unless it was occupied, Tom, his brother, Bill, my brother, Pa, and I took up residence for two years until the entire property was sold. The cost of oil was so low that we could easily afford to keep the central heating at a low temperature throughout the building during the two winters that we were there.

We only occupied the drawing room, which had three low sash windows facing directly south, taking full advantage of the breathtaking views. We did not use the original dining room on the other side of the outer hall. Although our kitchen faced north, it was very bright, once the overgrown area outside had been cleared. My bedroom was at the end of a long corridor. It was minimalist, with just a single bed and armchair, and had views unmatched anywhere on this planet. It would have made a perfect scene for a Beckett play, or *The Shining*.

On the downside, the absence of shutters and curtains meant that it was a little creepy. Perhaps the ghosts of the old nuns disapproved of the curious, often uncomfortable menagerie that replaced them. But in such an ancient landscape, there were magical moments too. During our second winter there, we had a month of icy weather. There was one morning in particular that I will never forget: I looked out at the entire surroundings clad in a blanket of snow; it was breathtaking.

Chapter Six

Adventures with Sir Henry Cotton

St Bridget's also provided us with one of our luckier escapes after we almost became accidental golf-course architects. This adventure occurred after Tom Brennan had met the architect Jack Collins at a golf outing. He was the perfect gentleman; he played off a two-handicap and later became Captain of Dun Laoghaire Golf Club. It was agreed that Jack would prepare a planning application for a small exclusive development of twelve detached houses on fifty acres of the land at St Bridget's. Alan Power insisted that each house would be individually designed on a minimum of four acres. This planning application was vehemently opposed by Dublin County Council, because they would not accept the proposed treatment plant.

I cannot remember who came up with the idea to convert the existing house and buildings into a hotel and develop an eighteen-hole golf course on the land, but Alan Power was obviously conscious of the need to have a well-known golf architect to highlight the golf potential of the setting to the planners and to the public. We contacted the great golf-course designer Henry Cotton, and he agreed to look the course over. Tom and I collected him at the boat in Dun Laoghaire, as he did not travel by plane.

At that time, Henry Cotton was the greatest English golfer: he would retain that status until the arrival on the scene of Nick Faldo. Mr Cotton won his first British Open in 1934 and his second in 1937, with the entire US Ryder Cup team playing in the tournament. That was his best season. Mr Cotton served in the Royal Air Force during World War Two. He won the Open Championship for a third time in 1948. He played in his first British Open when he was seventeen and his last in 1977, fifty years later. Henry Cotton designed golf courses and wrote several books. He rarely played in America, because he disliked flying. He set up the Golf Foundation, which encouraged thousands of young boys and girls to play golf. He made shrewd investments in property and bank shares, when banks behaved as banks should – unlike their casino-like behaviour in recent years. He received a knighthood in 1987, shortly before his death.

The morning began with cloud and heavy showers, followed by clear blue skies, giving the most spectacular views of the sea, the Scalp and the Dublin Mountains. Henry Cotton, Jack Collins, Tom and myself went to Enniskerry, a setting as good as any village in the Cotswolds, for a quick sandwich, as time was precious to this man. As we walked, he sketched and planned the eighteen holes. Mr Cotton insisted that we buy twenty-three acres of land from the adjoining farmer. He explained that the views would compensate for the hilly contours, and that it could be a commercial golf course or a private members' club, but not a championship golf course. That evening, Mr Cotton was more confident of the potential. On the way to the ferry that evening, Mr Cotton was more confident of the potential than he had been at lunchtime. We received full drawings of his design and layout within two weeks. It was a revelation. His fee for the day, including drawings, was £320 – a relatively small sum, considering the skills he brought to the project. Jack Collins got working on the drawings for the hotel and clubhouse, and within two months of providing additional information, we received full detailed planning permission. The farmer accepted the priest's house and £2,000 for the twenty-three acres.

Alan Power

Alan Power was keen to develop the hotel and golf course, at this stage called Kilternan Country Club. Jack Collins, a precise, honest and exact man, advised Tom and myself not to get involved, because it would require huge borrowings. This was not to mention the fact that we had no experience or training in developing or running a golf course, and had little knowledge of a big conversion job. So we decided to sell. It was a good decision. Arthur 'Chubby' Williams, a partner in Hamilton and Hamilton, valued the buildings, on 130 acres, at not less than £75,000. Ernest Ottewell and his friend Tony Hansen, a London solicitor who specialised in taking private companies to the stock market, exchanged contracts and paid £7,500 as a 10 percent deposit. Tony loved the setting and location but, after doing some research, realised that it would be a struggle to secure enough members for a private club, and decided not to go ahead with the purchase. Within months, it was sold to the brothers Johnny and Willie Opperman and a syndicate. They had experience in the hotel and leisure industry.

Alan Power suggested that he would provide finance to purchase land for residential development in established locations: we would build the houses, and all the profits would be shared equally. Colin Holohan introduced us to the vendors of thirty-six acres of good dry, level land inside the development area in Rathfarnham, directly opposite where we were building. The land had road frontage in a sought-after area beside public transport, and was only a short distance from Rathfarnham village. Since the vendors wanted a three-month completion and would not consider a conditional contract, Jack Collins arranged a meeting in the Planning Department of Dublin County Council. The planning officials told Alan Power and myself that the services in the area were overloaded owing to the delay in completing the Dodder Valley sewage project. They said that planning permission might not be achieved for up to ten years. It was a very negative and discouraging meeting. We considered that the risk of not getting planning permission was too high, and we did not proceed. Within eighteen months, however, the Gallagher Group opened a showhouse on this land, and were selling houses faster than they could build them. And that was the land for which we had been told we could not get planning permission for maybe ten years. Remarkable! Another lesson learned.

There was a great buzz in Dublin in the 1960s and 1970s. Apart from housing for the new generation brought up in the age of the Beatles, but still living in a country under the sway of Archbishop John Charles McQuaid, small and large office buildings were being constructed. The Stillorgan Bowl, opened in December 1963, was one of the templates of the new age. It was the first bowling alley in Ireland. Being modern and American and different, it took off immediately and became the 'in' place at weekends. During the week, it was always busy with league competitions. Separately, Metropolitan Estates & Separately, Metropolitan Estates and Property Corporation developed the first ever shopping centre in Ireland, at Stillorgan, County Dublin. The first ever shopping centre in Ireland, at Stillorgan, County Dublin. It was officially opened in 1966 by Dickie Rock, whose presence caused quite a fuss. We were moving on from the days where shopping crisscrossed all of the small corner shops – the butcher, the baker, the candlestick-maker – and the old bar, where tea and bread competed for space with Guinness and whiskey.

Chapter Seven

A Millionaire Before
My Twenty-seventh Birthday

One of the more interesting characters of the time was Ernest Ottewell, who specialised in purchasing houses on one to five acres, obtaining planning for low-density large houses or, sometimes, high-density townhouses. He would then sell the original house separately, and sell the sites to builders. As one can imagine, the residents who adjoined these properties hated Ernest for introducing this concept to Dublin. He continued his involvement in a few commercial developments in Dublin. His most cherished purchase was the freehold of Woolworths in Grafton Street for £70,000, financed by Lombard and Ulster Bank. His developments in East Midlands, and a few ventures with Tony Hansen in London, occupied part of his time, but ultimately, it often seemed to be the case that porcelain and china were his true love. Over the years, he built up one of the finest collections of Derby porcelain in the United Kingdom.

In Ireland, Ernest continued to have many involvements in exploits that he considered a success. One of those occurred when he agreed to buy Straffan House, on three hundred acres of land, from Mr Stephen O'Flaherty. Mr O'Flaherty, however, got annoyed when Ernest claimed that the sheep were included in the sale, and he asked for the return of the contract. Later that year, the property was bought by Mr Kevin McClory. Ernest, instead, bought the Hollybrook Estate on two hundred acres, outside Bray. Around 1975, he had a financial wobble, which was of his own making. He was brilliant at identifying opportunities, but unwisely relied on himself to tidy up and follow through on the final details. The banks insisted that he had to sell some of his assets. Richard Watson and David Maxwell, clients of Stephen Miley, bought the freehold of Woolworths from Ernest. They divided the building into three shops and made a heap of money. Still under financial pressure, Ernest felt obliged to protect Ravenstone Hall, his family home in Leicestershire. It was a magnificent house on fifty acres of parkland. The furniture and contents belonged to his wife, Elizabeth. He owned the clocks and porcelain, but needed time to raise £30,000 to clear the debt owed to National Westminster Bank.

He went to his solicitor's office in Ashby-de-la-Zouch and told the secretary that he wanted to check some boundaries on the title. Absentmindedly, he left with some of the title deeds, which upset the solicitor, as they were holding the title in trust for the bank until the loan was repaid. He remained in Ireland until he got the £30,000 together, which took a little longer than expected.

I still remember one occasion, in the spring of 1987, when I accompanied Ernest to view a stately home, Stapleford Park, near Melton Mowbray in Leicestershire, which he was hoping to buy with a syndicate. The owners, Lord and Lady Grattan, retained one thousand acres of the estate, where they had chosen a most attractive setting to build a home. They were very clever in building a lovely manor house which, while not too big, was practical, easy to run and large enough to house some of their beautiful family pictures and furniture. I remember that on the day of our visit to Stapleford Park, Ernest spent hours discussing their porcelain collection. I spent hours listening.

Back in the 1970s, despite the many adventures Ernest had experienced, Tom Brennan and I joined him in purchasing a 135-acre farm at Pilerton Priors, near Banbury in Oxfordshire, in 1973. Knight Frank Rutley, on behalf of the three of us, sold the farm, leaving the farm-buildings with five acres that, we hoped, could be developed at some time in the future. Years later, a local pig-farmer, who had a lease agreement with us, claimed squatter's rights. Our solicitor advised us not to get involved in litigation, so we settled with the farmer for £90,000 – a costly mistake. Still, for the future, we realised that English pig-farmers are not men to be trifled with.

You would think I might have learned my lesson, and that in future I would read all documents with care. But no! I was caught out on two further occasions – entirely through my own fault. The first was my failure to read carefully an undertaking given to Allied Irish Finance, and the second was my carelessness in not bringing a debtor's summons from Northern Bank to the attention of my solicitor. More about that later. Ernest Ottewell passed away fifteen years ago. He left us with many memories. He was a man of exceptional courage, and was a fund of knowledge. I miss him still.

Empire-building Begins

Colin Holohan had many solid connections everywhere. He has been involved in athletics with Donore Harriers all his life, and shared his love of motor racing with many people, including his solicitor friend, Stuart Cosgrave. Colin and Stuart introduced Tom and myself to John Healy and his brother, Joe, who farmed 113 acres on the Greenhills Road, exactly halfway between the Walkinstown roundabout and the village of Tallaght, in 1967. We were interested in purchasing this land, which was convenient to all services, for residential development. The Healys were hard-working dairy farmers, who did not want to be fussed. They needed time, and gave us their word that we would have first refusal when, and if, they decided to sell. Within months, an acquaintance had purchased a very nice farm near Straffan, in County Kildare. They suddenly got the urge to move out of Dublin and take their dairy herd with them. Colin and Stuart valued the land at £2,500 per acre, increasing by £100 per acre each year for five years, when the contract would come to an end, if we had not completed the purchase. The Healys would accept a small deposit, on condition that we had a letter from a bank, stating that we would be in a financial position to complete the purchase upon obtaining planning permission.

This was a development that would need serious financing. In that regard, Dan Miley took a set of accounts, prepared by Hugh Owens of Owens Murray, and a brief history of our business over the previous four years, to Ken Wall of Lombard and Ulster Bank. The following morning, Ken Wall arrived at the Laurels, our site at Terenure Road West. He was impressed with what he saw. We received his letter a few days later, stating that Lombard and Ulster would finance the purchase of the Healy land at Tallaght, once we had received planning permission.

Action Plan for One Thousand Six Hundred and Fifty Homes

The planning officials in Dublin County Council told Jack Keenan that the Healy land was part of the 230-acre action plan being prepared by the county council, and that a planning application for the 113 acres would not be considered on its own. Our decision was immediate. Colin Holohan, with the help of John and Joe Healy, arranged a meeting with Mr Gaye Crosby, another dairy farmer with about forty acres adjoining Healy's land. Mr Crosby was renting thirty acres from his father-in-law, Mr Steen, a real old-fashioned, proud man, on the Walkinstown side of Healy's land. We got on well with both owners and exchanged contracts to purchase their lands. This only left Pat Doyle's brother, Jim, who farmed one hundred and twenty acres, which a proposed new road would divide in two. J. P. & M. Doyle, valuers and estate agents, had their offices in a large building in the centre of Terenure. They also owned two of the largest and most successful cattle markets in the country, at Blessington and Maynooth; these provided them with a huge cashflow. The Doyle brothers had farms all over County Wicklow and County Kildare.

Colin Holohan arranged a meeting with the Doyles. We brought along all our drawings to the meeting, and told them precisely what our plans were. Jim Doyle immediately recognised that it would be much better for him to have fifty-five acres of his land adjoining the Healy land as part of the action plan. We agreed in principle that we could either buy the land or contract to build the proposed houses on his land. At our next meeting, he had decided to sell us the fifty-five acres, subject to planning. He told us that he was a farmer and auctioneer and did not wish to become a developer, as that could create a conflict of interest – a lesson in integrity and honesty.

Builders & Property Developers

"THE LAURELS", TERENURE

Telephone 905431

"PARKVIEW", CASTLEKNOCK

Telephone 300333

BRENNAN & McGOWAN LTD.

ST. BRIDGET'S, KILTERNAN, CO. DUBLIN

Telephone 893182

Thomas F. Brennan Joint Managing Director.

Joseph B. McGowan Joint Managing Director.

Messrs. Armstrong & Smith Ltd.,   November 28th, 1968.
108 St. Stephen's Green,
DUBLIN 2.

For the Attention of Mr. Colin Holohan.

Dear Sir,   KILNAMANAGH CASTLE, TALLAGHT, DUBLIN.

Having inspected the above land with Mr. Holohan, we would like to
submit our offer in writing. We will give £2,500 per acre if we
complete the sale before December 1969, £2,750 per acre if we complete before December 1970, £2,750 per acre if we complete our
purchase before December 1971 and £3,000 per acre if we complete
before December 1972.

We feel from our enquiries that Planning Permission will be forthcoming certainly within the next two years. At the moment this
land is outside the development area but our intention is to get
the Planning Committee to take this land into their draft development plan. The Contract will be subject to Planning Permission.
If you accept this proposition, please get in touch with our Solicitor,
Mr. Dan Miley, of Miley & Miley, 12, South Frederick Street, Dublin.

Yours faithfully,

JOSEPH B. MCGOWAN.

45

Armstrong & Smith Ltd.

Auctioneers & Estate Agents, Surveyors, Valuers.

DIRECTORS: COLIN J. W. HOLOHAN M.I.A.A.   JAMES A. JOY F.C.A.   BRYAN S. O'BRIEN

102, St. Stephen's Green,
Dublin 2.
Telephone: 58885/6

Daniel Miley Esq.,
Solicitor,
12 South Frederick Street,
DUBLIN 2.

December 9th, 1968.

Dear Mr. Miley,

re; KILNAMANAGH CASTLE, TALLAGHT, CO. DUBLIN.

I have been speaking to your client, Mr. Joe McGowan, of Messrs.
Brennan & McGowan, Building Contractors, in connection with their
proposed purchase of the land containing approximately 113 acres
at the above.

The Solicitor for the Owners has been in touch with me and informs
me that they are agreeable, in principle, to your client's suggestion
namely, £2,500 per acre, subject to Planning Permission as per the
contents of their letter of November 28th. The Solicitor whom you
should contact in this regard is Mr. Stuart Cosgrove, of Nicholas
Cosgrove and Son, Solicitors, 2 Clare Street, Dublin 2. He is
familiar with theprocedure regarding the purchase of land subject
to Planning Permission and he thinks his clients are agreeable to
a deposit of £2,000 being paid in lieu of the option contract.

Perhaps you might get in touch with me if you require any further
information.

Yours sincerely,

COLIN HOLOHAN, M.I.A.A.

H. T. Steen, Esq.,   December 10th, 1968.
"The Bungalow",
Greenhills Road,
TALLAGHT,
DUBLIN 14.

Dear Sir,

re: LAND AT TALLAGHT.

Further to our meeting last week, I am now in a position to
make you an offer on behalf of our Client. He will give you
£2,500 per acre, if the Sale is completed before December '69,
£2,750 if completed before December 1970, £2,750 if completed
before 1971 and £3,000 if completed before 1972.

We feel from our enquiries that Planning Permission will be
forthcoming within the next two years. At present this land
is outside the Planning Area but it is their intention to have
it drafted into the Planning Committee development Plans.

Should you agree to the above terms, Contracts will be subject
to Planning Permission.

                        Yours faithfully,

                        BRYAN E. O'BRIEN.

BO'B/mm

47

We now had all the land for the proposed action plan in our control, or at least contracted to purchase, on receiving planning. We sent a letter of thanks to Ken Wall. (Apart from being a good banker, he was a top-class squash player.) We were single-minded about carrying out this development without giving anything away, particularly any equity. We knew that we had Alan Power to fall back on, if necessary. When we eventually got our planning permission, we did not need any financial partners.

In 1969, Brennan and McGowan had completed the Laurels, Terenure. Pat O'Toole and Greenmount Properties were in full flight at Terenure Road East, while Mike Brennan and Grange Developments were getting on with Pine Valley, and doing well. We were progressing slowly at Parkview in Castleknock. Tom Brennan himself bought one of the houses at Parkview, before moving to his farm at Hilltown near Clonee. His neighbours at Parkview included George Redmond, Brian Lenihan TD, Jim Gleeson, Michael Downey, and Noel Keating, the founder of Kepak. George Redmond had a senior position with Dublin County Council and played his golf at Hermitage Golf Club, quite often with Tom, and sometimes joined by Jim Gleeson's brother, Pat, a wealthy landowner on the Meath-Dublin border near Clonee. When George, who was notoriously thrifty, wasn't spending hours looking for a lost ball, they had small bets on horses owned by Tom, myself and the Gleesons, and enjoyed the excitement, especially if they had a successful flutter. Tom took the odd day off midweek to play golf, and I started hunting with the Galway Blazers. At this time, Tom joined his brother Bill, Jack Foley, Bernard Cooke and Jimmy Lyons to start Oak Park Developments. This company went on to build houses for thirty years in the Leixlip and Swords areas.

A Mother's Concern

During the summer of 1968, my mother came to stay for a week at St Bridget's, Kilternan, County Dublin. Every day during that week, she walked to Kilternan to pray in the 'Blue Church', as it is known locally. One evening, as we walked through the fields, my mother made it absolutely clear to me how upset and disappointed she was that my brother Pa was not a shareholder in all that was happening. 'Your partner, Tom, told me that he admires Pa's work ethic,' she said: I explained to my mother that Pa would continue working with Tom and myself, until I found the correct opportunity for him. She said, 'I'll keep reminding you in my letters.'

Connections

One other key member of our 'circle of enterprise' was Edward Campion. I had known Edward 'Ned' Campion, Commanding Officer of the Army Equitation School, and his wife, Eva, since they had bought one of Uncle John's houses in Churchtown in 1962. I cleared and left the large garden tidy before they moved in. They are still living in the same house, having reared their family. They always arranged to meet me at the RDS Horse Show, usually on the Saturday after the Nations Cup 'Aga Khan Competition'. Ned introduced me to many people, including Tommy Wade, and his wonder-horse, Dundrum, who wasn't much bigger than our mule at home in Mayo. I will never forget my excitement when Ned took me to the bar where the competitors entered and left the arena. It was known as the Pocket, where the competitors waited their turn. It was there that Ned introduced me to Frank Dunne, Noel O'Dwyer, Noel Fox and many others.

Noel Fox, a chartered accountant and a barrister, was a partner of Oliver Freaney & Company, Chartered Accountants. He was reliable, and thoroughly straightforward. I mentioned to him that Ken MacDonald had identified forty acres of building land inside the development plan, near Lucan. I explained to Noel that my money was tied up for the moment, and that I was not in a position to move on this land. I told him that I felt it was too good an opportunity to miss. Noel told me that he had institutional connections, and we arranged to meet the following evening. I immediately shared the same respect for Noel as many others had. I brought plans, sketches and information on previous developments to the meeting, and suggested that we inspect the land the following day.

Noel was rock-solid and helpful, providing me with encouragement and expert advice. Having established our style and policy, we signed heads of agreement, handwritten on Shelbourne Hotel notepaper. I went into action immediately. Ken MacDonald negotiated the purchase at £4,500 per acre, with completion in twelve months, or £4,750 per acre for a two-year completion. This land was included in the development area, and all the services were available. Liam Bourke, a civil engineer who had been working in the Middle East before returning to Dublin, together with architect Jack Keenan, prepared detailed drawings.

After submitting additional information to Dublin County Council, we received full planning permission a year later, in 1969, for 350 houses. We instructed the reliable Jim Hodgins to do the infrastructural work. Jim Hodgins started immediately on the roads and services infrastructure. Noel Fox arranged the finance for my brother Pa and his partner, Peter MacDonald, a brother of Ken. They had the showhouse completed within three months. Hooke & MacDonald were the selling agents, and they received twenty-five booking deposits within ten days. A feature of this development was that it was, as far as I know, the first estate to have its own sweeping equipment, which kept the place tidy.

Pa and Peter inherited good subcontractors from Tom and myself, and were fortunate to have John Groarke as a site manager. The new housing development was named 'Beech Park' by Ken MacDonald. Beech Park is just two hundred yards off the Lucan Road, which was the main road to the west. It was close to primary and secondary schools, buses, shops and recreational facilities. It was a striking example of a good design and prudent planning. The four-bedroomed semi-detached houses were good value: the houses had full oil fired central heating, garages and walled gardens, and were realistically priced, at £8,250.

Hartstown House

Captain Des Ringrose, one of the leading showjumpers with the Army Equitation Centre, had represented Ireland at home and abroad, and took early retirement from the army. He joined Murphy Buckley & Keogh Estate Agents. Des knew I was looking at Paddy Thornton's Hamwood Stud outside Dunboyne with Robin Palmer and Denis Mahony of Keane Mahony Smith. However, my focus soon switched when Des Ringrose told me that George Malcolmson, one of their clients at Murphy, Buckley & Keogh, had put his 145-acre farm, known as Hartstown House, Clonsilla, County Dublin, on the market. I was immediately interested, and moved quickly. Within days, we arranged a viewing of the house and stables. The farm was triangular in shape, with two fields fronting the Clonsilla–Mulhuddart Road, and extended for half a mile to the Ongar Stud on the back road between Clonsilla and Clonee. The long narrow avenue, with a mature blackthorn hedge on both sides, led to the magnificent copper beech tree at the gable end, which divided the two entrances: left to the house, and right to the stable yard and sheds.

The 145 acres were divided into nine fields. The middle field had twenty-one acres, and the hedges were well maintained, and provided great shelter for livestock and bloodstock. The gates to all fields, although narrow, opened and shut properly without the support of wire or bailing twine. That in itself was a rare phenomenon on an Irish farm. The octagonal building, with its galvanised roof, was an example of superb craftsmanship, and was in perfect condition. It was built in 1902, when the previous owners had two stallions and visiting mares. When I walked the farm with Oliver Freaney, Noel Fox and Tom Brennan, Oliver remarked that we could have two or three football pitches on any of the beautiful level fields. Both Oliver and Noel had won All-Ireland Gaelic football medals playing with Dublin. Noel was extremely impressed with Hartstown, and was adamant that we not miss this opportunity, especially when I told him that the vendor did not wish to complete the sale for a year. Tom said, 'Don't miss out on this farm. You fellows will have plenty of money in twelve months' time.'

Hartstown House had it all: character and innate honesty, nestled in the heart of the best grassland in the country. The hall was welcoming and compact, with four main rooms downstairs and four bedrooms, with one bathroom. A boot-room had been added to the back of the hall. We discovered that there was an underlying thematic similarity about all these Georgian houses in the area: Coolmine House, Corduff House, Huntstown House, Lohunda Park, Clonsilla House and Ongar House Stud, at that time owned by the Aga Khan, and the Swjeder family house. Brian O'Halloran, an architect, suggested a few changes and alterations, keeping it simple and understated. We started on this work after we had completed the purchase.

Donald Pratt, a partner of T. G. McVeagh, Solicitors, acted for Noel Fox and myself in the purchase of Hartstown. Since we were in the middle of our second bank strike, Noel Fox arranged with Ted O'Driscoll from Allied Irish Finance to get a sterling draft for £18,000 from Allied Irish Banks, London. This was our 10 percent deposit. Donald arranged to meet Mr McGuinness of Fred Sutton, solicitors, the next day at 7 AM to pay the deposit and exchange contracts. The reason for the early-morning meeting was that George Malcolmson was a steward at the Dublin Horse Show and had to be at the RDS early in the morning.

Meanwhile, we were making considerable progress at Beech Park, Lucan: thirty houses were occupied, and booking deposits had been taken on another forty. Hooke and MacDonald sold eighty sites to Sean Reilly, a very good builder. We also gave him an option on another eighty developed sites, provided he completed the purchase within eighteen months – which he did. This left us in a good financial position.

A non-residential farm of eighty-three acres between Portmarnock and Malahide came up for sale after we had signed the contract to purchase Hartstown in August 1970. Agricultural land in this area rarely came on to the market. This land was very close to Oliver Freaney's farm. Noel Fox exchanged contracts and completed the purchase in four weeks. He immediately applied for planning permission to build a family house. Getting planning permission was a mere formality. Noel built a fine house with great detail, supervised by John Groarke. When the house was finished, it looked as if it had been there for years. The interior was relaxed and cosy. The lawns and garden were well laid out and easy to maintain. Noel, however, on reflection, felt that it would be wrong for him to become a property developer. He suggested that I should take full ownership of Hartstown, and that he would be happy with his farm and house. Thus I became the owner of Hartstown House, on 145 acres, and Noel had his house and farm in Portmarnock, with very little borrowings on either properties.

I have to say that Donald Pratt's most noticeable quality, apart from being a good solicitor, was his desire to help others. He was a natural athlete, like his uncle George McVeagh. Both men captained Ireland at cricket. George McVeagh played tennis for Ireland, while Donald was Irish squash champion for ten successive years. In 1974, Donald left his legal practice to join his wife, Hilary, to purchase Avoca Handweavers. Later, joined by their children, they built up a successful business.

Chapter Eight

Kilnamanagh: The Best Residential Development Ever

Meanwhile, Dublin County Council had also granted us full planning permission to build a new town between Walkinstown and Tallaght. The suburb, Kilnamanagh, stretched from the Greenhills Road to the Belgard Road. Tom Brennan and I owned Kilnamanagh Estates Limited, a company that completed 1,650 houses in just under five years. The 230-acre site, with the foothills of the Dublin Mountains as its backdrop, was self-sufficient, consisting of a shopping centre, a bank, a pub, a church, schools and a community hall. The Catholic Archbishop of Dublin asked George Redmond to get Tom Brennan to accept £2,500 an acre for the seven acres of land allocated to the church and schools. We agreed, on condition they commenced work without delay. Tom and I had our first proper office, a refurbished two-storey house on the Greenhills Road, almost directly across from the Cuckoo's Nest pub. We had outgrown the old mobile office.

In developing Kilnamanagh, we were lucky to have on board Ken Woodley, an accountant, who came to us from Owens Murray Accountants. He became our general manager and was in charge of sales and advertising. He was excellent. Donal O'Carroll, another chartered accountant, loved the buzz of co-ordinating the sub-contractors. Equally important to our success were the accountants, Tony Skinner and Sheila Nolan. Tom O'Doherty, a neighbour from home, looked after the company's materials in the compound. I should mention that my mentor, Dan Miley, entrusted his son, Stephen Miley, who had just qualified as a solicitor, with all the legal aspects of the Kilnamanagh development.

Disaster Averted

At the beginning of 1974, the first two hundred houses were occupied. We were now on the second phase, with a hundred and fifty houses at various stages of construction. These houses had all brick frontage and upmarket kitchens, and were selling at £8,000 each. Then, in a forerunner to our current housing crisis, the economic difficulties that followed the oil crisis led to a mortgage famine. Even our own source at the Irish Permanent Building Society had become a dribble. One Sunday afternoon, we realised that our sales and completions had slowed down because the purchasers could not get mortgages. In business, liquidity is blood, and in bad times an otherwise healthy company will bleed out. We suddenly realised that we would become financially stretched and might have difficulties repaying our loans within the specified time. We arranged to meet at the office on Monday morning at 6.30 AM. Ken Woodley had a startling ability to get to the core of a situation: he pointed out that local-authority loans up to a maximum of £4,750 were available. All the prospective purchasers had at least £1,000 for the deposit. Tom Brennan arranged to meet his golfing friend, Mr Brian Butler, from United Dominion Trust. A few days later, Brian Butler told Tom that United Dominion Trust would provide up to £1,200 to suitable purchasers over ten years, secured on a second mortgage. We built a house with basic essentials to sell at £7,000, made up as follows:

Dublin County Council Mortgage	£4,750
Local Government Grant	£250
United Dominion Trust	£1,000
The Purchaser's Deposit	£1,000

On the Monday of our 6.30 AM meeting, the foundations were dug and the concrete poured for a new showhouse. We were probably the first builders to introduce concrete floors and other cost-cutting measures that allowed us to sell the houses at £7,000 each. Two weeks later, we advertised our new showhouse. Ken Woodley stated in the advertisement that his formula was very simple: 'We just give very good value for money.' He added that the Kilnamanagh houses were within a price-range that allowed the purchasers to take advantage of the £4,750 loan available, and that this loan was for a period of twenty-five to thirty-five years and was at a fixed rate of interest. In addition, a second loan of between £500 and £1,000 was available to suitable applicants. It was a superb marketing strategy; this was probably the first time that people had had to queue outside a showhouse.

The *Irish Independent* Property Editor, Mr Frank Cairns, reported: 'This house has been produced to sell today, not tomorrow or next week or when the bank rate drops or the building crisis is over or when the Minister for Finance returns from his holidays. It is today's house for today and, in terms of value for money, will be hard to repeat.' We sold 114 houses in thirty-six hours. Two weeks later, the remaining 136 houses in sections seven and eight were also sold, bringing us to a total of 250 houses sold. This success was clearly due to a combination of factors, but the key to success was that the properties were priced at a level at which loans were available during a mortgage famine. The team at Kilnamanagh engineered a masterly campaign that was envied by many builders. Some builders thought that we were losing money when, in fact, our margins were above the prevailing rates at that time. Families from the city of Dublin could afford to buy houses at Kilnamanagh. Ken Woodley would often say at our weekly meetings: 'I have taken two more families off the housing list this week.' United Dominion Trust provided a second mortgage of up to £1,000 on six hundred houses in Kilnamanagh and they didn't have a single bad debt.

We were fortunate that John Nolan, Jim Savage, Joe Russell and their team had the roads and services completed on sections seven and eight. They took pride in their work and didn't take shortcuts. They were always at least a year ahead of the foundations team. John Nolan, a farmer from County Carlow, arrived on site every morning at 7.30. He used to say, 'Joe, here's the shovel, you have to keep fit for that racing.' I would like to thank all those marvellous men with whom I worked in Kilnamanagh. They got enjoyment watching, and sometimes going to the races to watch, our good horses. They were my friends. When I look back on my life, these were my happiest days.

I was delighted when Frank Dunne, on behalf of the Dunne family, agreed to purchase the shopping-centre site in Kilnamanagh for £250,000. Frank Dunne and the Dunne family were a huge help in introducing me to influential connections. They often invited me to join them for lunch at their Mitchelstown stud farm outside Athboy, County Meath. The gossip at that time was that Frank Dunne was our financial backer. I did not confirm or deny these rumours. Frank Dunne has a great personality and is an astute businessman. To the outside world, he was the quiet man. Frank had great vision, and was saddened by the sudden death of one of his right-hand men: Denis Keane of Keane Mahony Smith Estate Agents. I used to meet them at the races and gymkhanas around Dublin when Frank was competing with his showjumpers, Henry Street and Cornelscourt.

Maintenance and Completion

Kilnamanagh, with one thousand six hundred and fifty houses, was nearly a constituency in itself for politicians. It became the hunting-ground for hopeful aspirants to political power and for one or two half-established politicians. They were constantly dropping leaflets into every household, asking them if the householders had any complaints; if they did, the politicians would provide legal action at no cost to the householder. In fact, Liam O'Halloran, an all-round tradesman, and Joe Staunton, a carpenter, were the perfect team to take over full-time maintenance of Kilnamanagh and our other developments. They had very few complaints from the residents, who for the most part were simply delighted to own their own homes. Some had genuine minor teething complaints which were dealt with. There was one particular family, however, who sent us a solicitor's letter every two or three months, complaining that their chimney was not working properly. They were never at home when Liam and Joe wanted to inspect the chimney, but the legal letters continued to arrive. After two years, the householder produced documents that more or less indicated that the house had to be rebuilt. In the High Court, they were awarded £2,800, half the original purchase price of their house, and we had to pay their costs.

Willie Connor RIP

We were having terrible delays getting the open space on our developments taken in charge by Dublin County Council. The landscape contractors we employed did a good job of levelling and seeding the land; however, their work was not acceptable to Michael Lynch of the Parks Department. We met Willie Connor, who was a supervisor in the Parks Department of Dublin County Council. Willie suggested that we agree with the council the cost of doing this work, give them a cheque, and let Michael Lynch do it himself. This saved us money, time and litigation. Michael Lynch is undoubtedly one of the most hard-working, conscientious men I have known.

In February 2017, I received a call from Dr Peter Staunton, telling me the shocking news that Willie Connor had passed away following an unfortunate accident while cutting overhanging branches on a tree. Willie, from outside Claremorris in County Mayo, was loyal and trustworthy, and an entertaining companion at all times. He travelled the length and breadth of Ireland to cheer on the Mayo footballers at all levels. I remember when he bought his first house investment on North Circular Road in 1969. I will miss him dropping in for discussions on many topics, but Mayo football in particular. He was proud and happy when Mayo got to Croke Park, whether for the semi-finals or the final. Weeks before Willie's accident, as he left our house, his last words to Anne and me were: 'Ah Joween, don't worry we'll bring Sam home before we die.'

Frank Cairns, Karl Jones and some other property journalists appreciated what we were achieving. However, there was a certain amount of negative reporting, which ultimately had no damaging effect whatsoever on sales at any of our developments. Such journalists tended to regard builders as corrupt and insincere, despite the shifting and questionable practices of other professions – which included bad reporting without investigating. Not a single reporter asked Tom or myself, or any of our team, to give our version of events at that time: I regard this as unprincipled behaviour. None of them took the trouble of visiting our showhouses, but instead relied on desk research. Rather than denigrating our companies for not completing the open space on time, they should have bought one or two of these houses themselves as an investment. I would refer the cranks who peddled negative criticism about the quality of our work, without gathering the facts, to an article published in the *Irish Independent* on 26 November 1974, quoted at the beginning of the next chapter.

Chapter Nine

'Tallaght to Be a Beautiful City'

'Tallaght is one day going to be a beautiful city, not a town, and the people are going to be proud of it.' That was the message of the Dublin County Council City and County Manager, Mr Matthew Macken, last night. He was speaking at a special meeting called to consider the development of the three new towns at Blanchardstown, Clondalkin and Tallaght', *Irish Independent*, 26 November 1974.

He told councillors who had been critical of the new developments: 'Remember, this is your plan. You accepted it. You need not be ashamed of it at all.' Mr Macken said that four years ago they had neither plan nor planners for Tallaght. He said they were sorry they could not provide amenities, but they had schemes for providing them within a reasonable time.

He continued: 'We ask the people of Tallaght to be patient, and in so doing counter the disgrace that has been brought on other areas, such as Ballymun.' He hoped that as regards the other two new towns, the carping criticism would not develop. The provision of the Development Plan was that the bulk of the population increase would be housed in the three major growth areas, each taking approximately a hundred thousand people.

Karl Jones reported in the *Irish Times* in November 1975: 'At the Kilnamanagh estate at Greenhills Road, County Dublin – where the 1,000th house has just been sold – general manager Mr Ken Woodley, Brennan and McGowan, said yesterday that the development of the company's residents' community "is now nearly five years ahead of original target."'

'Mr Woodley said that development of the estate started in March 1973. "At that time, we targeted for house sales of one hundred in the first year, and two hundred in each of seven succeeding years. In fact, we have just sold our 1,000th house, and the entire development will be completed by next September," he said.

'The selling programme started at Kilnamanagh with a showhouse priced at £6,400. Mr Woodley said that "an indication of the appreciation since is the recent private resale of one of these first houses, which made £9,800."

'He added that the thrity-two-classroom school at Kilnamanagh is now completed, with pupils installed and landscaping finished. Work is to start after Christmas on a 54,000-square-feet shopping complex, which will be completed some time after Easter next.

'"When the entire community development is completed next autumn, appreciation in housing values will be strongly apparent," Mr Woodley said, "By then, 'first-generation' Kilnamanagh houses will be worth up to double their original cost."

'He presented an interesting property conundrum, based on Kilnamanagh. "Where, in Dublin," he asked, "could you buy a neo-Georgian home for £14,000 complete with six bedrooms, two bathrooms, two kitchens and four reception rooms?"

'The answer, he suggested, lies in the neo-Georgian showhouse which opens to the public for the first time today at Kilnamanagh. The price of the first phase of these houses is £7,295, with higher prices for later phases. And it would be possible to buy a pair of the semi-detached units with all of the space and facilities listed above for £14,600. "That would make it the cheapest and best-appointed new house in Ireland for the larger family, and there is the alternative of living in one and letting the other to produce income," Mr Woodley said.

'In all, Brennan and McGowan will build 230 of the neo-Georgian semi-detached houses. When the company released a new house type last year, they sold over 140 in the first three days of the marketing programme, and Ken Woodley said yesterday that "he confidently expects to beat this record with the neo-Georgian."

'The builders at Kilnamanagh are now averaging twenty-two new houses per month, completed and ready for occupation, and the workforce expects to continue this average through the winter months.

'With a construction and marketing target several years ahead of schedule, Brennan and McGowan have had to create a land-bank which will provide continuity when Kilnamanagh is completed. A company spokesman said yesterday that they have two major housing developments at the preparatory stage, "one for 740 houses, and one very much larger than this."'

It is only now that I fully realise what Tom and I and our team achieved forty years ago, providing affordable houses at values that will never happen again. I was twenty-nine years old and Tom Brennan was thirty-four. We were selling houses in Kilnamanagh at £7,200, which was approximately four times the average annual industrial wage. The average selling price for new houses in Dublin in 1974 was £9,200. The average selling price of a house in Kilnamanagh today is £280,000; the average industrial wage in 2017 is £37,000. In 1974, Dublin County Council's mortgage was £4,750 and the purchasers got a grant of £250. This worked for us because our land cost was £700 per plot, undeveloped. This was 10 percent of the sale price, and there were no financial contributions or onerous planning conditions, and no VAT on the sale of new houses.

Tallaght Today

Tallaght offers a strong return for limited risk in both residential and commercial property. Tallaght, with all amenities, including an ultra-modern hospital, is within easy reach of the M50 motorway and the new light-rail transport system, Luas. Kilnamanagh, within walking distance of Tallaght, has two entrances, one from the Greenhills Road and the other from the Belgard Road, and is within easy reach of Junction 10 on the M50 motorway. Conveniently located for Dublin city and Dublin Airport, the 1,650 family homes, interspersed by open green spaces and sporting facilities, are unmatched in any other part of the country. Kilnamanagh, with its mature trees and excellent facilities, has the Luas stop, between Kilnamanagh and Kingswood. The Luas stop is in the centre of where Jim Doyle's farm was – half of which he sold to us in 1968. All this adds up to an eviable lifestyle.

I attended a concert in the Kilnamanagh community hall in the autumn of 2016. Tommy Moore, one of the many original purchasers, recently showed me around the schools, the church and the estate with pride. He told me that houses in Kilnamangh were selling for between £325,000 and £425,000, with only three 'For Sale' signs in the whole development. The critics of the original development claimed that the open spaces and facilities were rat-infested, and wrote awful nonsense about the standard of building. It would give me great satisfaction if these critics took time out to visit Kilnamanagh today: they would regret not having bought a house or two as an investment.

Gerry Tierney, Managing Director of Northern Bank Finance Corporation

Gerry Tierney, Managing Director of Northern Bank Finance Corporation, a subsidiary of the Midland Bank in England, was about to play a role in our expansion. In this regard, I must thank Frank Fitzpatrick, a prominent and established solicitor in Belfast and Dublin, who introduced Tom and myself to Gerry. Gerry was a specialist in taking companies to the stock market: He is a man full of presence and brimming with confidence; he introduced Tom and myself to Ray McLoughlin. Ray acquired vast experience working with the IDA worldwide. In particular, Ray learned the importance of teamwork from his rugby days with Ireland and two tours with the British and Irish Lions. The Lions were the perfect mix of old and new, of romance and tradition, before the advent of the professional era. Ray and Willie John McBride got their first Caps on the same day in 1962, away to England. Ireland improved in

1965: they won two out of four games that season in the Five Nations. I still don't understand what goes on in the scrum, but the following statement from Willie John McBride's autobiography best describes Ray McLoughlin: 'He is a highly intelligent man, a deep thinker about the game, who brought special qualities to the Irish teams at that time. I would say that under him was the first time we looked at a properly organised, disciplined side which understood what was required to be successful. First of all, you had to be fitter and stronger. Ray believed that it all started with the scrummage: "Get that right and then you could think about developing from there. Without a power scrum, you have little chance in rugby. This holds true even to this day. If your scrummage is right, the whole game is right." Ray brought a streak of steel into the team.'

Most of our developments were under-capitalised. This can lead to disaster in the building industry, especially when profit margins are tight. We were nearly crippled on a few occasions by a lack of cash. Ted O'Driscoll of Allied Irish Finance showed unswerving loyalty to me; once committed, he was unwavering. He never failed to provide us with bridging finance, sometimes with only our personal guarantees acting as security. We never let him down. Ray McLoughlin explained to us that if we became part of a PLC, we would not be under-capitalised. One of the advantages of being a PLC was that finance was more available, and was offered on better terms.

Tony O'Reilly, Vincent Ferguson and Nicholas Leonard took control of Crowe Wilson, a PLC. They used Crowe Wilson to take over and merge with other companies: they acquired a 30 percent stake in McKone house-builders in this way. Sean, Eddie and Nicholas had a good reputation and built affordable houses in Dublin. After going to and fro for months, Hugh Owens and Tom realised that being a public company had some disadvantages, especially when profits dipped for periods; this was extremely likely to happen in the building industry, which lacked consistency. Ray understood the commercial, economic and political policies which dictated business conditions. Ray and I have remained good friends, keeping in touch all the time. In fact, Ray had offered me financial support during those difficult years – support which, as things turned out, was not needed. In retrospect, all our assets comprised future development land; we could have divided our huge cashflow between buying land and investments. Property is not just a business, it is a profession.

Old Bawn

Not everything in business happens on the golf course, but sometimes a great deal does. One example of this occurred when Tom Brennan was playing golf with Michael Anglim, an executive with McInerneys PLC, and George Redmond. They talked about the introduction of the Certificate of Reasonable Value and VAT on the sale of new houses. McInerneys were considering selling one of their sites at Old Bawn, Tallaght, in County Dublin. They had expanded their house-building interests in the United

Kingdom and had been told by the banks that they would have to sell some of their land-bank. Tom told Michael that he would talk to our bank and, if they agreed to provide the finance, we would buy the site, which had planning permission for the construction of nine hundred houses. Tom arranged to meet Ken Wall and told him that we had only two years' work left in Kilnamanagh, with nine hundred houses already occupied; Greenmount Properties was also going well, with sales on Belgard Road in Tallaght. Lombard and Ulster had financed Grange Developments at Pine Valley in Rathfarnham, probably the most sought-after residential development in Dublin at that time. Ken told Tom he would strongly urge Lombard and Ulster to finance this purchase. When I got back from Galway, there was a message for me to telephone Tom. I was surprised and delighted that McInerneys were considering Tom's offer. Michael Anglim telephoned Tom a few days later to let him know that his offer of £720,000 had been accepted.

The site layout comprised around 10 percent four-bedroomed detached houses, 75 percent three-bedroomed semi-detached houses, and 156 percent three-bedroomed terraced houses. This site represented one of the last remaining residential-development opportunities in an established area. We had no hesitation in giving our personal guarantees to Lombard and Ulster, who were providing nearly 100 percent of the finance, to confirm our complete commitment to the project.

Ken Woodley and the rest of the team opened two showhouses looking onto a small area reserved for a children's playground. We had a good radio advertising campaign. At first, Tom and I baulked at Ken Woodley's sharp radio advertising idea. Our campaign turned out to be an outstanding success. This was our advertising slogan on RTÉ Radio: 'Call in and chat to one of our building team about construction details, and enquire as to when we can have a home ready for you. Someone will be on hand to advise on mortgages, or simply come and have a look. Join us for a glass of wine.'

Meanwhile, Dublin County Council produced a draft development plan in 1971 that showed nearly one thousand acres in the Clonsilla and Mulhuddart area zoned for residential development. House-building could not commence on this land until the services were available. Shortly after I had completed the purchase of Hartstown, on 145 acres, John Finnegan, Liam McGonagle and Ken O'Reilly Hyland purchased the adjoining land, covering 146 acres, known as Castaheany. Gerry Tierney had agreed to provide finance to Kilnamanagh Estates to buy land for future development. In 1972 and 1973, Tom and myself were negotiating with Pat Geoghegan of Geoghegan O'Rourke Estate Agents to purchase the land at Castleheany. We eventually agreed a price of £600,000. Gerry Tierney contacted his pal, Ken Wall, to see if Lombard and Ulster Bank would allow Kilnamanagh Estates Limited to put £100,000 from the sale of the shopping-centre site towards the purchase of the Castaheany lands. Ken Wall confirmed within days that his board, which included Fergus Smith and Pat Pendergast, would agree, as they had plenty of security. This arrangement meant that Kilnamanagh Estates Limited would require a loan of £500,000. Gerry Tierney had the authority to lend up to this amount, without seeking approval from the

Midland Bank board in London. We paid off the loan within the three years, from our cashflow.

This left Tom and myself with Hartstown and Castaheany: it amounted to 291 acres in our ownership. Dublin County Council had bought Coolmine House on 150 acres for development. Lohunda Park, Clonsilla House, the Swjeder farm and the non-residential Castaheany farm were bordering my land. My land, now zoned residential, increased in value from £1,250 an acre to £4,000 an acre: a remarkable increase! So here I was, almost a millionaire before my twenty-seventh birthday, not in cash, but in assets, and that was when a million was a million. Later, when we bought the Swjeder farm, Kilnamanagh Estates Limited had 460 acres and Grange Developments had 120 acres.

Our success was helped by Mike Brennan, who completed every development within budget. One weekend, Tom, his brother Bill, and I walked the farm that Mike had just purchased, which was within walking distance of Clonee village. It was nearly all in pasture, with very little plough, and no large woodlands. Mike, his wife, Ann, and their beautiful daughters moved from their Killiney house to their very smart new farmhouse. Mike bought his young cattle, usually at the Doyle-owned Maynooth cattle market, fattening them on the rich grass, and getting them ready for the factory. Around the same time, Bill Brennan had bought his first one hundred acres of agricultural land in the heart of County Meath. Bill, however, took time out to buy young cattle at the marts in Mayo – which had replaced the Fair Days – to fatten them on the rich agricultural land in County Meath.

Mike Brennan, who knows his own mind, prevailed upon Tom and myself to purchase Clonsilla House on 120 acres, zoned residential, for Grange Developments Ltd. We agreed to get the funding sorted before approaching Captain Des Ringrose of Murphy Buckley and Keogh to negotiate on our behalf. To arrange finance, we met Mr Jack Stanley, Brian Collins, Peter Hooper and John Kenny, senior executives in the Bank of Ireland, Corporate Banking. Having inspected our accounts and cashflow projections, they came on a tour of our completed site at Pine Valley and two other developments which were under construction in Rathfarnham; they were happy to provide us with the finance we required. Captain Ringrose agreed a purchase price with Colonel Byers, the owner. We went ahead and completed the purchase with a loan of £570,000 from Bank of Ireland. We told the gentlemen from the bank that we would pay off the loan within three years, which is what we did.

The Gallagher Group

One evening, Frank Dunne and I dropped in to the Ashbourne Hotel on our way home after schooling a few horses in Noel O'Dwyer's yard the far side of Ratoath, before the Dublin Horse Show in 1972. Frank introduced me to Patrick Gallagher and his father Matt Gallagher, who owned one of the largest property and house-building companies in Dublin. These were building legends who were linchpins in the evolution of a new Dublin. Matt Gallagher and his brothers Patrick, Charlie, James and

Hubert were born in Cashel, County Sligo, a few fields from the Feeley family, into which my aunt Molly married. Matt Gallagher made his seed-money after World War Two in England, before returning to Ireland. The Gallagher brothers built two factories in County Sligo, GWI Joinery and Basta Locks, which employed many people in the area. James Gallagher was the Fianna Fáil TD in the area. Charlie Gallagher built up a hugely successful construction business in England. The brothers Charlie, Patrick, James and Hubert joined forces for their commercial development at Earlsfort Terrace.

I recall Matt Gallagher saying to me: 'So yourself and that other young fellow, Brennan, purchased Morgan's Land outside the Phoenix Park; that was in my patch.' I told Mr Gallagher that he was building 350 houses on land in Rathfarnham that the planners had told Alan Power and myself might not be built on for ten years. He laughed, and then asked me: 'Where are you getting the money to expand so fast? You now have more building land in the Dublin area than McInerney and my companies put together.' After these exchanges, we got on very well and often met for coffee in Myo's Pub, Castleknock. We were all saddened when Matt Gallagher died suddenly less than two years later. Patrick was only twenty-two when he took over the family business. Patrick expanded into banking and formed a separate construction company to build their commercial developments. He also expanded his interest in the bloodstock industry.

A Forty Million Plan

All the house-builders knew that over one thousand acres from Tallaght for two miles on the Blessington Road were in Dublin County Council's New Draft Development Plan. Carroll Joinery, Frank O'Toole, Tom and Frank Woods, established house-builders, and Hugh Mulcahy, took options on three hundred acres of this land. Oak Park Developments and Grange Developments together had options on one hundred acres. We were fortunate to have a good connection with the Tuohy family, who owned 140 acres in a commanding position sloping down to join the other plots. Colin Holohan's uncle, Jack Holohan, and Mr Tuohy had emigrated together to America. In the 1930s, Mr Tuohy returned to Ireland, and purchased fifty acres with his savings. Later, he purchased two other holdings, finishing up owning 140 acres. The Tuohy family were approached by builders and agents but would only sell to us. Our company, Greenmount Properties Limited, agreed to pay £4,000 per acre for the 140 acres, subject to planning permission.

So this whole parcel of land, consisting of 530 acres, had six different owners. The developers, who had contracts or options at different prices per acre, were finding it difficult to reach an agreement to apply for planning permission on the 530 acres. Any individual application would not be considered. This led to meeting after meeting to reach an agreed working system. Tom Brennan had the temperament for these long, tiresome meetings. There were meetings with the clearing banks and the merchant banks. There were more meetings with the accountants, the solicitors and the tax experts. And there were even more meetings to discuss new proposals with surveyors, engineers, architects and officials from Dublin County Council. It was eventually agreed that each participant would provide sufficient cash on a pro rata basis to pay for the professional costs, because it was vital to get the architects and engineers working on the action plan.

Tom Brennan enjoyed the challenge. I knew that the mountain of work that Tom had put into this project was not fully appreciated. When the action plan was agreed and full planning permission was granted for 3,700 houses, Dublin County Council indicated that they would like to purchase a chunk of this land for their own social-housing requirements. At first, two members of the syndicate were reluctant; they felt that this might reduce the value of the remaining land. The syndicate negotiated the sale of 230 acres to Dublin County Council. All the remaining lands were then transferred to Fortunestown Holdings Limited, financed by Gerry Tierney and the Northern Bank Finance Corporation.

I was uncomfortable with the idea of developing the remaining lands with so many different views within the syndicate. The atmosphere was uneven, and members were nervy. There seemed to be shifts as to what the targets and objectives were. The situation seemed to me to be becoming increasingly byzantine. One day I told the meeting that Patrick Gallagher of the Gallagher Group was interested in buying the remaining lands at Fortunestown for the Gallagher Group. Frank O'Toole was all for it, and so was Tom Woods, brother of Frank. After discussions, the syndicate agreed that I should meet Patrick Gallagher to negotiate the sale of the remaining land on terms acceptable to all parties. I agreed a price with Patrick Gallagher that was acceptable to the syndicate. But a week later, Patrick Gallagher told me that the bank was forcing him to sell Hollywood Rath on 540 acres before they would finance the purchase of the land at Fortunestown.

The syndicate agreed to give the Gallagher Group a lockout agreement on the deal for a month, in order to organise the finance. On the same day, Patrick Gallagher asked me if I would consider buying Hollywood Rath myself. I told him that to do that, I would have to sell Dollanstown Stud on 320 acres, which was owned by Anne and myself, with no borrowings. A few days later, Patrick Gallagher told me that their bank would agree to accept Dollanstown Stud as part-payment for Hollywood Rath. We went to Bob Carroll's pub in Lucan and valued Hollywood Rath at £2,000,000; we valued Dollanstown Stud at £1,300,000. Anne was completely opposed to leaving Dollanstown, and she had the support of our close friends. I told Anne that I could get planning permission within the next twenty years on some of the land at Hollywood Rath. She very reluctantly agreed. There are moments in life to savour; this was not one of them. The story of Dollanstown is told in Part Three, but at this stage I have only one memory of that time: it was the most costly blunder of my life.

When the sale to the Gallagher Group was completed, it was the opinion of Don Reid, tax consultant, and John Caldwell, solicitor, that a figure of £1,800,000 should be deposited for payment to the Revenue. The Revenue Commissioners eventually accepted the figure because that was all that was due to them in the first place.

Profit-taking

Pat O'Toole, Tom and I, equal shareholders in Greenmount Properties Limited, decided to take some of the profits from Greenmount Properties. With the proceeds, Pat O'Toole bought a farm near Maynooth. Tom carried out improvements to his stud farm and bought a few mares with good pedigrees to breed from. With my share, I reduced my bridging loan with Allied Irish Finance by £350,000, and they released the title deeds to seventy acres on the Finglas-Ratoath road.

We had companies that had grown quickly from 1964 to 1982 through hard work and avoiding mistakes. Derek Mulligan of Smith Griffin, later Hamilton Osborne and King, and now Savills, had no difficulty persuading Tom and myself to purchase an unoccupied house in ruins on just over an acre on Eglinton Road, Donnybrook, in 1969 for £30,000. For this purchase, we used profits from our development at the Laurels, Terenure Road West.

Acting Against Good Advice

Both Gerry Tierney and Ted O'Driscoll advised us not to build on this good site on Eglinton Road. They were right, of course, but I foolishly ignored their advice. The value of the site increased to £200,000, and we often used it as collateral for short-term bridging finance. We built twenty three-storey townhouses there, and struggled to sell them for £35,000 upwards. When the houses were sold, we got back the residual value of the site, but without any building profit. To me, this will always be one of our mistakes: building on this site in the middle of a recession when we didn't have to. On reflection, it was ego on my part: wanting to be involved in upmarket houses. Up to then, we had very wisely been associated with affordable homes. Eglinton Road should have been locked away in a trust, in what Gerry Tierney called 'a little black box'.

Lynwood in Dundrum

There was one exception to this trend. Kilnamanagh Estates Limited built one hundred houses at Lynwood, only a stone's throw from Dundrum village, in 1977–78. Ken McDonald negotiated the purchase of twelve and a half acres on our behalf from the Pembroke Estates. The demand for these spacious four-bedroomed semi-detached houses was unbelievable. The timing was right. The purchasers had no difficulty selling their three-bedroomed houses and trading up. Hooke and MacDonald were the selling agents, and prices started at £20,000. This was the only profitable upmarket development we achieved.

Pine Valley, Rathfarnham

There were still successes during this time of trial. Mike Brennan's heart was always set on purchasing the best residential site in Dublin. The eighty-five-acre Ballinteer Hall, at Ballinteer Road, Rathfarnham, was owned by Mr Bill Kavanagh and his family. Mr Kavanagh was a substantial but low-key property developer who owned development sites throughout Dublin. It was very unusual for the freehold of agricultural land not to be owned by the landowner, but the freehold to this land was owned by the Pembroke Estates. The policy of the Pembroke Estates was to offer the freehold interests in the land to the leaseholder before putting it on the open market. When the leaseholder was not prepared to pay £120,000 for the freehold, John Finnegan, of Finnegan Menton, who was acting for the Pembroke Estates, put the freehold on the market. I persuaded the five directors of Grange Developments to purchase the freehold for £120,000. Jimmy Lyons was hesitant, until Bill Brennan told him that he would buy his share. Bill Brennan was extremely confident about this country's future; he continued buying land in County Meath. Later, Mr Kavanagh said to me, 'I am happy that you lads have the freehold and not some outlier.' Twenty-four years later, I met Geraldine Kavanagh and her husband, David Cantwell, at one of the rugby pitches in Willow Park, Blackrock, and it was agreed that Niall O'Donoghue, Geraldine's brother-in-law, and I, on behalf of the five directors, would value the freehold. It just so happened that the new Grange Road extension divided the Kavanagh land, leaving seventeen acres on the Pine Valley side of the new road and sixty acres on the Ballinteer side of the road. Niall and I reached an agreement that the directors would convey the freehold interest to Angel Kavanagh, Geraldine's mother, or her nominees, on the sixty-eight acres, and that Angel Kavanagh would convey the benefit of the leasehold interest on the seventeen acres to the five directors. When capital-gains tax was reduced to 20 percent, and the value of building land had rocketed, it was the time to sell. It was the best investment we ever made.

Smyths on the Green

At this point in time, we also moved into the upmarket territories of St Stephen's Green, when John Finnegan negotiated the purchase of the leasehold interest on Smyths of the Green for us, for £450,000. He agreed to buy the freehold for £120,000 from Metropolitan Estates and Property Corporation (MEPC), a leading British-based property and development business that developed and built the first shopping centre in Ireland, at Stillorgan. On the morning that we were to exchange contracts, John Finnegan telephoned to say that the syndicate which owned the leasehold would pull out of the deal if the contract was not exchanged at the agreed time, 11.30 AM. Tom and Nuala Brennan were on holiday, and I had no way of contacting Tom. To get over the problem, John Finnegan said that he would take Tom's share, in the event of Tom not being happy about the venture. Stephen Miley and I paid the £45,000 deposit and signed the contract for the leasehold.

When Tom returned, we agreed with John Finnegan that we would take one third each. A month later, Hugh Owens suggested that, since the freehold was owned outside the country, we should leave it outside. Canio, a Jersey-based company, bought the freehold from MEPC. This was the beginning of a new partnership, comprising John Finnegan, Tom Brennan and myself. Smyths on the Green was a deep, irregular-shaped building with good access to Anne's Lane, off South Anne Street. Brian O'Halloran Architects got planning permission for an arcade of shops, which dramatically increased the value of the property.

Ken MacDonald arranged a meeting at Finnegan Menton's, Merrion Row, to purchase the freehold of Lynwood in Dundrum. The stylish offices were the last word, with gilt lettering on spotless glass; the staff, friendly and attentive, were turned out impeccably. William Forward, a director, and John Finnegan, the sole estate agent for the Pembroke Estates, agreed to sell Tom and myself the freehold. John Finnegan, may he rest in peace, was a cutthroat competitor when steering his yacht in dragon-racing championships. He had one of the best property brains in the country; time spent in his company was usually illuminating, reflecting a humour that was deep and to the point. He used his connections to negotiate the largest office letting at Central Park, Sandyford, to Eircell, in 2002, at a rent of €5,200,000 per year.

Jim Gleeson was negotiating the purchase of eighty-nine acres of land in Sandyford on our behalf. He was the right man for this job. If Tom and I, as builders, appeared, the asking price might increase.

Meanwhile, Finnegan Menton put 'Smyths on the Green' up for sale, with the new planning permission for a shopping arcade. It sold quickly and for a very good price: that gave us enough cash to pay for the Sandyford land.

Catch a Falling Star: The End of the Age of Optimism

Fine Gael Finance Minister Richie Ryan was a man possessed of an understated sense of humour. It was needed, for he was pilloried on a weekly basis as 'Red Richie Ruin' on the famous *Hall's Pictorial Weekly* TV show, which did more to 'take out' the 1973-77 Fine Gael-Labour coalition government than their political opponents, Fianna Fáil. Few, though, were smiling when, at the official opening of Norfin House, the new headquarters of the expanding Northern Bank Finance Corporation, the Minister for Finance announced the introduction of capital gains tax and a new wealth tax. Like many other taxes, it was a good idea in theory. But it did not take sufficient account of people who had significant assets but lacked sufficient income to pay this new tax. Gerry Tierney was furious, and said: 'If I had known that the Minister for Finance was going to announce the introduction of a wealth tax and a capital gains tax at the official opening of our new offices, I would have asked somebody else.'

When Fianna Fail was behind, and struggling, in the 1977 general election campaign, they promised the electorate the sun, moon and stars: they would abolish rates on residential houses, and get rid of motor tax. The result, unsurprisingly, was a landslide victory for them in the election. It took a decade to recover from this recklessness. Mismanagement and overspending by successive governments crippled the Irish economy. Our budget deficits soared and the national debt spiralled out of control. Public-sector employment was a third of the total workforce. Despite Mr. Haughey's warning about 'living way beyond our means', wage inflation and excessive consumer spending continued.

The development at Kilnamanagh

Chapter Ten

Bitterness and Resentment: The Ultimate Defeat

In the late 1970s, Tom and I discussed various methods of giving Donal O'Carroll, Ken Woodley and Tim Miley a share of the profits. In the end, we agreed to form three new building companies: Milewood Construction, Lansdowne Construction and Windsor Park Homes. Tom and I each held a 15 percent share in each company. All three companies got off to a great start, building affordable houses on land we owned in Tallaght and Clonsilla. The three companies purchased land at market value in Templeogue, Glenageary, Monkstown, Newtownpark Avenue, Mount Merrion and Woodbrook. We were halfway through building luxury houses on these sites when the recession started. Trouble with a capital 'T' was waiting around the corner.

After two decades of a mostly perfect business career, Tom and I were about to experience our time of difficulty. As in all falls, we were the victims of our own flaws. We ignored the warning signals and continued on in the same old way in a different world. Space and time were critical factors in an economy where property prices were in freefall. In what was a mini-post-Celtic Tiger collapse, the price of agricultural land dropped by 25 percent and building land halved in value. Let me give a good personal example: the best offer we received for the sale of two hundred fully developed sites at Hartstown in Clonsilla, ready to build, was £700,000. These two hundred developed sites were valued, and could have sold for £1,900,000 six months before the Gallagher crash. This offer was rejected. Our borrowings never exceeded 40 percent of asset value until the sudden drop in values because of the Gallagher collapse.

Tom and I became worried that we could be exposed with personal guarantees that we had given to companies that had borrowings. We arranged to meet Luke Mooney, managing director of Trinity Bank, a personal friend, to discuss our situation. He told us that we were wasting our time trying to negotiate with the banks ourselves. What we needed, he said, was a professional who would act on our behalf. He said: 'The person for that job is a friend of yours, Joe.' I thought for a moment and replied: 'Only if you ask him, and give him all the details.' The man he was proposing was my friend Laurence Crowley.

Laurence went through the accounts for all the companies with Sheila Nolan. Tom and I took him on a tour of all the sites. He wrote to the institutions, informing them that we were solvent, and only needed time in order to have our overdrafts and personal guarantees cleared in full.

Our companies had made profits year by year. We never told any creditors anything but the truth. If we had to tell people that they would have to wait a month or two for payment, we told them. Our track record enabled us to persuade the builders' suppliers, including Roadstone and Readymix Concrete, to extend our credit period when necessary. We made absolutely sure that our sub-contractors were always paid up to date. They all responded favourably, except Allied Irish Finance.

We needed cash, and fast. We got it, too. Grange Developments paid us £400,000 for the twenty acres of land on the Malahide Road that we had bought from Mr Dickie. Uncle John paid me £320,000 for the seventy acres on the Finglas/Ratoath Road, near Mulhuddart. None of these lands had borrowings, but we borrowed £650,000 from Lombard and Ulster Bank; we worked day and night to get those houses built and sold. The money began pouring in, from the sites at Glenageary, Monkstown, Newtownpark Avenue, Rathfarnham, Mount Merrion and Woodbrook, to clear the debts and personal guarantees.

Chapter Eleven

Disappearing Millions – and a Mareva Injunction

I had agreed with Allied Irish Finance that if there was ever a shortfall in my personal guarantees, we would give Allied Irish Finance up to a maximum of £800,000 when we developed or sold the eighty-nine acres at Sandyford. At this stage, the eight-nine acres were zoned residential with good freehold title, and free of any encumbrances. Allied Irish Finance were very unhappy about sharing the title deeds with Lombard and Ulster Bank, so they carried out a valuation on the eighty-nine acres. It was a very low valuation, because Dublin County Council was undecided as to which of two routes the M50 would take. Option one was straight through the middle of our land in Sandyford; the second option was down by the Leopardstown Racecourse. At first, the Racing Board was completely opposed to the route interfering with their property. Tom Brennan arranged to meet Jim Bolger, a member of the Racing Board. Tom brought all the relevant drawings to the meeting and pointed out the advantages of having the M50 beside Leopardstown Racecourse. He also advised Jim that the racecourse could get a significant amount of money in compensation claims. Once it had been ratified that the route for the M50 would go by Leopardstown, the value of our eighty-nine acres was now clearly established. The intervention of Tom Brennan and Jim Bolger speeded up a decision to take the Leopardstown route – something that was likely to happen anyway.

I first met George Russell in 1965, when he was acting for Stephen Tracy, a farmer who lived between Sandyford and Glencullen, County Dublin. George began acting for my brother, Pa, after I purchased the Lucan land with Noel Fox. George Russell also worked on several transactions for us over the years, including the purchase of Dollanstown and Hollywood Rath. Uncle John also transferred his legal work to George Russell. George was everyone's idea of a country solicitor: courteous and kindly, with a calm sense of humour. He sat behind a desk piled with files, looking more like a farmer than a solicitor. There were photographs on the walls of him receiving rosettes at the RDS, showing some of his pedigree Hereford cattle, and as a young motorbike-racing enthusiast in the Isle of Man. If I wanted advice, he was always approachable, and infinitely painstaking about what I was setting out to do.

Allied Irish Finance threatened to take court action against George Russell. We were preparing to take on Allied Irish Finance in court, if necessary, when George Russell served a Mareva Injunction on Kilnamanagh Estates Limited. This was the most extreme method to take. A Mareva Injunction is a freezing order, usually considered to be the beginning of the end of the defendant – the defendant, in this instance, being our twenty-two companies. We were required to make a full and frank disclosure of all material facts of each company in an affidavit to the court. This was pressure like never before; to make matters worse, our own solicitors, Stephen Miley, and John Walsh were abroad on holidays. We retained another firm of solicitors. They had never acted for any of our twenty-two companies and were not familiar with the background. Tom and I gave them as much information as we could recall, and they soon got to grips with our business. After four gruelling days, I signed the Affidavit for the High Court for the following Monday morning.

In the High Court, Gerry Danagher, barrister for George Russell, wanted me to be held in contempt of court for not disclosing two companies: Canio and Gasche. Mr Justice Costello asked my barrister if I could attend the following Monday. I jumped from my seat to tell my barrister that I was here now. I wanted it over and done with. I explained that Mr Russell acted for both companies, Canio and Gasche, on behalf of Bedell Cristin, so why would I tell a barefaced lie, since Mr Russell knew and acted for both companies? Mr Justice Costello accepted my apology when I told him of the enormous amount of work that had had to be done in preparing the affidavit in such a short time.

Stephen Miley and John Walsh returned, and resumed as our legal team. At this point, the colourful Gerry Danagher, Counsel for Mr Russell, said that the plaintiff was concerned about the 'disappearing millions'.

It did not take long for our travails to reach the media world. This headline-grabbing article appeared in the *Phoenix* magazine on 6 December 1985, under the headline 'DISAPPEARING MILLIONS':

Monday December 9th is the date for the next stage in the High Court drama that looks like challenging the Bula saga for the title of Commercial Controversy of the Year.

In the High Court again will be that celebrated construction twosome, Tom Brennan and Joe McGowan. Last August, Dublin solicitor, George A. Russell, secured an order requiring the boys to disclose full details of all companies with which the duo are associated. Unfortunately, the existence of two companies – Canio Ltd and Elvy Ltd – seemed to slip their mind when making the disclosure, and on Monday a motion for contempt of court against them is due for hearing.

But the really fascinating part of this case is the rate at which *millions* have been disappearing – or so 'tis claimed. The plaintiff has stated in court that over ten million has disappeared from the list of joint assets since December 1983.

Goldhawk will be pleased to receive full information on the background to this saga of the disappearing millions.

Roger Kenny, our barrister, said: 'This is pure sensationalism. I have been acting for these companies for almost twenty years and I know perfectly well they don't have a million to spare, never mind ten.' I only wish that the 'disappearing millions' were real. Our legal team and ourselves presented sufficient details to the High Court to ensure that George Russell was unsuccessful in getting a Mareva Injunction against Kilnamanagh Estates. In the meantime, Allied Irish Finance had taken court action against Kilnamanagh Estates, Tom Brennan and myself, to repay the outstanding loans. Allied Irish Finance should have taken this course to begin with, instead of getting George Russell trapped between Kilnamanagh Estates and the bank. We were particularly fortunate to have the backing of Grange Developments, which had spadefuls of cash from the sale of the 120 acres, with planning permission, to the Abbey Group. We were set to go.

On the second day in court with Allied Irish Finance, and before Ted O'Driscoll and myself were to be questioned on the undertaking of the £800,000 from the sale of Aiken's land, the barristers agreed to an adjournment to see if a settlement could be reached. We agreed terms that had been proposed by Laurence Crowley two years previously. Allied Irish Finance would receive 50 percent of the proceeds from the sale of Hollywood Rath instead of the £800,000 from Aiken's land.

Time and again, I used to drop in to George Russell to update him on the progress that we were making to resolve this misunderstanding. Our monthly lunch in Buswells continued. I am convinced to this day that there were quite a few who regretted their inability to come to terms with our survival. We paid George Russell £125,000 to cover all their legal costs, without sending it to the Taxing Master. When everything was settled, George thanked Tom and myself.

One story from this time illustrates the importance of luck. Anne was at a lunch party in the beautiful Corbally Stud, Maynooth, then owned by Sean and Hanna Collins; she knew most of the guests there, including Donald and Hillary Pratt and Ken and Nuala Wall.

Ken told Anne to get me or Tom to telephone him as soon as possible, about an urgent matter. I phoned him early the next morning and he told me that a professional person in Dublin was about to buy our Kilnamanagh debt of £650,000 from Lombard and Ulster Bank. I phoned Tom and he told me to get in touch with his brother, Mike, immediately – which I did. Mike said: 'I'm not going to have that f**ker take over land which could be worth ten million, for six hundred and fifty thousand.'

Within hours, Mike went to the Lombard and Ulster Bank offices and gave them a cheque to clear the debt.

Chapter Twelve

Showing Cause in Bankruptcy

One Monday morning, I left Dublin for a meeting in England. That evening I was in the George Hotel in Stamford with Richard Watkinson, estate agent, when Stephen Miley telephoned me to say that I had been declared a bankrupt in the High Court that morning, with no legal representation. He told me not to panic, but to get back to Dublin in the morning, so that we could do something about the situation. That was easier said than done. It was not very fashionable to be a bankrupt in 1989.

This all happened because, due to an oversight, I had failed to respond to the debtor's summons from the Northern Bank in Grafton Street to repay a loan of £32,000. It was the only personal debt I had, other than the personal guarantees.

In the context of things, I could have – and should have – paid it off. Stephen Miley, who used to ride out at Hollywood Rath two or three mornings a week, was preparing to ride in the Madhatter's Charity race, and assured Anne that everything would be all right. When I reached Dublin Airport, my farm manager, George Dowling, was there to collect me. I arrived home mid-morning and had tea with Mr Murray, a perfect gentleman, who had been asked by the official assignee to do an inventory of the contents of Hollywood Rath. The official assignee certainly didn't waste any time. I produced documentation which clearly stated that Anne Marie owned the entire contents, and that was the end of that.

Stephen Miley and John Walsh, a partner in Miley and Miley, and Esmond Smyth, barrister, prepared an exceptionally good case for the following Monday, before Judge Hamilton in the High Court. Judge Hamilton agreed that I should be allowed to show cause in bankruptcy and not be declared a bankrupt. My solicitors also pointed out that the highly respected Laurence Crowley was now effectively running the companies until our personal guarantees had been satisfied. There is a distinct difference between showing cause and being a bankrupt. 'Showing cause' allowed me to operate a bank account and continue as a director in twenty-two companies in Ireland and a few in the UK. During five years of 'Showing Cause' in bankruptcy, every transaction had to be approved by the official assignee.

Bankruptcy is best for those who come to it in debt with assets worth less than their market value. Our assets, even though their value had fallen, were still worth more than our borrowings. Every six months we appeared before Justice Hamilton in the High Court to bring him up to date on our progress. The official assignee, on a few occasions, requested the court to declare me a bankrupt. Justice Hamilton refused each time. He said that, as significant progress was being made, and as the official assignee had to approve each transaction, there was no need to interfere. Tim Gwyn Jones, David Johnson and Roger Wreford wrote to the official assignee, confirming that they were my sponsors and that I worked for Millkirk Limited. The assignee then asked me who was paying our children's school fees. I happened to have with me a list of the people to whom I was sending Christmas cards in Ireland and the UK. He was surprised at some of the names on my list. I told him that any one of these people was prepared to help me. I still have the list of names. The interview ended.

Showing cause in bankruptcy was probably one of the best accidents that happened to me. It slowed everything down and allowed us time to sell what we had to sell and look after what was left. I remain grateful to John Walsh, Stephen Miley, Esmond Smyth, and Lorcan Hand from Grant Thornton, for producing document after document. The official assignee, Mr G. N. Rubothan, and I even exchanged Christmas greetings in December 1993.

During this time of transition, Anne and I were attending sporting occasions in England and accepting invitations from some of the people we had entertained at St Clerans, one of our original homes, and at Dollanstown. Tim Gwyn Jones was joint master of the East Galway Hunt, and I was joint master of the Galway Blazers. You will read all about the hunting, racing, point-to-pointing, Royal Ascot and more in Part Three. I have to emphasise at this stage that Tim Gwyn Jones, together with Roger Wreford, David Johnson and Jim Beardsley, played a huge part in my survival and recovery.

I first met Tim Gwyn Jones at Lough Cutra Castle, Gort, County Galway. It was the beginning of a friendship that has lasted since 1972. Tim is a meticulous person, who reads relevant papers carefully and has amazing powers of retention. He has a remarkable instinct for property and is a man of means, with a significant collection of paintings. He attends and gives the best parties, and enjoys skiing.

Roger Wreford hates overheads, takes his responsibilities seriously and is never fazed by anyone. Anne and I were guests at his chalet in Meribel, France, on many occasions. We had met Roger and his wife, Roz, with David Johnson, during a skiing holiday in 1975. Roger had shares in a textile business with Trevor Boardwell and has income from industrial units he developed at Slough, off the M4.

Jim Beardsley is another person whose friendship and support I must acknowledge. Jim was an engineer in coal mining before starting Beardsley Theobold Estate Agents and Financial Consultants in the East Midlands. They expanded to over twenty offices and sold to the Halifax Building Society for £18,000,000 in 1986. Sadly, Jim fell off his horse and died of a massive heart attack while hunting in October 1989, just after the European three-day event in Burghley.

he two-storey house built by my father and his brothers: Opposite the farm buildings and the old ouse, now the granary. My father with Rocky (Marciano).

om Doherty (Tom the shop) with his children: Rosearie, Stephen, T.J. and Joan.

om Doherty's niece Patsy Dermody (Patricia Kennedy).

I married Anne
Marie Berkeley a
the Augustinian
Church, John's
Lane Dublin, on
September 197

Anne Marie with
father Christoph
entering the Joh
Lane Church.

...he Shelbourne Hotel, St Stephen's Green following our marriage. Jim McGowan, Mrs. Margaret ...keley, Christopher Berkeley junior, Madeleine Berkeley, Frank Dunne, best man, bride and groom, ...emary Berkeley, Pa McGowan, Mrs. Kate McGowan, Roger Berkeley, Christopher Berkeley snr, ...ry McGowan, Pageboys and Flower Girls, John O'Dwyer, Margaret Toolan, Mary O'Dwyer, Anthony ...abe.

...stown House and farm, Clonsilla County Dublin - our first home, 1971.

St Clerans, Craughwell, Co Galway, 1973.

St Clerans dining room. The hand-blocked Japanese wallpaper, the breakfast table at large bow window. At night, candles were the only source of lighting.

Frank Dunne, Dot Tubridy,
Senator Ted Kennedy, Anne Marie, Senator
John Tunney, Anne Marie Achmann,
Pat Lawford and self in the library in
St Clerans.

avy Lad (Dessie Hughes) jumps the last hurdle clear of the Queen Mother's horse, Sunnyboy, to win
e Sun Alliance Novice Hurdle at Cheltenham 1975.

avy Lad (Dessie Hughes) passes Tied Cottage (Tommy Carberry), and Sommerville (Jeff King) to
n the Cheltenham Gold Cup, 1977.

Davy Lad and Dessie Hughes are led into the winner's circle by Anne Marie to a deafening receptio from the Irish on St Patrick's Day, 1977.
Below, being presented with the Cheltenham Gold Cup by The Marquess and Marchioness d'Aulan. Mick O'Toole, the trainer on far left.

Taoiseach Liam Cosgrave, presenting me with the bronze trophy (by Gary Trimble) in the Phoenix
rk after winning the Madhatters Race in July 1973. Also Sir John Arnott and Basil Brindley who
shed third.

rtstown's powerful finishing speed up the Cheltenham hill won by three lengths and was installed
ourite to win the Champion Hurdle the following year.

rkhill (Dessie Hughes) jumping the last hurdle to win easily at Leopardstown. Three weeks later, he
n the Sun Alliance Hurdle at Cheltenham 1976.

Bessie Hughes and Parkhill, the favourite, with Anne Marie in the winner's enclosure, after winning the Sun Alliance Hurdle at Cheltenham, 1976.

Anne Marie leading in Hartstown (Niall Madden) the winner, and favourite, of the Waterford Crystal Novice Hurdle at Cheltenham, 1981.

Catherine, our eldest daughter, at pony camp Burghley 1990.

Van de Vater with Catherine and Joseph at Badminton 1989.

Joseph, our son, at Pony Camp Burghley 1990.

Anne Marie and Hermon, competing at the Ward Union Hunters' Trials at Abbeyville.

Joseph in his Willow Park rugby gear.

Stephen O'Shea tennis coach with Christine.

Anne Marie, Catherine and Joseph 1987.

Captain Mark Philips designed an exciting and successful cross-country course for the Championships at Burghley, 1989

Joe's Bad Day

SPLASH!

That all is not plain sailing on the event scene was demonstrated by Joe McGowan and Private Deal at Punchestowns. Of course if Joe really wanted to go sailing he should have brought a boat. As for swimming, well he wasn't really dressed for the occasion. However, there is no doubt that whatever he intended, this time out Joe took a bath on Private Deal!

was my mistake, approaching the water jump much too fast.

rode Poulinargrid to win the Joseph O'Reilly Memorial Hunters Chase at Fairyhouse, 1979.

Thornacre and myself winning a Point-to-Point at Fairyhouse 1981.

Nancy Twomey with her pride and joy, Private Deal, 1987.

Anne on her favourite hunter, Disney, at Raymond and Joan Keogh's Ward Union Stag Hunt, Lawn Meet, 1978.

At Centaur's Leap, Burghley in 1989.

Our best performance so far, at the British Olympic Selection Trials at Holker Hall, Cumbria, August 1988, to finish 10th.

at Gallagher, Lurga, Charlestown, Catherine
n my shoulders, Mrs Pat Gallagher and
my uncle John Dolan. Pat and uncle John
orked together for many years.

hristine with Safety Pin and Jane Kennedy,
fter coming third in the Pony Championship
DS, 1995.

Tom Brennan had a half share in Hartstown.
My brother Pa with Tom, studying the form
before the race at Cheltenham, 1981.

With Kevin Molloy and John Wright, 2017.
Anthony Kenny and Jim Gleeson, 2009.

Van de Vater riding Priva
Deal in the dressage at
Punchestown, 1994.

With Bill Buller and
Stephen Miley at
Hollywood Rath Horse
Trials, 1987.

Facing; Queen Elizabeth
congratulating Van de
Vater on finishing 2nd,
riding Fenella Freya, at
Windsor Park.

Sonya Rodgers presenting Tom and Nuala Brennan with the trophy, John Kirby, Nuala's nephew on ri[g]

At home, L to R: Justin Williams, Roy Pettey (distinguished artist), Brian O'Halloan,
Raymond Keaveney, Trevor Stewart, Anne Marie, Van de Vater and Nora Pat Stewart.

My other loyal friend, David Johnson, inherited over one thousand acres in Lincolnshire and supplied the supermarkets there with potatoes and vegetables. David used to complain about the supermarkets squeezing his tight margins. He built a state-of-the-art crisp factory at Corby, and sold out for a very good profit. Appletree House, in Brancaster, was the perfect package for David's getaway weekend. The house, on the edge of the village, had been discreetly modernised, and overlooked the Broads, with views across to the Royal West Norfolk Golf Club, a natural links course, ranked seventeenth in England. The tennis court and heated outdoor pool were hidden in five acres of gardens. Anne, our children and myself spent the last week in July at Appletree each summer. David was a true friend. Sadly, he died in 2001, aged sixty-six, after a brief illness.

David Johnson agreed to make available to Dollanstown Limited, the company that owned Hollywood Rath, £380,000 to completely clear my bridging loan with Allied Irish Finance. Allied Irish Finance would not release the title documents until all the loans by the various companies and our personal guarantees were cleared. Anne and I had equal shares in Dollanstown Limited, the company that owned Hollywood Rath on 470 acres. I remember that, at the time, both David Johnson and Roger Wreford advised me to put Hollywood Rath up for sale, while I was still in control. I followed their advice. I appointed Anthony Wardell and my good friend John Inge, a senior partner with Knight Frank Rutley, as joint selling agents, with Willie Coonan Auctioneers of Maynooth. They came to inspect Hollywood Rath. The purchaser would have an option to buy an additional 170 acres.

Dermot Weld introduced a syndicate from the United States; they were the only overseas people to express an interest in Hollywood Rath. The syndicate brought various advisors to inspect Hollywood Rath. I met them in London on two occasions. At our second meeting, they produced an option document with many conditions, all favouring themselves. The syndicate would pay £1,000 for a twelve-month option, and would complete the purchase only if they could raise the £2 million finance required. George Russell and I got the impression that they were very rich. We rejected their ridiculous proposal and withdrew Hollywood Rath from the market at that time.

Chapter Thirteen

My Introduction to Building in England

Anne and I attended the wedding of Anne-Louise Ottewell at King's Newton Hall in Leicestershire. We sat at the same table as Jim and Mary Beardsley. When I told Jim that I was finding it difficult to get into the London property scene, Jim stressed that the property market and building industry was not confined to London. I spent the following weekend with Jim and Mary at their home, The Vicarage, in Laxton, just off the A1, between Newark and Retford in Nottinghamshire. On Saturday, we looked at different opportunities, including an eight-acre site at Tuxford, just off the A1. The site had two entrances and all the services laid on from phase one that had been developed and completed four years previously. I could put music to this, I reflected.

Jim took me to Spencer Estate Agents in Retford on Monday morning and instructed them to advertise the land for sale by tender. Jim held 50 percent of the company that owned the land. Five weeks later, Jim, and Dereck Whitehall, a director of the company that owned the eight acres, went to the estate agents to open the tender envelopes. We were the highest bidders, but what surprised me was that there was a difference of only 5 percent between the highest and lowest tenders. Jim then said to the agent: 'This man, Joe, has given me some of the best hunting days in Ireland.' Jim then introduced me to solicitor Gary Reynolds of Hunt Dickens, and to architect John Finch. Roger Wreford formed a company called Millkirk Limited, and David Johnson and Tim Gywn Jones became directors and shareholders with him. Millkirk Limited provided the finance to purchase the land. I did not become a shareholder of Millkirk because I was still sorting out my financial difficulties in Ireland.

The architects, John Finch and Richard Rogers, produced a very good layout of the site, with four different designs, two bungalow types and two house types. The agents were confident that this mix would meet the demand for houses in that part of the country. The single-storey bungalows were tailored for people who were down-sizing. I was lucky to find an excellent foreman, Jim Parker. He was a sports fanatic, and a happy family man, with experience and confidence. This was like starting all over again. I got the same satisfaction in opening the showhouses as I did at Foxrock in 1964. It was pure magic. Roger Wreford checked the progress and accounts every month. David Johnson attended the occasional monthly meeting. When I met Tim Gwyn Jones socially, he would sometimes refer to Millkirk: 'Are we making money? Have you found another site? Well, get on with it.'

Powerscourt

Fintan Gunne telephoned me one evening in 1992. There was great excitement in his voice: 'I have a big one for Roger and his wealthy friends, a partnership with the Slazenger family to develop Powerscourt.' In 1961, the Powerscourt Estate at Enniskerry, County Wicklow, was bought by the Slazenger family. The house was severely damaged by a fire in 1974. They replaced the roof and carried out a temporary renovation on two reception rooms to accommodate functions and weddings. The Slazenger family received full planning permission to construct an eighteen-hole golf course and build two hundred houses on the part of the estate nearest the village of Enniskerry, and to convert the stables and outbuildings to residential. There was a condition that the building of the houses and the restoration of Powerscourt House would take place at the same time. This required huge funding, so the Slazenger family were looking for a partner. Roger Wreford and David Johnson found it hard to believe that such a place and such an opportunity existed so near to Dublin. Roger was so excited that he was already planning in his mind – as Roger always does – which of the courtyard houses was best positioned for himself. David and Roger got confirmation from their banks in London that they had funds to develop this exciting, once-off opportunity.

Fintan Gunne took Roger, David and Michael Slazenger to Patrick Guilbaud's for lunch. As things turned out, however, we did not go through with the project. It was my fault: I made the awful blunder of undervaluing the residential land. This was due to my lack of confidence in the property market, which was still recovering from the recession. I take the blame for the deal not proceeding. Fintan forgave me. The Slazenger family retained full ownership and have made a huge success of the Powerscourt estate.

Chapter Fourteen

How We Almost Sent Dublin County Council Officials to Jail

In 1978, we became embroiled in an extraordinary dispute with Dublin County Council, which almost resulted in us sending the council to jail! It began around 1972, when Paddy Langan, estate agent, introduced Tom and myself to Mr Dickie, an extremely prosperous tillage farmer in the Swords-Malahide area. We purchased from Mr Dickie twenty-one acres on the Malahide Road for £165,000. The location was good, convenient to Dublin Airport and Dublin Port. After receiving detailed planning permission to build two factories on the twenty-one acres, we offered the property for sale. We accepted an offer of £450,000, and exchanged contracts with Page Bar, an English PLC. Two days before the completion of the sale was due, in April 1974, one of the English banks appointed a receiver to Page Bar, and so the sale fell through. This was the only setback that we experienced during the very bad economic period brought about by the energy crisis in 1973.

Meanwhile, Mike Brennan and Tom Brennan had purchased fifty-one acres from a few different landowners adjacent to the twenty-one acres we had purchased from Mr Dickie on the Malahide Road. This gave us a land parcel of seventy-one acres, on which we planned to build affordable houses. Dublin County Council refused to grant planning permission. Grange Developments Limited appealed this decision to An Bord Pleanála. Again, planning permission was refused. We then applied to the High Court for compensation. The High Court rejected Grange Developments' application. Grange Developments Limited then appealed to the Supreme Court, and the Supreme Court overruled the High Court decision, which meant that Grange Developments Limited was entitled to compensation. In July 1988, the arbitrator, Mr Sean McDermott, valued the compensation due to Grange Developments at £1,750,000. Getting the compensation money, however, proved to be a prolonged process. The following article from the *Irish Times* explains the compensation saga:

RECEIVER APPOINTED TO BANK ACCOUNT OF DUBLIN COUNTY COUNCIL

The High Court appointed a receiver over the bank accounts of Dublin County Council at a special sitting in Dublin yesterday. This followed a decision by the Council at a meeting on Tuesday night not to authorise the expenditure required to pay a planning compensation award of £1,900,000 made to the property developers, Grange Developments Ltd.

Mr Justice Murphy also decided to send papers in the case to the Director of Public Prosecutions following claims by the plaintiffs that the Council was in contempt of court.

Mr Stephen Miley, solicitor for Grange Developments, was appointed receiver over the accounts of the Council at the Allied Irish Bank, Nos 7–12 Dame Street, Dublin, until the compensation bill was discharged. On the question of contempt, Mr Justice Murphy stated he was not saying that the Council or any of its officers or officials or elected representatives had committed such a criminal offence, but it was appropriate for him to send the papers to the DPP.

The Council had been directed on March 14 to pay the money within seven days, and this ruling was upheld by the Supreme Court. The High Court yesterday refused to grant any further stay on that order.

The Grange case arose out of a 1980 decision by the Council to refuse planning permission for a large housing development on seventy-one acres of agricultural land at Mountgorry near Swords, County Dublin. The company's compensation claim was opposed unsuccessfully through the courts and their solicitor yesterday put the amount now due, including interest, at £1,871,917.

An affidavit read to the court by Mr Miley stated that he had spoken by telephone with Mr George Redmond, manager of the County Council, who, he said, confirmed to him that the Council had resolved to refuse to pay the amount of the judgement and that he, as County Manager, had no authority to pay the plaintiffs.

Counsel for the defendant, Mr John Gallagher, barrister-at-law, said that Mr Redmond disagreed with the terminology used by Mr Miley. The elected members of the Council had not defied the court; they had simply refused to pass a motion authorising the excess expenditure required to pay the compensation.

Mr Justice Murphy said that the law of the land must be obeyed by everybody. Legislation as enacted by the Oireachtas was often complex but when the rights and duties of the parties were made clear, then it was manifest that the laws must be obeyed. Anything else was anarchy, he said.

Mr Miley's affidavit, which was submitted yesterday morning, stated that on Tuesday night the elected members of the County Council voted against the advice of their law department and refused to pay the compensation.

It was just, equitable and convenient that the court should exert its authority to the fullest extent in the speediest way possible with a view to publicly demonstrating that the law must be obeyed.

The persistent refusal to pay Grange Developments had caused the company severe financial embarrassment and had placed it in financial jeopardy. In a separate case, it had consented to a judgement against it from Allied Irish Banks for £176,000 on the basis that Dublin County Council would pay the compensation.

'The resolution of the elected members evidences a clear intention to defy the orders of the court,' the affidavit said. The unconscionable delays to date, the financial position of the plaintiff, the availability of funds to the defendant and the urgency of the matter meant that it was now imperative that a receiver be appointed over the defendant's funds.

Mr Nial Fennelly, SC, for the plaintiffs, explained that Grange Developments was seeking a receiver to be appointed until the compensation bill was discharged.

Mr Justice Murphy adjourned the case until the afternoon to allow the Council to respond. He added that there was another course open to the plaintiffs and that was to apply for a committal. Mr Fennelly replied: 'We want our money.' He added that committal proceedings might be what the county councillors wanted.

At the resumed hearing, Mr Gallagher said the terms of the motion put before the meeting on Tuesday night had asked the council to authorise excess expenditure of £1.900,000 in the current financial year.

They had not defied the court, as reported. They simply refused to pass that motion. He asked the court not to appoint a receiver, in order to allow the County Manager time to convene another meeting of the Council on the matter.

Mr Justice Murphy said that day in day out, the courts encountered husbands who were unable or unwilling to make maintenance payments as ordered by the court. These were often people in unfortunate circumstances and emotional distress but they had to be told that orders of the court must be obeyed.

'The law of the land must be obeyed by everybody and, if they don't, they go to Mountjoy,' Mr Justice Murphy said.

Mr Gallagher asked that no receiver be appointed and that the application be adjourned to April 3, to enable the manager to call another meeting of the elected representatives.

Mr Fennelly, for the plaintiffs, said they had applied for compensation in 1981. They got a judgement from the High Court on the 14th of this month. The Council then sought a stay and had been granted seven days, which meant the money was now payable.

Day in, week out, the Council, as a public body, applied for orders and invoked the jurisdiction of the courts. How could they credibly ask for such an order again?

Accusing the Council of 'a dishonest charade', he said the only thing the plaintiffs could do in the circumstances was to ask that a receiver be appointed over the bank accounts of the Council.

The Council were asked to pass a resolution and 'with their eyes open' at a five-hour meeting they had decided not to pass it. 'They have cocked a snook at the courts,' he said. The courts' time had been wasted for several years past. Always at the back of the Council's mind there had been the intention: 'we won't pay anyway'.

The 'correct, just and practical remedy' was to send in a receiver. The sheriff could be sent in but it would be a long process for him to collect £2,000,000 in County Council chattels. Mr Justice Murphy said that his order of March 14 had given the plaintiffs liberty under Section 41 of the Arbitration Act to enforce an award made by Mr Sean McDermott, the property arbitrator, on July 20, 1988 in the same manner as if it were a judgement or an order of the court.

He had been asked at the time by the Council to put a stay on the order. He had explained that effectively this was a request to the court to prevent Grange from collecting the monies due to them. It would have been illogical to grant a stay by way of interim injunction. He had not wanted to create unnecessary difficulties for the parties and had granted a stay of seven days so the matter could be mentioned in the Supreme Court. The Chief Justice had refused to extend the stay.

It had been said the Council was deliberately and consciously defying the order of the High Court and the Supreme Court. Copies of newspapers had been put in evidence to this effect. The crucial passage with regard to allegations of flouting the courts was set out in the affidavit of Mr Miley, where he made a very serious allegation over what he claimed was said in a television conversation with the county manager.

Counsel for the defendant informed him there was a misunderstanding of what the manager said to Mr Miley. It would be impractical to ask Mr Redmond to prepare and swear an affidavit. He would not entertain the request for another adjournment and accordingly he would accede to the plaintiff's application to appoint a receiver by way of equitable execution.

Costs were reserved and the hearing concluded. Grange Developments Ltd were represented by Mr Nial Fennelly sc, instructed by Mr Stephen Miley, solicitor. Dublin County Council were represented by Mr John Gallagher, barrister-at-law.

Some newspaper reports were confusing, and I can fully understand the outrage as a result of the largest compensation claim of this type ever. Grange Developments got the £1,900,00 compensation and still retained ownership of the land in question. All this compensation could have been avoided if the council had granted us planning permission in the first place to build affordable homes on the seventy-one acres of land at Grange Developments. Ten years later, Owen Kirk, Michael Cannon and

MILEY & MILEY

SOLICITORS
COMMISSIONERS FOR OATHS

35 MOLESWORTH STREET
DUBLIN 2

TELEPHONE NOS.
(01) 785122, 785626, 785956
FAX 619935
D.D.E. 8

PRESS RELEASE

DANIEL O'CONNELL MILEY
ALEC DIAMOND
STEPHEN O'CONNELL MILEY

UNA FLYNN
JOHN G. WALSH
TANIA SLESS
PETER McGUINNESS
PATRICIA BOYD

OUR REF
YOUR REF

At approximately 3.00 p.m. yesterday 22nd March, 1989 the High Court appointed me Receiver by way of Equitable Execution (without salary or security) over the Bank Accounts of Dublin County Council at Allied Irish Banks Plc., 7/12 Dame Street, Dublin, 2 and over the Rates due to Dublin County Council to such extent as the funds in the Bank Accounts may be inadequate to satisfy a Judgment of Grange Developments Limited obtained on the 16th March, 1989 in a sum of £1,871,917 together with interest thereon.

At my request the Manager of Dublin County Council, Mr. George Redmond and the Council's Chief Financial Officer attended my office at 6.00 p.m. yesterday evening. They were accompanied by two members of the Council's Law Department and three members of Allied Irish Banks Plc., including Mr. Rory O'Connor, the Bank's Law Agent.

Following a brief meeting a cheque in the full amount due to Grange Developments Ltd., in respect of the Judgment was tendered and accepted by me.

I anticipate an Application will be made later today to the High Court to discharge me as Receiver of Dublin County Council. I will consent to such Application provided I have received value for the cheque before the Application is made.

DATED THIS 23RD DAY OF MARCH, 1989.

STEPHEN O'CONNELL MILEY.
RECEIVER OF DUBLIN COUNTY COUNCIL

Cathal Cannon purchased the shares of Grange Developments Limited, including the seventy-one acres. When they received planning permission for a residential development, Dublin County Council recovered the £2 million compensation paid to Grange Developments, but without interest.

During the controversy, one letter, by a Terry Sudway, to the *Irish Times* caught my attention. Titled 'Mr Flynn's Bill', in reference to the then Environment Minister, it said:

Sir, I write in relation to your editorial entitled 'Mr Flynn's Bill' published in the *Irish Times* (July 25).

For many years now as a practitioner in the field of compulsory purchase and planning compensation, I have read in the newspapers and listened on radio and television to reporting which endlessly talks of loopholes in the Planning Act. It is difficult to find time to begin to reply fully to the nonsense trotted out by reporters in both the newspapers and the television, but when one reads an editorial in your paper, which seemingly has taken on board the nonsense in relation to planning compensation, then one despairs of ever achieving sanity in the planning compensation process.

Firstly, there is no loophole in the Planning Act and secondly, the Act is not flawed. Obviously, none of the people who consider these two points to be arguable have ever been at the receiving end of the planning process nor had their property compulsorily acquired from them. I acted in the Viscount Securities case and I can assure you that the Planning Act is not flawed in regard to that case and its decision. What I suggest is flawed, however, is that local authorities continue to expend public money running endless cases to the High Court and the Supreme Court on points of law, which have been more than adequately answered by those bodies, in a wilful effort to negate a right given to the landowner under the laws of this country.

It is not good enough, Sir, to read in an editorial in a quality paper expansive adjectival descriptions of compensation such as 'vast compensation'.

Vast sums of compensation have not been paid under the Planning Act and I would refer you to analytical detailing on this point, available from the Department of the Environment, and, should you have any difficulty in finding it, I will be happy to supply the relevant information to you.

Compensation, for the uninitiated, and I include you in this, Sir, is only payable where someone has their constitutionally guaranteed property rights alienated in such a way as to render his land incapable of beneficial use, and for interpretation purposes, one must differentiate between designation and reservation for a purpose. Popularly and colloquially, designation is called zoning, although the word does not appear in the Irish Planning Act and reservation for a particular use for the public circumscribes, in an unfair manner, the rights which a landowner would – and is entitled to – expect to normally apply to his land.

If society must, or feels it must, impinge on these guaranteed property rights, then it is proper that society should do so but, as a corollary, it is also proper,

I submit, that if you take away a right, which is available to any citizen of the State, then it is only proper that that person should be compensated adequately for the loss inflicted on him to serve this common good.

I wonder is this concept too conservative for you, your reporters and the rest of the media. I would suggest it is not too much for the politicians to take on board and perhaps that is why legislation has not been brought forward to date to amend the legitimate right to compensation for people who have had their property interests infringed for the common good.

This is notwithstanding the fact that there has been a consistent effort on behalf of the media to influence the matter, obviously without full knowledge of the subject matter on which they are so articulate, and just to point this up for you, zoning is a non-compensatable ground for refusal of planning permission. Need I say more?

You might also like to take on board the fact that if lands are of such high amenity a special Amenity Order can be made and this is not compensatable. What more do you want?

In conclusion, let me say that if the accuracy of the other matters reported in your paper is as accurate as your reporting on planning compensation, then Heaven knows what we are reading.

– Yours, etc., T. L. Sudway, FRICS, MIAVI.

It was, even by Irish standards, an extraordinary affair. The mischievous part of me wonders how I would have coped with sending the council to jail. I would hope that the more charitable element of my personality would have spared them the jailer's key. We shall, alas, never know. I would, of course, meet John Gallagher again in even more surreal circumstances.

In 1988, I decided that the value of my share in the eighty-nine acres at Sandyford, zoned residential, had more potential than my share in Hollywood Rath. I put Hollywood Rath back on the market and received my asking price. My share of the sale cleared the personal guarantees with Allied Irish Finance.

I recall from my time at Hartstown, Clonsilla, how much my father enjoyed staying with us for the first two weeks of June every year. It was his favourite house, manageable, and surrounded by the best limestone land in the country. He used to say: 'You can see the grass growing.' When it rained after a dry spell, the result was unbelievable growth. If you left a slating lath in a field, the growth of grass would have covered it in two days. It was the very best land.

The hedge-cutting contractor, Simon Quinn, had a very good system and left all the hedges tidy. My brother Gerry would top the fields. Uncle Tom checked the cattle every day with his dog, Rover, a 'pennyfeather'. Anne McCann from Dunboyne looked after the few horses we had at the beginning. While Uncle Tom went to the pub at weekends and on Wednesday evenings, my father read and listened to the radio and told us stories. He was very comfortable pottering around with the scythe, cutting the weeds.

When my father came to visit us at Dollanstown in July 1976, he only stayed a few days, not to return for the next six years of his life. He made lame excuses for not coming back. The truth was, as my brother Pa told me, he left Dollanstown not just upset, but heartbroken at the acres of lawn that he felt cattle should be grazing. It nearly killed him to learn that our three full-time gardeners required extra help during the summer. Coming from East Mayo, where every inch of land had to be used for productive purposes, he saw this as awful waste.

My father spent the last five years in the home-place. He sold the cottage and twelve acres that went with it, and gave the entire proceeds to my brother Gerry, to help him purchase a forty-five-acre farm of good land. Gerry and his wife, Hilary, were thrilled with their good farm at Curry, County Sligo. Sadly, however, Hilary died of a brain haemorrhage within three years, at the age of thirty-one. It was an awful shock to us all. Hilary's people, Brian and Kathleen Moran, her parents, her sisters, Justina, Martina and Muriel, together with our mother and my brother Pa, helped Gerry bring up three wonderful children: Alma, Gerard and Martha. They have the same gifts of understanding, generosity and work ethic as their mother, Hilary, had. All the Morans are caring and lovely people. Gerry loves the land, cattle-dealing, and in recent years playing with his grandchildren.

Towards the end, back in the family home, my father could barely take a few steps owing to his asthma, and he died in March 1982, a month before the arrival of our first child, Catherine – the start of our family. I remember my father as a man who watched every penny, and took pride in his small collection of sovereigns. His motto throughout was: 'Pay as you go and if you can't pay, don't go.'

Part 3
A Sporting Life

Chapter Fifteen

The Galway Blazers Hunt across the Fields of Athenry

I owe a great debt of gratitude to my mentor, Daniel O'Connell Miley, solicitor, who launched me into a generation of contemporaries drawn from every background and every persuasion. This was a period of tremendous opportunities – opportunities that required finance, cool nerves and hard work. Connections are so important in life. Phil Fitzsimons, the flamboyant estate agent, and his jovial partner, Pádhraic Hassett, always kept in touch. Peter White, I consider a lifelong friend. It was Peter and his cousin, Jeremy White, who introduced Tom and myself to our very first land purchase in the heart of Terenure. I was lucky, too, meeting in my very early days Colin Holohan and Ken MacDonald, who were to play a significant part in my future life. Other friends I made were Captain Des Ringrose and the self-assured John Mulhern.

The building business is tough; politicians and purchasers only see the finished showhouse. The creation of that house is an exciting challenge: securing suitable land, meeting solicitors and occasionally barristers, architects, engineers and town planners, the hard-working sub-contractors, the frostbitten hands of the bricklayers and their helpers. From the very beginning, while working with Uncle John during my summer holidays, I knew that this was what I wanted to do for the rest of my life.

Despite our long working hours, we still attended the rugby dances at Lansdowne and Old Belvedere. Brittas Bay was the 'in' spot during the summer for the set that went to the rugby and tennis club dances. Brittas Bay, in County Wicklow, has a vast area of sand dunes and a wide stretch of beach. It was bumper-to-bumper on Sunday evenings returning to Dublin on the old roads. Then there was beagling with the Goldburn, black-tie dinner-dances, and later, the hunt balls during the Royal Dublin Horse Show, without doubt the social event of each year.

One of my friends, Jack Foley, returned to Ireland from Chicago in 1965, and introduced me to my greatest passion. While living and working in Chicago for almost ten years, Jack spent most of his leisure time with farming friends who bred and broke young horses. In the spring of 1966, I was twenty-three when Jack introduced me to horse-riding at Springfield House, Kilbride, County Wicklow, a short distance from Brittas Bay. My only previous experience was riding our mule, Speedy, bareback when I was growing up in County Mayo. Jackie Beever supervised a very well-organised riding school and she arranged that I would ride out a well-trained horse, accompanied by one of the gorgeous sisters, Vivienne or Joy Alexander, while Jack went out with the more advanced riders. One Sunday afternoon, I got my chance to ride with the advanced riders: David Kendrick was unable to ride his grey horse, Bond, and I replaced him. We hacked along for half an hour before entering the wood leading to the Coillte forest. Bond lived up to his reputation, going faster and faster; I lost control rounding the second bend, and went straight ahead into nettles and briars. I got up, scratched, and spent most of the afternoon searching for the horse. I survived – and the experience only made me more determined.

Dan Miley introduced me to the hunting set at Bel-Air, Ashford, County Wicklow – where I did not immediately fit in. At first I felt uncomfortable with a few university-educated professionals who had a way of reminding me that I hadn't been to university. I remember many expressions that Father O'Neill, Principal of Coláiste Pádraig, taught us: 'Be a good listener'; and if you are not sure of something, say, 'That sounds very interesting but I need time to think about it.' This advice helped me on many occasions, especially in my early days in sport and business. The Grafton Street set were always impeccably turned out in their hunting gear on their well-groomed horses. They didn't seem serious riders to me: after just a short appearance at the hunt and having jumped only a few obstacles, they would retire to the comfort of the hotel.

The Horseshoe Bar in the Shelbourne Hotel was the social spot for the medical and legal profession, entrepreneurs and politicians. The barmen, Jimmy Kelly, Sean Keating and John Fitzpatrick, were gifted hosts, and they had the full background of their clients. Their clients included Mr and Mrs Ben Dunne Senior; Frank Dunne; Margaret Dunne and her husband, Dr Andrew Heffernan, a racing enthusiast; John Mulhern; Jim Gleeson; Jim Stafford, the merchant from County Wexford who dealt in property and fine art; David Austin, who worked with Jeff and Michael Smurfit; Tom Kavanagh, the grain merchant from Maynooth; Daniel O'Connell Miley; and Owen Brady, who was dating the beautiful Yvonne Murphy.

At the other end of the Shelbourne Hotel was the famous Saddle Room and, in between, was the restaurant overlooking St Stephen's Green, where you would see plenty of upper business types and some of the old money. The food was consistently outstanding, with excellent service and realistically priced. Tom Brennan and I had lunch in the Saddle Room at least twice a week, when we were in Dublin for meetings. It was known as 'the Brennan and McGowan Dublin office'.

One evening, Owen Brady introduced me to his future parents-in-law, Mr Joe 'Tayto' Murphy and his bubbly wife, Bunny. Mr Murphy said to me, 'I understand you are in the construction business' – to which I replied, 'Not exactly. Tom and I are house-builders.' He then asked me, 'What section of the market are you involved in?' I told him mainly the cheaper end – to which he replied, in a sensitive manner, 'Oh, Joe, you must never use that word "cheaper". You could say "lower end of the market" or "for first-time buyers".' I have never used the word 'cheaper' since. He was surprised and impressed when I told him that I had pledged at my Confirmation that I would abstain from alcohol until I was twenty-five. In August 1968, Anne and I were invited to Joe and Bunny Murphy's Christmas party at their magnificent home in Glenageary. It was without doubt the hottest invite during the Christmas and New Year celebrations. We sat at a most interesting table with Michael and Norma Smurfit, Eamon and Joan Donnelly, and Gerry McGuinness, chairman and largest shareholder in the new Sunday newspaper the *Sunday World*, and his wife, Alma, whom Anne knew well through work. Gerry himself was responsible for the gossip section of the *Sunday World*, known as 'The Chairman's Column', where I featured for the first time. This was the beginning of invitations to the best parties.

My first outing with the Galway Blazers was at Athenry in October 1969. On the Monday night before the hunt, Captain Des Ringrose, Frank Dunne, Brian O'Connor, Lawrence Crowley, Declan Collins and John Mulhern, all of whom influenced my business for the next twenty years, stayed in the Great Southern Hotel beside the railway station in Galway. On Tuesday morning, I tried to be calm, though I was terrified of making a fool of myself. I hired an experienced grey hunter from the Daly brothers, while John Mulhern and the others got their hunters from Willie Leahy. We were not members of the hunt, so, as visitors, we paid a 'cap fee' of twelve pounds. Membership was by invitation.

Athenry, with its small fields and dry stone walls, is the perfect hunt for a beginner. On that first hunt, the rain cleared in late morning. The fox ran from a small forest; it was a very fast forty-minute run, covering some five to six miles. I don't know how many stone walls we jumped, but whatever about the song 'The Fields of Athenry', I will never forget the hunting fields of Athenry. I soon became hooked on hunting, and I planned my working life around horses. Frank Dunne, a very experienced showjump rider, bordering on international standard, introduced me to Noel O'Dwyer, whose father, Major Jed O'Dwyer, was one of Ireland's greatest showjumpers with the Irish army. Noel got me involved at novice level, riding at the gymkhanas, which brought order and discipline to my riding.

The first time I saw Anne Marie Berkeley was in the old Brown Thomas's on Grafton Street; I saw her again at a reception in the Shelbourne Hotel. That was it. My friend Jeremy White was dating a friend of Anne's, and he arranged for us to meet in the Hibernian Hotel. Then, as always, Anne dressed stylishly. Her clothes were beautiful, uncomplicated and really chic. A year later, when Anne was in New York doing an advertisement for Aer Lingus, she visited my Aunt Mary and her family in New Jersey. This is the letter my aunt wrote to my mother:

359 McCloud Drive,
Fort Lee
New Jersey
U.S.A.

August 1st '67.

Dear Katie,

I hope you are not angry at me for not writing to you sooner. Rose sent you a few lines last week. I thought Paddy would write and have some news about John coming down. I sent him a package a few months ago; there were a few things in it for you. I hope you got them. The sweaters you sent me are just beautiful; everybody wondered how you could do such beautiful work, so many different stitches. It must have taken a lot of time to make one of them. When I get straightened out with all the expenses I have this year, I'll send you something for your expense and work. This has been a busy year with weddings and I'll have two new grandchildren, Elaine in Nov and Eileen in December. They are both feeling fine. Maureen is busy buying furniture. They have found an apartment near us and it's very nice, in a two-family house, three rooms and yard. They know the people they are renting from.

We had the pleasure of meeting Anne Marie when she was here. She called me and Maureen, and Eddie picked her up at her hotel and we took her to her plane Sat night. She is just beautiful in every way. Everybody said she was the nicest girl they ever met. Joe must never let her get away. She said she enjoyed her visit down in Mayo. She must come from a wonderful family. I wrote to John after I heard from you last. I didn't receive an answer yet, but maybe he has got his problems too. I think Lena hasn't been feeling well, don't say anything about it if they don't tell you. Anne Marie said that John and Lena were going down next month. I think Paddy is getting restless if they don't decide something soon. I guess Pa might be home by this time, he sure gets around and is having a ball. This country is going to wreck and ruin, race-riots every night in all the big cities, nobody knows where and how it's going to end. Kathy's husband is OK so far and with God's help will be home by Christmas. She met him in Hawaii for a week and he looks wonderful. She gets letters every day and it keeps her busy answering them and then she's got her job to keep her busy. If you get a chance write to me.

Love,
Mary.

Anne and I got engaged in January 1971. My family were delighted, as indeed were Uncle John, Dan Miley and Tom Brennan, but especially my mother, when she realised that Anne spent most summers with her grandmother, her Uncle Roger and her Aunt Kay in Monasteraden, four miles the Boyle side of Ballaghaderreen. She said, 'Sure isn't she a country girl.' Tom Brennan married Nuala, the eldest of the attractive Moynihan sisters from County Limerick, in 1969. Anne has two sisters, Rosemary and Madeleine, and two brothers, Christopher and Roger. Christopher Berkeley, her father, worked hard to provide a comfortable upbringing for his family. He was creative, a man of natural refinement, and an entertaining companion at all times. Margaret Casey, Anne's mother, born in County Sligo, had strict traditional family values, and is a homemaker with great determination. They enjoyed their children's achievements in education, music, singing and athletics.

Our wedding in September 1971 took place in the Augustinian Church, John's Lane, unquestionably one of Dublin city's most outstanding examples of church architecture. John Ruskin (1818-1900), writer, critic, artist and philosopher, called this church 'A Poem in Stone'. Anne Marie's brothers were singing in the church choir. Anne wore a beautiful wedding dress created by Matt O'Donoghue. Margaret Toolin, Anthony McCabe and the twins John and Mary O'Dwyer were in attendance. The bridesmaids, Rosemary and Madeleine, wore silk dresses with autumnal colours. Frank Dunne was my best man, assisted by my brother Pa and Owen Brady. After the ceremony, the reception was in the Shelbourne Hotel, for 350 guests. Our wedding attracted press attention, as Anne was a successful fashion model.

The estate agent, Arthur 'Chubby' Williams, arranged that we could spend part of our honeymoon at Inverlochy Castle in the Scottish Highlands. On our arrival there, the housekeeper took us to a large comfortable bedroom. When we came downstairs to the library, we were greeted by the owner, Mrs Hobbs, a gracious woman with charm and a free spirit. The next morning, Mrs Hobbs took us around the grounds and gardens. Anne had developed a great interest in gardening as a child during her summer holidays with her uncle Roger, who was the head gardener at Coolavin House, in County Sligo. Inverlochy gave us a picnic basket for lunch when we visited the Glenfinnan Viaduct, a work of art now known as the 'Harry Potter bridge'. Inverlochy was beautiful. On the sixth day we left for the Cotswolds, staying with Jim and Mary Beardsley in Nottinghamshire on the way, then on to Bunratty Castle in County Clare, where Anne had been one of the musicians in the summer of 1967. Major Jed O'Dwyer, Anne and I received a great welcome at the banquet in the castle.

Then on to the Great Southern in Galway, where I had arranged a morning cub hunting with the Galway Blazers. We started at daylight, 6 AM; Willie Leahy provided me with a young horse that jumped well. It was a long morning and I was certainly hungry when we got back to the kennels at 8.30 AM. The next day, Anne and I went to Connemara, where Willie Leahy and his family organised the Connemara trail for visitors from every part of the world.

We spent our first Christmas at Hartstown House. Anne decorated the tall tree in the back porch, with the gifts underneath. On Christmas Eve, we had drinks for friends and neighbours. On Christmas morning we attended early Mass at Porterstown church, and called in to Jack and Aileen White for a moment. Anne's family joined us for Christmas lunch. We had a perfect Christmas, which included visiting my family in County Mayo.

Three months later, in March 1972, the sudden news that Anne's father Christopher had suffered a massive heart attack and had little prospect of survival was the first severe jolt in our lives. Roger, Anne's youngest brother, was twelve, about to start secondary school; Christopher was in second year; Rosemary had a good position in Player Wills;

Madeleine worked in the Guinness Brewery office while waiting for her call to join the RTÉ Orchestra full-time. It was sad that Mr Berkeley was not around to watch his son, Christopher, retain the Irish pole-vaulting record for nine years and his brave attempts training in South Africa, before injury, for the Los Angeles Olympics. Had he lived, he and I would surely have had good conversations about Davy Lad, Parkhill, Hartstown and Private Deal – our best horses.

Margaret Berkeley's deep faith helped her recover from the sudden loss of her husband. She guided her children, especially Roger and Christopher, still at secondary school, through college. Later, she enjoyed every moment with her grandchildren. She supported their interest in music and sport, and enjoyed the summers in England, helping our three children during pony camp at Burghley. Margaret had the time of her life travelling to the horse trials, including Badminton and Burghley, set in some of the finest estates in England, meeting our friends and the competitors, in particular Van De Vater. She took pride in her own dressmaking but cherished the suit and coat made by Hawkins of Cavendish Row, Dublin: a present from her children and myself for Christmas 1973. She appreciated the tweed bespoke tailoring, the art of coat-making and years of master cutting. They were still like new when she died on Christmas Eve 2006, thirty-three years later.

Now came a new turn in my life. The year was 1972. Charlie Bishop and Tim Gwyn Jones were joint masters of the East Galway Hunt. Livi Bishop had broken her arm and leg after jumping a solid boundary wall into a gravel pit. John Mulhern visited her in Galway Hospital. She suggested to John that he and I should buy St Clerans, owned by John Huston, the filmmaker, which had come on the market. I agreed, and within days John and I had negotiated the purchase with Laurence McCabe, who was a partner with Jackson Stops and McCabe. On exchanging contracts, Gladys Hill, John Huston's secretary, asked for a six-month completion. She needed time to decide what to sell, and to facilitate packing what they decided to keep. Gladys Hill cancelled the proposed auction of the contents when we agreed to buy what was on the list. Shortly before completion, John Mulhern took the opportunity to acquire more shares in Findus Foods; this gobbled up his spare cash, and he didn't wish to proceed with his share of St Clerans. I went ahead with the purchase on my own. I was fortunate to be in a financial position to do so. I was now the owner of the famed St Clerans, and I was only twenty-eight years old.

The previous owner was a far more famous individual. In 1951, just before starting work on *The African Queen*, John Huston came to Ireland for the first time, on an invitation from Lady Oonagh Oranmore and Browne, to attend the Galway Blazers Hunt Ball in the Gresham Hotel. That weekend John Huston stayed at Luggala, Oonagh's place in County Wicklow. He returned to foxhunt with the Kildare and Meath Hunt and, two years later, brought his wife, Ricki, and their children to Courtown House, Kilcock, County Kildare, which he leased. John Huston and his family used to drive to Galway, and on one of these journeys they saw a house in the distance behind a ruined tower. Some months later, John Huston's wife Ricki, while staying with Derek and Pat Trench for the Galway Races, had a good look at a beautiful old place, St Clerans, located between Loughrea and Craughwell.

It had cost John Huston little to buy St Clerans from the Land Commission, but it took three years – and a small fortune – to restore it. The house was in a state of utter disrepair, but the proportions were perfect and the stonework was beautiful. The setting, on one hundred acres, was unbelievable. From the attractive narrow entrance, you drove on the gravel path through the trees and over the bridge of the St Clerans river and the two weirs. On one section of the estate there was a thirteenth-century tower, the groom's quarters, stables, and the steward's cottage. There were two spacious lofts above the garages and stables: one was John Huston's studio, and Gladys Hill, his assistant, lived in the other.

St Clerans itself has two storeys over the lower floor. It is surrounded by a stone wall that allows full windows and full light to the lower floor. The famous Japanese bathroom, which we never used, is on this floor, together with a gallery for pre-Colombian art, an office for the estate manager, a wine cellar, a storeroom, an apartment for staff, and a lovely room called the 'television room', where everybody watched sporting events. The front part of the house was added in 1820. Galway marble paved the spacious entrance hall, with the imprint of oyster and other fossil shells and plants, white against black.

The dining room and the drawing room off the entrance hall were long and wide, identical in size, with bow windows. There was a large inner hall, with the study on one side and the kitchen on the other. Off the kitchen were the pantry and the staff room. On the first landing there was the 'grey room' – a woman's bedroom. The other bedroom was called 'the Napoleon Room', because of the canopied empire bed. The top landing had three bedrooms and a drawing room. All the bedrooms were large and all had fireplaces – even the bathrooms. The dining-room table was a twelve-foot-long Georgian three-pod with chairs of the same period, which we still have.

Prior to taking over St Clerans in 1972, Gladys Hill, to ease us into our new environment, arranged for Anne and myself to meet prominent local members of the Galway Blazers hunt. We arrived early to meet the staff. I will always remember the expression on Mrs Creagh's face when she met Anne for the first time: 'Oh, you are so young – such a beautiful girl.' Her husband, the butler Willie Creagh, gave a great sense of calm and serenity to the proceedings. Mrs Creagh took us to the north wing, approached by its own stairs, where they kept the Sacred Heart lamp burning at all times. We had tea with the Creaghs, Mary Bodkin, Margaret and Paddy Coyne in their bright dining area, overlooking the river and garden. We waited in the study, enjoying the smell of the turf fire until the guests arrived. Mark and Mrs Scully were the first to arrive, then Lord and Lady Hemphill, Derek and Pat Trench, Tim Gwyn Jones, Jack Mahoney, Charlie and Livi Bishop, Anne and Oliver Stoney, secretary to the Blazer Hunt, and Charlie and Monica McCarthy, treasurer to the hunt.

We had dinner by the light of candles only, with the fire burning brightly. Most of the guests were older, and very grand. Lord Hemphill and John Mulhern discussed racing and pedigrees; Lady Hemphill talked of her involvement with the pure-bred Connemara Pony Breeders Society. Tim and Derek Trench talked about grand houses of Ireland and their contents. Séamus, the elderly Irish wolfhound, barked and cried until Willie Creagh allowed him to sit, where he always did with his master, John

Huston, at one end of the dining table. Séamus, happy that he would continue to own St Clerans, fell asleep at my feet.

Even though John Mulhern and I had met the guests at hunt meets, it was interesting to hear behind-the-scenes stories of what they were really like. Before we left, Gladys took Anne's arm and whispered, 'Mrs Creagh really likes you, and they will be delighted to stay on at St Clerans, and Séamus has fallen for your husband, his new master.' We arrived back at the Great Southern Hotel before midnight. John and I talked a bit about everything for hours.

The parties in County Galway during the Christmas period were renowned. Mrs Creagh prepared us for our first party in St Clerans, on St Stephen's night, after the hunt at Craughwell. Anne welcomed the guests as they arrived: the Hemphills, Tim Gwyn Jones and his house guests, Monica and Charlie McCarthy, Brigadier and Maria Mahoney from Kilchreest House, Men and Didi Mahony from Hollypark, Charles and Olivia 'Livi' Bishop from Raford House, Maureen Smith from Cooliney House, Shirley Ringly-North and husband, Jack Mahoney, joint master and huntsman, Merrick and Jeannette Coveney, Claud and Chantal Forde, Michele and Chantal Deon, Anne and Oliver Stoney, Kathy Lydon, Derek and Pat De Paor Trench, John O'Driscoll and Ernest McMillen from Northern Ireland, Andrew and Nicki Greenwood, John Mulhern, Jean-Danielle and Jacqueline Evette with their son, Paul-Jerome, and daughter, Delphine, and guests, Lady Ampthill, Michael Hanna, Bill King from Oranmore Castle, and Colonel Dick Lovett and his wife Bee. Lord Hemphill said a few words and asked everyone to raise their glasses and drink to Anne and Joe for continuing the Stephen's Day party tradition that John Huston had maintained for years at St Clerans. Anne then said a few words in reply.

Other party-givers at that time were Charlie and Livi Bishop, who entertained guests and friends in the full Christmas spirit. Their home at Raford, near Athenry, was more than just a fine manor house. It represented their way of life – a way of life that revolved around horses and hunting, and the occasional visit to London to meet their stockbroker. Charlie was joint master of the Blazers, where he learned much from Captain Brian Fanshawe, who was popular with the farmers, and a most talented horseman. Brian had been master and huntsman of the Warwickshire hounds before arriving in County Galway. Charlie Bishop became joint master of the East Galway Hunt, accepting the challenge of hunting the hounds together with Michael Dempsey. Charlie was an excellent horseman, good with hounds and really good with people. Livi Bishop has a superb eye and understanding for the countryside; she can assess a field quickly and find the best way to keep up with the hounds.

The traditional New Year's Eve party was always given by Jean Daniel Evette and his wife, Jacqueline, at Creganna Castle. They lived in Paris, where Jean Daniel had a well-established architectural practice that involved commissions in Saudi Arabia. Jacqueline was much sought after as a landscape architect. They enjoyed at least four breaks a year at Creganna. The Evette family used to go to Roscommon to shoot with friends, where snipe gave the guns great fun. One of Jacqueline's greatest pleasures was training and working with her dogs. A local farmer took care of their working dogs in their absence.

Other great parties were given by Charlie and Monica McCarthy. They entertained in the true traditional family way, always helped out by their five children: Noel, Ian, Yvonne, Lorna and Audrey. Forty-two years later, our youngest daughter Christine, recently chartered, is fortunate to have Ian McCarthy, chartered surveyor, as her mentor, just like Dan Miley was to me.

Chapter Sixteen

The Ghost of St Cleran's and Other Country Tales

St Clerans was a world apart. One evening, Willie and Mrs Creagh told Anne and me the exciting story of Daly, the resident ghost at St Clerans. Even John Huston was enthralled by the story. Almost two centuries earlier, a man by the name of Daly was accused of shooting at the gamekeeper, who was also the bailiff at St Clerans. For an Irishman to fire a gunshot at such a public servant was punishable by death. Daly's defence was that he was such a good shot that, if he had wanted to kill the bailiff, he would not have missed. He insisted he was innocent. The Judge, a Burke, who owned St Clerans, condemned Daly: he was to hang.

The gallows was about a mile away from St Clerans on top of Seefin Hill. The ladies in the Burke family secretly watched the execution from two windows of an upstairs bedroom on the south side. After the hanging, the windows were blocked so that there was no view of the hanging ground from the house, and they remained so until the restoration of St Clerans. Michael Scott, architect and artist, persuaded John Huston to open these windows again, despite warnings from the locals that if they did so, Daly's ghost would surely come into the place – and that's how we inherited him.

After Daly's death, his mother pronounced a widow's curse upon the Burkes. 'No Burke will ever die peacefully in his bed again,' she said, 'and no rooks will ever again nest at St Clerans.' I understand that the Burkes tended to meet violent deaths to the end of their tenure there, and although there are rookeries all round St Clerans, the birds never build nests on the estate proper. Whether this is after the fact or not, I don't know. I do know that the grass never grows on the spot where the gallows stood.

A priest in Loughrea told John Huston that another man had, on his deathbed, confessed to having shot at the bailiff. Yes, Daly was innocent. The priest also advised John Huston against writing anything on the subject, as it was too soon to bring this matter up again – two hundred years later. We never heard or saw a ghost. The only sound we occasionally heard was that of a gale-force wind from the north, howling down our bedroom chimney like haunting music.

Anne's sister, Madeleine, on returning from a music scholarship in Switzerland, spent a week in St Clerans. She slept in the large bedroom called the grey room. On the first night, sleep came to her fast but it was interrupted by creaking from the outer door to her bedroom. She shivered; all she heard was a deep groan. The inner bedroom door creaked open and a satanic sound of guttural breathing surrounded her. Frozen in a flurry of sweat, her eyes stared wildly into the darkness. She jumped up to turn on the bedside lamp, having felt warm breathing on her shaking arm. Séamus, our Irish wolfhound, had come to welcome Madeleine, and he protected her for the rest of the week. The ghost of Daly didn't appear at all. But that is not the end of the story.

A few years after I had left St Clerans, I happened to be having a cup of coffee in Aggie Madden's pub in Loughrea. The place was quiet, with just one other customer. After glancing in my direction a few times, he approached me.

'I know you,' he said. 'You used to live at St Clerans. I often saw you out with the Blazers.' 'That's right,' I said.

He asked me, 'Did you ever see the ghost of Anthony Daly in St Clerans?'

I told him that I knew the story of Daly's hanging, but that I had never seen the ghost.

'You'll be interested in this,' said my newfound companion. 'You probably know Cregg Castle; it's only a few miles from St Clerans. You must have seen it when you were out with the hunt. Anyway, after Daly was hanged, his friends captured a man called Geoghegan, who had sworn false evidence to convict Daly. They took him to the abandoned castle at Cregg, where he met the same fate as Daly. They say Geoghegan's ghost haunts the place. Some people claim to have experienced strange, unearthly feelings of sheer terror in the place, and had to run out of it. I'm telling you I wouldn't go in there for love or money.' He suggested, though, that we could drive out to see the castle – from the outside, of course.

I turned down his offer, as I had to collect Anne, who was meeting friends in Galway.

Daly was hanged in 1820. So in 2020, around Seefin, Craughwell, Loughrea and Kilreekill, where Daly is buried, they will be marking the two-hundredth anniversary of his execution. We can look forward to renewed interest in the ghost of St Clerans, and indeed, the ghost of Cregg Castle.

An Eccentric Gentleman

During my time hunting with the Blazers, I met wonderful characters, some of whom were quite eccentric; none more so than Colonel Dick Lovett. Dick was tall – very tall – and he joined the British army. His story was never told, but what I do recall is that

Dick was taken by the Japanese on the Burma Road and spent time as their prisoner of war. This is where Dick's height came to haunt him. The Japanese saw his height as a target: as a prisoner of war, he spent much of his time on his knees, so as not to overshadow his captors. What else he suffered he never told.

Many, many years later, I met Dick in Galway through the Galway Blazers. He was an avid horseman and trainer, and gave much of his time to coaching young riders at Pony Club in Tulira Castle with his good friends Peter Patrick and Ann Hemphill. He lived quietly with his beautiful wife Bee, in a cottage in the grounds of Kilcolgan Castle. Bee, in later life, got cancer that took her from Dick, who in his inimitable way, and no doubt because of his army experience, handled Bee's passing as a matter of fact: life hits you, and you have to deal with it. Yet his war experience, which he always kept to himself, did on occasion raise its head.

His good friend Peter Patrick Hemphill used to collect Dick at his home in Kilcolgan on many an occasion. Peter Patrick (in the good days) always drove a smart Mercedes, but as we know the good days are interspersed with the bad, and in one such cycle Peter Patrick replaced his Mercedes with a less expensive but nonetheless luxurious Toyota. Dick was perceptive, and when he was collected in this new car, he complimented Peter Patrick, who replied: 'It's a superb car. It's Japanese, you know.'

Dick quietly asked Peter Patrick to pull over, and he got out of the car without a word. We will never know just how Dick's height upset his Japanese captors. Dick passed away many years later in a car accident in Kilcolgan: he was driving a French Citroën 2CV. A gentleman.

Entertaining at St Clerans

Moving to St Clerans was a huge challenge for me. During John Huston's time, it had become a great gathering place for the Big House people of Galway and for poets and artists from the US, including such people as John Steinbeck and Arthur Miller, one of Marilyn Monroe's husbands. And here was I from humble Charlestown about to become the lord of the manor. Of course, I was nervous, but I tried not to show it. Anne, on the other hand, was composed; she has the natural grace that enables her to be at home in any company. As one of the top fashion models of that time, she showed Irish haute-couture collections in the Georgian houses of Irene Gilbert, Wolfangle, Matt O'Donghue, Pat Crowley, and Clodagh and Ib Jorgensen. Their clientele included Lady Clague of Newbury Stud, County Kildare, Mrs Meg Mullion of Ardenode Stud, County Kildare, and Sonia Rogers of Airlie Stud, County Dublin, prominent racehorse owners and breeders. Others she met were Jacqueline O'Brien, wife of Vincent, the greatest racehorse trainer of all time, Eileen Mount Charles, Mary Williams, Eileen Plunkett, Anne, Countess of Rosse, and Miranda, Countess of Iveagh. Anne helped Pat Crowley show her clothes in London, Paris and North America. Anne's career in the fashion world enabled her to deal with any occasion, and gave me encouragement when it was needed, as I moved into a new way of life.

Anne and I also had a wide circle of friends coming to stay with us at St Clerans during the hunting season. Those in turn introduced us to many interesting people. I can't remember all of them, but there is something special about Dot Tubridy. Her late husband, Michael, a well-known County Clare GAA Star, joined the army equestrian school with Bill Mullins from County Kildare. They immediately became household showjumping names. Bill Mullins took early retirement and remained involved in three-day eventing, representing Ireland at international competitions, including the Olympics. Later, he gave much of his time to the administration of the sport. I served on a Punchestown three-day-event committee with him, and admired his discipline, hard work and lack of pretension. Michael Tubridy was on many winning teams at home and abroad. He won the Dublin Grand Prix at the RDS in 1946 and 1953 and was on the Aga Khan winning team. Michael, on leaving the army, accepted a position with Séamus McGrath's racing stables at Glencairn, in Sandyford, County Dublin. Sadly, within a year, Michael died in a fall while riding a young horse.

In the early 1950s, the McGrath family invested heavily in Waterford Crystal, which prospered for decades. Dot Tubridy became their successful ambassador, marketing the luxury crystal in North America. Dot often stayed with the Kennedys while promoting Waterford Crystal. She effectively became an adopted sister to the Kennedy sisters and really enjoyed campaigning for the three Kennedy brothers, Jack, Bobby and Ted. Dot, herself a frequent visitor to St Clerans, was so impressed by the seclusion and beauty of the place that she arranged for Ted Kennedy to holiday at St Clerans with his family, their children's school pals, his sisters, Pat Lawford and Mrs Shriver, and Senator John Tunney. I knew plenty about the Kennedys. However, I had to read up on Senator Tunney's background. Senator Tunney had been a friend of the Kennedy family since his college days, when he had shared a room with Ted Kennedy. And he was, of course, the son of the great Gene Tunney.

Senator John Tunney's grandparents, Mary and John Tunney from Kiltimagh and Westport, County Mayo, emigrated to the United States in 1880. Their son, Gene, excelled in both athletics and academia. He had a special interest in Shakespeare's plays and could recite from memory many of the famous soliloquies. He began his boxing career at the age of sixteen. Although he won his first fourteen professional fights, his father still would not go to see him fight, and he and Gene's mother continued to hope that their son would study for the priesthood. Gene's exceptional record in the ring allowed him to challenge for the world heavyweight championship title. The two fights with Jack Dempsey were the most memorable of his boxing career. He beat the great champion in a ten-round decider before a crowd of 112,757 – the largest crowd to witness a boxing match up to that time.

A year later, Tunney and Dempsey met in Chicago before an even bigger crowd, of 145,000 people, in a rematch that became famous as the 'Battle of the Long Count'. Dempsey was more popular than Tunney. The crowd roared when he knocked Tunney down in the seventh round, but the knockdown count by the referee was delayed as Dempsey did not return to a neutral corner, as required by the Illinois rules of boxing. The delay gave Tunney enough time to recover from Dempsey's stunning punch to his head, and Tunney went on to win the fight on a split decision. When he retired from the ring at the age of thirty-one, he devoted himself to his other great interest and became a lecturer on Shakespeare at Yale University.

Saint Brendan's Cathedral, Loughrea

The Kennedy party enjoyed their two weeks at St Clerans, making no demands on the staff. Mrs Creagh anticipated all their needs; she was very knowledgeable on the local area, and advised the guests on places worth seeing. She was delighted when Dot Tubridy, Senator John Tunney and the Kennedy sisters spent a morning in Loughrea. They met interesting locals in Aggie Madden's pub. But the highlight of the day – in fact, the highlight of their entire stay in Ireland – was their visit to St Brendan's Cathedral in Loughrea. The cathedral is a treasure house of art, with Irish-made stained-glass windows and beautiful wood carvings. Saint Brendan's was the first cathedral in Ireland to have all its stained-glass windows made in Ireland. The works of great artists contributed to its splendour: A. E. Child, Sarah Purser, Michael Healy, Catherine O'Brien, Hubert McGoldrick and Evie Hone. Evie's magnificent 'Stations of the Cross' were created for Kiltullah parish church, just down the road from St Clerans. Edward Martyn of Tulira Castle was the driving force behind the native Irish stained-glass movement; most stained glass for churches had previously been imported, mainly from Italy. St Brendan's Cathedral is well worth a visit if you are in the area.

Dinner with the Kennedys

Dot Tubridy invited Frank Dunne, myself and Anne to join the Kennedy party one evening at Dún Guaire Castle, Kinvara, for dinner. They wore their Aran sweaters, and that set the tone for a cheerful and chatty evening. The Kennedy sisters were great company. Ted Kennedy gave the impression that, as my children would say nowadays, he was 'cool'. Lord Hemphill and Frank Dunne discussed Irish and American politics with him, while Lady Hemphill told Senator John Tunney and the rest of us all about the breeding of the Connemara ponies.

During the dinner, Lord Hemphill told us that when the original owner, Lady Ampthill, bought Dún Guaire Castle, the roof was gone, but it still had the original fireplaces. While Lady Ampthill was supervising the restoration, with skill and imagination, a stranger appeared. She told the story that he pleaded with her to allow him to pay the entire cost of the new roof, but she never told anyone who he was.

Lord Hemphill – a natural storyteller – was in his element as he continued with the colourful story of Lady Ampthill. Lady Ampthill (née Christabel Hart) was born in 1895. Her father was a career soldier – a Colonel in the Leinster Regiment – and her mother was from a well-connected Scottish family. Christabel was educated in France. She first learned to ride when she was five – the beginning of a lifelong passion for horses, riding and, above all, hunting. Christabel Hart, aged twenty-two, married John Russell, son of Lord and Lady Ampthill, in 1917. Her husband received a very small allowance to supplement what he earned in the navy. Five years later, their divorce attracted huge publicity, as her husband's family, Lord and Lady Ampthill, were challenging their grandson's paternity. Her husband, who had brought the case against her, claimed that the child could not be his, as she had never allowed the marriage to be consummated. She insisted that she had never had sexual relations with another man. The jury failed to reach a verdict and were discharged.

The rehearing of the case began in March 1923, before a different judge and jury. After four hours' deliberation, the jury reached a verdict. They found the respondent guilty of adultery with a man unknown. Christabel lost on appeal, but had the verdict overturned on a further appeal to the House of Lords, which ruled in 1924 that no child born after marriage could be declared illegitimate merely on the testimony of his mother or father. The scandal led to the enactment of the Judicial Proceedings Act 1926, which prevented detailed evidence in divorce cases appearing in newspapers. When the Ampthills' son, John Russell, brought the case against Christabel, they did not allow for her enormous courage, and probably hoped that she would give way or climb down rather than allow her private life to be fully exposed to the media.

Christabel and her mother raised capital of five hundred pounds and opened a dress shop in Curzon Street in London, in 1922. It continued to be a success despite all the publicity. Christabel was a woman of extraordinary courage who did what she had to do. She was a gifted, hard-working business woman. From 1960 onwards, she spent more and more time in Ireland, eventually making her home in Galway.

Hunting

Hunting with the Galway Blazers got me more involved with, and familiar with, everything associated with fox-hunting. The huntsman has a demanding position, supervising the stables, and feeding and taking care of the hounds. A large kennel might have fifty to sixty 'couple'. Hounds are counted in twos, making a couple, as are foxes, with two making a 'brace'.

Hunting begins in October with the Galway Blazers and goes on until the lambing season begins, at the end of February. The hounds are only as good as the huntsman. A hound with a good nose, drive and cry is indispensable. There is no point in having a hound that stands on the line and babbles; you want one that gets on with it. The hounds are put into the covert, encouraged by the voice of the huntsman; when they pick up the scent of a fox, the leading hounds will 'speak'. The 'whippers in' – so called because their main task is to bring stray hounds back to the main pack – are posted around the covert to watch for the fox breaking cover. The hounds suddenly whimper and the whole pack breaks into full cry, a music that, once heard, can never be forgotten.

Once all the hounds are clear, the chase starts. It may be a burst of thirty minutes or so, with hounds running. The pack may catch its fox in the open – or the fox may get the better of them and go to ground in an 'unstopped earth', where the terrier men hadn't filled in the fox's earth. The huntsman blows 'gone to ground'. The terrier man is no longer allowed to dig out the fox for another chase. Not every day gives the field (the hunt) the supreme excitement of a long, fast run lasting an hour with a few checks. Coverts may hold no foxes and be drawn blank. Scent may be poor, and there will be much pottering about. Often, during those quiet hunting moments, I would find myself thinking of Charlestown: my days in Tavneena National School, my five years at

Coláiste Pádraic, my days working in the bog, saving hay in the meadows, visiting the forge, and all the events and people that made up my childhood and early youth. And I would begin to wonder about life's twists and turns. How, for example, would my life have turned out if Uncle John had not taken me under his wing all those years ago?

Riding to hounds is without doubt the ultimate objective of every keen horseman. I remember Jack Mahoney saying to me, 'Remember, you and your horse are out for a day's hunting, so train yourself to get as much pleasure watching the hounds working as galloping across country.' Lady Hemphill had given a framed page to John Huston, outlining seven basic pieces of advice for his hunting guests to read at breakfast before the meet:

1. The coat should be neither too long nor too short.
2. The rider should always turn out smartly.
3. If hounds pass you on a road or narrow lane, always turn your horse's head towards them.
4. Don't jump fences unnecessarily, and give the rider who has jumped before you time to get clear.
5. Nurse your horse as much as you can throughout the day's sport.
6. Remember that the horse is a noble animal and that 90 percent of horses are good. We cannot say the same about the riders.
7. Finally, if the landowner or farmer is sporting enough to allow the hunt to ride over his land, it is up to all followers of the hunt to be courteous, to show their appreciation by showing consideration for him and his livestock.

Now that I enjoyed fox-hunting, the next step was to acquire a horse of my own. This would be much better than hiring a different horse for each meet. Major Jed O'Dwyer, one of the Irish Army Equitation School's first recruits, recommended that I buy the exceptional chestnut horse Limerick Lad from Michael Buckley, master of the Limerick Harriers. The horse was perfection, with a fine intelligent head and large bold eyes set well apart; he was a brilliant jumper with several gears. I never thought Anne would be interested in hunting, but she surprised me. One morning, herself, Maureen Smith and Monica McCarthy followed the hunt in a jeep. Anne said afterwards that watching and listening to the hounds at work was exciting, and that her pulse quickened to their music in full cry. She loved every second of it. From that moment, she was hooked.

Monsignor John Wilson, who had stables in Castleknock before he left to study for the priesthood at Clonliffe College, told Anne: 'Take lessons at the Kellet riding school on Mespil Road beside the canal. I wouldn't like to see you galloping out of control in the park, as happened to Joe twice.' The indomitable Lady Ampthill of Dun Guaire Castle was a prominent member of the Galway Blazers hunt. She hunted side-saddle, but after a few mishaps she retired, approaching her eightieth birthday. It was on Lady Ampthill's horse that Anne had her first hunting experience with the Blazers. That was on St Stephen's Day at Craughwell, in 1972. She performed very well and impressed Lady Hemphill, who told her that she was a natural rider. Anne was delighted.

Charlie Bishop and Tim Gwyn Jones and Michael Dempsey, the joint masters, sometimes arranged a Sunday meeting with the East Galway hounds. We had a small turnout on the Sunday before Christmas 1972; it was cold but dry. It looked like another blank day, but suddenly on our way back to the trailers, out popped the fox from a small area of gorse. Most of the field were left behind at our first check. I remember Tim Gwyn Jones, Sarah Glynn, Livi Bishop, our guest Raymond Keogh, master of the Ward Union hunt, and Miley Cash, uncle of Walter Swinburn, always looking for and choosing the best place to jump. The light was failing, but the hounds kept on with the fox, and we had big jumping in the dusk until Miley Cash, an experienced horseman who knew the country well, told us it was too dark and dangerous to continue. Some hounds were found the next morning.

During our years at St Clerans, we had several hunting people as guests: Bert Firestone, owner of the Giltown Stud before selling it to the Aga Khan, John Corcoran, a well-established property dealer, and his wife Anne, Sir Hugh Fraser, Basil and Maureen Brindly, Renata and Cecil Coleman, Captain Des and Bernice Ringrose, John Mulhern, Galen and Hilary Weston, John O'Driscoll, Ernest McMillan, Jim Beardsley, Eamon and Eileen Walsh, Patrick and Susan Gallagher, Demi O'Byrne, P. P. Hogan, Eddie Crotty, and of course Frank Dunne.

Willie Leahy produced two experienced hunters for John Wright and Kevin Molloy for their first day's hunting with the Blazers. What John's horse lacked in looks, he made up for in his jumping over the more demanding Loughrea country. Kevin Molloy parted company with his big grey hunter a few times, but his bravery was never in doubt: he jumped everything that came his way. John Wright finished the hunt with the inside of his knees quite raw. Kevin was all set to hunt the following day with East Galway, but Willy Leahy did not have a suitable horse. They still recall that weekend – only the jumps get bigger and wider with the telling.

One of the most remarkable riders that stayed at St Clerans and hunted with the Blazers was the great Iris Kellett. Iris was a star of the sport of showjumping, winning major competitions during her long career. Iris Kellett decided to retire after winning the Ladies' European title at the RDS in 1969: the same year, she spotted the exceptional talent of the twenty-year-old Eddie Macken. Iris trained, and allowed Eddie Macken to ride her good horses for the next six years; Eddie won two silver medals at the showjumping world championships with Pele, owned by Iris Kellett, in 1974, and on Boomerang, in 1978. He also won a record four consecutive Hickstead Derbies. Suzanne Macken, Eddie's wife, is well known for her ability to bring on young horses.

Becoming Joint Master of the Blazers

In 1974, I felt especially honoured when Lord Hemphill invited me to become a joint master of the Blazers. In July 1975, Lord Hemphill, Eamon Walsh and myself attended the Heythrop Hunt Puppy Show at Chipping Camden, Gloucestershire. Lord Hemphill introduced Eamon and myself to Captain Ronnie Wallace, who had been master of Fox Hounds for fifty-eight consecutive years, twenty-five of those with the Heythrop hunt. On the same day, I caught up with Captain Brian Fenshawe, one of the judges of the puppy show, who had spent three seasons as joint master and huntsman with the Galway Blazers. I asked him if he remembered the hunt we had at

Gurtymadden, near Loughrea. He replied: 'You mean the rainbow day. How could I forget it?' On that morning in October 1974, Captain Des Ringrose, John Mulhern and myself had a hearty breakfast in Hayden's Hotel, Ballinasloe, before arriving at the meet. Willie Leahy was there with horses for visitors, including ourselves.

Brian Fenshawe and his hounds hacked to the first covert at 11 AM sharp, and the hounds were soon away, covering four to five miles for forty minutes, over thirty stone walls for every mile before the fox went to ground. That afternoon, in rain and sunshine, we had our second run over the best hunting country in the world, with an uninterrupted view of many dry stone walls, separating field after field. The fox in the distance, hounds in full cry, sixty mounted riders in pink and black jackets across the countryside, as a magnificent rainbow lit up this scene in front of our eyes. It just was mesmerising, like a giant spotlight in a vast stage. I have never seen such a sight since, not even in any of J. H. Herring's paintings of fox-hunting scenes. Later, back in Ryans' pub, at Gurtymadden crossroads, Brian, as always, made time for everybody. I remember him saying, 'Galway and the Blazers is a special part of my life.' It is a special part of my life too.

Demi O'Byrne, veterinary surgeon, who is now a key part of Coolmore Stud, the largest bloodstock enterprise in the world, and his wife Catherine, had some good days with the Blazers. On one of those days, at Ardrahan, Demi was joined by the well-known Timmy Hyde and his wife, Trish, and Eddie Crotty, a big farmer from County Waterford. Timmy was a successful National Hunt jockey, riding winners at Cheltenham, Punchestown and Fairyhouse, and winning the Ulster National a few times. He was master of the Golden Vale hunt for ten years and the Tipperary Fox Hounds for eight years. He is very well known in all bloodstock circles.

Timmy's presence, hunting with the Blazers, excited all the members, Willie Leahy made sure we were well mounted. The hunt members insisted that Timmy, Demi, Eddie and myself join them in Paddy Burke's pub in Clarinbridge. It was well dark when we got back to St Clerans, joining Anne, Trish, Catherine, the McCarthys and the Anglo-Irish Michael Hanna, with the posh accent, from Kilmadoony (nicknamed 'the Earl of Mayo' by John Mulhern). As the night progressed, the hunting stories, the gambles that came off and the ones that didn't, and the jokes got better and more colourful. They got a breather when Karen, Willie and Mrs Creagh's daughter, a champion Irish dancer, swept the floor with her dancing to the music of 'The Harvest Home', a hornpipe, and 'McLeod's Reel', played by Anne on her fiddle.

Later that year, Demi O'Byrne organised a Sunday hunt with Eddie Crotty and his neighbouring farmers at Ballinaclough, County Waterford. This was different. There were no fixed times or advertised places for these meets; only locals 'in the know' were aware of what was happening. Eddie started from his farm with three couple and was joined on the way by other farmers at different stages, with one or two couple. Farmers, solicitors, bank managers, shopkeepers, and sometimes clergy, joined the hunt at different stages. We met wonderful characters: one follower told us, 'This is a county where the horse is worshipped.' He was hunting the same horse for eight seasons, and hoping the horse would take good care of his granddaughter for another eight years.

Eddie gave Anne and myself two quality horses that galloped and jumped. When we returned to his house after the hunt, we were welcomed by the biggest logs I have

...na, Princess of Wales, presenting me, with the bronze medal after the Irish Team finished third at the ...opean Championships in Burghley, 1989.

At Burghley 1988.   Vets' inspection 1989.

Arriving with Sir John Major at Trinity College Dublin in 2007.: where the Auditor of the College Historical Society, Mr Timothy Smyth delivered his inaugural paper, "Overcoming Conflict and the Legacy of History".

Back Row; Michael Brennan, Gerry Harnett, Bill Brennan, Bernie Cooke, Pat O'Toole, Tom Brennan. Front; Jack Foley and Jimmy Lyons. They all returned from Chicago in the early 1960s (with money)

Presidents celebrating their childrens'
...ing Cert results at our home in 2000;
...ident Mary McAleese with Christine,
...atrick Hillery, Mark Cummins, Partrick
...ry, Joseph and Catherine; Emma
...leese, John Staunton, Sarah and Justin
...leese, Michael, David and Sarah Jane
...ry, Caitlin Nic Gabhann and Ian Cummins.
...w: Dr Martin McAleese and Mrs. John
...ry.

...s. Michael Cannon and Mrs. Roger
...rkeley.
... Peter Staunton and Dr John Hillery at
...therine and Barry's wedding reception.

President Mary McAleese with Mrs. Peter Staunton, Mona McGarry and her husband Mr Tom Dillon at our house warming in 2007.

Lady Sarah Camden, Exton Hall, Leicestershire with Christine, 2005.

Anne Marie with her mother, Mrs. Margaret Berkeley, at Exton Hall before Christine was born, 1989.

ebrating the
rriage of
y Murphy
of Mr and
, Patrick
phy to
herine, our
est daughter,
t Mary's
rch
dyford
ge, 2012.

Catherine with
her Bridesmaids,
Mary Canty,
Sarah Jane
Hillery and her
sister,
Christine.

Joseph and I, bride and groom, Anne Marie and Christine, October 2012.

With Owen Brady, Kevin and Colette Dempsey.

With Timothy and Harry Smyth.

Anne Marie and Catherine.

Diarmuid Murphy, Patrick Murphy, bride and groom, Mary Murphy and Padraic Murphy.

With Gerald Steinberg and his wife, Maris, at the wedding reception, 2012.

Joseph and Jenny Hobdell, his fiancé, at the wedding of Gerard McGowan and Edelle Kennedy at Tourlastrane Church, Co Sligo, 2015.

Sarah Wilson, Jenny Hobdell and Christine McGowan with baby Sophie, our Granddaughter, at Foxrock Church, December 2017.

Joseph and I, Gerard, my nephew, and Gerry, my brother, 2012.

Martin Kelly, Una Kearns, Denis Creaven, Anne Marie and myself at the Patrick Kavanagh memorial lecture delivered by Paul Durcan, hosted and sponsored by the Institute of Education, Mrs Marie Heaney and John O'Doherty also attended.

With Michael Cannon at the American Embassy, 2014.

Ernest O'Brien, Barry Murphy, Lorraine O'Brien, self, and Fintan Flannelly, 2012.

Mrs Margaret Berkeley and Mrs Kathleen Moran with the McGowan families. My mother Kate, Catherine, myself, Gerard, Alma, Joseph, Christine, with Martha seated; on holiday in County Mayo, 1991.
With Christine in Croke Park for the All Ireland final between Dublin and Mayo, 2017. Another heartbreaking day.

The Willow Wheelers set out from Blackrock College on their annual 100 mile charity cycle led by Mr Christopher McDaid, 2010.

Christine, Dr Peter Staunton, Nicholas Power, Marita Staunton, Peter Staunton junior and Jenny Hobdell, celebrating Christmas 2017.

Ed Cunningham and I, accepting the Coronation Bowls in the Irish handicap doubles from Patrick Delaney, (President Carrickmines Croquet and Lawn Tennis Club), with his wife Ma and Evan Newell, the Irish croquet handicapped 2007.

Alan Looney, President of CCLTC with Simon Williams the Irish Open Champion 2016.

Andrew Johnson, one of Ireland's leading croque players and Irish Open Champion 2017.

Michael Shaughnessy and Anne Marie McGowa had a narrow victory over Linda Newell and Pats Fitzgerald in the Strokestown Park Handicap Doubles 2016.

an era where the boot was king, Ireland owed a lot their success to the phenomenal goal-kicking of Ollie mpbell - Peter Bills.

Dave Terry, Owen Kirk, self, Christine and Joseph, Michael Foley and Paddy Lyons arriving at Cardiff, supporting Munster to win their first Heineken Cup in 2006.

Fergus Slattery, one of the best open side rugby players ever - skilful and ferocious.

Lunch with Renata Coleman at her Irish home in County Wicklow, self, Mickey Herbst, Renata, Wendy Herbst, Anne Marie, Ivor and Susan Fitzpatrick, Summer 2016.

With Willie Norse, Ollie Campbell, Bill Beaumont and Dr John O'Driscoll at Old Belvedere, 2017.

h Colin Holohan and Ken MacDonald at Hooke & Donald's offices Dublin 2, on the 9th March 2018. have remained very good friends since 1964.

ristine and Niamh Coveney after winning the Doubles at william Lawn Tennis Club.

ristine with Martin Smith, tennis technician from Norwich, npeting in Germany 2003.

ristine captained the CBRE team, winners of the Irish Times veyors Tournament for the first time at Donnybrook Tennis b, 2017.

Philip Young, Alistair McDonald, Peter McGill, Frances Lyons, Ronnie Regan celebrating the Award for the Best Residential Development in the North West of UK, 2011.

Leaving home to attend a function in Old Belvedere, in honour of Sir Anthony O'Reilly, at the invitation of Frank Hayes, Hon Secretary of the Club, April 2018.

With Pat Lam, Noel McCarthy, Ian McCarthy and John Muldoon, celebrating Connacht's rugby achievement at a lunch in Lough Cutra Castle, Gort, November, 2016.

Uncle Jim Dolan, Uncle Paddy Dolan, Uncle Tom Dolan and my mother Kate, with her sister Mary Whooley, home on holidays from New Jersey. Summer, 1967.

James, Kathleen, John and Nuala Dolan, my first cousins, gave me one of uncle Paddy's clocks (1880), for my 60th birthday. It is an 8 - day American Dropdial Wall Clock. The 12" white dial has black roman numerals, beautifully cut hands in a lovely solid mahogany case.

This photograph with my brother Gerry on my knee, and Pa, taken Charlestown, 1950.

ever seen in a blazing fire. Elizabeth, Eddie's girlfriend, had the most delicious Irish stew waiting for us. Eddie's ambition was to hunt a recognised pack. Demi quietly assured me that Eddie was ready to take on the Galway Blazers. I respected Demi's opinion, and put Eddie's name forward to become a joint Master and Huntsman to the Blazers. The reaction of Lord Hemphill and the committee to my proposal was: 'Who is this man Eddie Crotty?' This was quite understandable, as Eddie had no experience with a recognised pack. I suggested to Lord Hemphill that Eddie should spend a week with the Galway Blazers at the kennels in Craughwell before the committee made their decision. Eddie grasped the opportunity. After the week, the committee was so impressed that they had no hesitation in appointing him.

Charlie Haughey

Richard Duggan, a very good friend, invited me to Abbeville, where he was part of a Saturday-morning clay-pigeon shoot. He introduced me to Mr Charles Haughey as the new owner of St Clerans. Mr Haughey was surprised, and quick as lightning said: 'McGowan, there must be money in this building business.' After that, he always addressed me as McGowan. Mr Haughey and his wife, Maureen, enjoyed a good day with the Blazers. John Mulhern, and Lord and Lady Hemphill, looked after them. On another occasion, they came to St Clerans for lunch.

Thanks to Father John McNicholas, my good English teacher at Coláiste Pádraig long ago. I still remember some of Marc Antony's famous speech in *Julius Caesar*, one of Shakespeare's greatest plays. Standing over the body of the dead Caesar, Marc Antony declared:

The evil that men do lives after them;
The good is oft interred with their bones.

I would like it if the reverse of this statement were true – if we could inter a man's faults and wrongdoing with his bones and remember whatever good he may have done. Of course, a great deal of negative commentary has been made about Charlie Haughey. I am not going to add to it. But I must say that he did great positive things: the Succession Act, the Adoption Act, the Criminal Justice Bill. He encouraged the growth of the bloodstock industry by abolishing income tax on stallion income. He removed income tax on artists, and he set up Aosdána. He introduced free travel for pensioners. He listened to good ideas from inside and outside the party, and then implemented them. The best example is the success of the International Financial Services Centre. The IFSC has become one of the largest providers of wholesale financial services in the EU, directly employing almost forty thousand people, on an average salary of €60,000 – some legacy. I believe that while acknowledging his flaws, we should be big enough and, indeed, mature enough to remember and admire his achievements. I cannot conclude the Haughey story without paying tribute to his wonderful wife, Maureen. I knew her well; she was a gracious lady, with a brilliant mind.

When we hunting people meet socially, we recall various occasions. On one such occasion after a meet at Athenry, we were gathered in our hunting gear in a pub. The place was packed with locals, talking about lambing and cattle prices. Frank Dunne and John Mulhern ordered drinks for the house. One local, on his stool near the turf fire, had been listening and watching for a long time. After a while, he thanked John and, winking at me, said to him: 'Do you mind me saying to you, sir, that that thing in your hand would make a fine handle for a spade' – referring to John's Havana cigar.

We had three glorious years owning St Clerans, but then inflation began. St Clerans, as a weekend retreat, was becoming a burden. It became too expensive to run. The price of central-heating oil and petrol almost trebled. Our home was still in Hartstown. On top of that, the introduction of a wealth tax made it difficult to justify owning a place like St Clerans. My work and all other activities were in the Dublin area, and we spent less and less time visiting St Clerans. It wasn't difficult to make up our minds whether to live in County Galway or somewhere that was convenient to Dublin. We put St Clerans on the market with Robin Palmer and Denis Mahony of Keane Mahony Smith. It wasn't easy parting company with Mr and Mrs Creagh and the staff, who were the heart and soul of the place. Anne and I gained a lot from our time at St Clerans, things money couldn't buy.

After St Clerans, Anne hardly missed a day with the Ward Union stag hunt from 1973 to 1985, riding such good horses as Hermon, Millhouse, Egan and especially Disney. The hunt had a lot of followers on foot, some on tractors and others in motor cars. The meet was at 1 PM on Tuesdays and Fridays; this allowed farmers to get work done in the morning. Disney had it all: appearance, personality, temperament and above all good manners. He was the outstanding horse across country with the Meath and Ward Union stag hunt: leading the way, gaining lengths, jumping the big hedges, and measuring the yawning ditches, always under control, enjoying every moment.

Anne introduced Disney to Gervaise Maher, a friend and a member of the Ward Union stag hunt during our last season hunting from Hollywood Rath. Anne told Disney that he would receive the same love from Gervaise on her farm in Clonee, and promised that she would visit him as often as she could in his retirement. Anne kept to her word, taking Catherine and Joseph to visit him. When I recall the great times Anne and I had with the Ward Union stag hunt, I always think of another horse, Dusty, owned by Jack Foley. What a horse: he hunted twice a week for fifteen seasons without an injury.

Chapter Seventeen

A Mad Hatter's Introduction to the Sport of Kings – and Polo in the Park

I might never have got involved in racing or eventing if I hadn't taken part in two point-to-points in County Galway. Charlie Bishop had no trouble in persuading John Mulhern, myself and other members of the East Galway Hunt to take part in a point-to-point race at Eyrecourt in the spring of 1973. This race was confined to genuine hunters only. Charlie Bishop won by a distance, and John finished a poor second, with Tim Gwyn Jones and myself tailed off.

Two weeks later, the legendary Molly Cusack Smith, master of the Birmingham North Galway hunt, had her point-to-point on the old Tuam racecourse. I entered my best hunter, Limerick Lad (almost a thoroughbred), in the open feature race. My horse loved the good ground and flew over the fences. We finished third. It was pure magic.

Returning to Dublin, John Mulhern, Anne and myself dropped into the Grasshopper in Clonee and joined Tommy and Pamela Carberry, Ray and Rosika Lyons and Sir John Arnott, owner of the Phoenix Park racecourse. The chat and the banter were lively. That night marks a significant moment in my sporting career. The idea of riding under rules had never entered my mind; all that changed when John suggested that a charity race similar to what was happening in England be held at the Phoenix Park racecourse. Within days, Sir John Arnott got permission from the Turf Club to hold a charity race, but only if the Turf Club was happy with the conditions.

John Mulhern contacted Basil Brindley, and they decided that it would be a one and a half mile race for four-year-olds and upwards that hadn't won a race, and the minimum weight was to be twelve stone seven pounds. Each of the twelve riders had to donate £200 minimum, of which £800 would be donated to the Drogheda Memorial Fund, £800 to the Jockeys' Accident Fund and £800 to the Apprentice Jockeys' Education and Welfare Trust. The winner was to receive an impressive bronze sculpture by Gary Trimble.

The race would be called 'The Madhatters Private Sweepstake', and it was scheduled for Saturday 31 July, at the Phoenix Park racecourse. Basil Brindley, John Mulhern and Mick O'Toole already owned horses which were suitable to ride in the race. Frank Dunne purchased King Charles, a four-year-old, and since I couldn't lease Great Ben, who had finished second in a two-mile bumper race at Leopardstown the previous week, I bought him. Both King Charles and my horse, Great Ben, were trained by Dermot Weld.

Peter Russell, travelling head man with D. K. Weld, and a National Hunt jockey, was a huge help in getting me ready for my first race. This race got media attention for three months and, of course, in our circle scarcely anything else was discussed. I rode out two mornings a week at the Curragh and trained very hard on the bicycle. I remember clearly the final gallop at the Curragh two days before the race: Frank Dunne rode his own horse, and Peter Russell rode Great Ben, carrying twelve stone seven pounds. They worked with two other horses on the mile grass gallop. Charlie Weld, Dermot's father and myself were surprised that Great Ben finished the gallop on a tight rein while the others were flat out. Mr Weld was going to Ascot on the Saturday with Renata Coleman, who had a runner in the King George and Queen Elizabeth Stakes race. Dermot had several runners at the park, including our two. Charlie Weld said, 'J.B., put a ten-pound bet on Great Ben for me', and in the next breath said, 'J.B. make that twenty.' John Mulhern always called me 'J.B.', which seemed to stick with the racing set. He called me other names if I made a mistake.

We didn't know much about the two English-trained horses owned by Sir Hugh Frazer and Stanley Threadwell. Peter Russell told me that, when he was on form, Great Ben was the best horse in the race. Peter got permission that I did not have to ride Great Ben in front of the stewards, in case he would take off with me. Great Ben seemed happy enough in the parade ring, but after a leg up, he got giddy. The tape start was at the back of the stands. The race itself could not have gone better. The field took off as if it were a five-furlong sprint. I settled Great Ben and, rounding the bend, gained valuable lengths and quickened to win with ease.

Anne was standing at the entrance to the winners' enclosure; she just shook my hand, with tears rolling down her cheeks. We got a tremendous reception. Many punters had every reason to be pleased, having backed Great Ben from ten to one, to five to one, as second favourite. Mrs Noel Griffin presented each rider with a Waterford Crystal vase. An Taoiseach, Mr Liam Cosgrave, himself a keen hunting and racing man, presented me with the trophy.

Dave Baker, writing in the the *Irish Field* on Saturday 4 August 1973, described the race as follows: 'In the concluding Madhatters Private Sweepstakes, a fairly light-hearted race resulted in a win for the youngest competitor, Joe McGowan, who steered a tight course all the way to beat Sir Hugh Fraser on Le Doyen and Frank Dunne on King Charles. Both first and third are trained by Dermot Weld, while the second is from Barry Hill's stable. Favourite, Breve, ridden by Stanley Threadwell, ran out of "gas" in the straight after having every chance. Running to the top of the course, Acey Deecy, Le Doyen, Jack Frost and Breve went clear of the others; Mick O'Toole and Jack Frost went to see what the traffic was like on the main road as the other three turned across the top. On the final bend, Le Doyen, Breve and Acey Deecy all went wide and Joe McGowan came through on the inner early in the straight for an easy win.'

Polo Proving Increasingly Popular as a Spectator Sport

Polo was very popular in the 1970s, attracting new names. Galen Weston, John Mulhern, Cecil and Renata Coleman, Michael Herbst, Declan Collins and Lawrence Crowley brought good, professional players to their teams. John Mulhern, when he undertook something, went all out to excel. He built up a good string of polo ponies within a few years.

Before the Madhatters race was ever thought about, John Mulhern asked me to join his polo team, 'The Wild Geese', for the 1973 season: Jamie Mackay and Hughie Higgins from Australia completed the team. John Mulhern had a polo pit, a wooden horse set in the middle of a stable, with sloping sides and a heavy mesh to prevent the ball hitting the walls. He would practise three or four nights a week at different shots, hitting the ball against the mesh. One freezing-cold night at Christmas 1972, John told me to get on the wooden horse. After twenty minutes, I was exhausted, but I continued the exercise three times a week.

Charles James's article in the *Irish Field* described the opening of the 1973 season: 'For those people, who appreciate the game, last Sunday provided a real feast. The opening game in the league between the Wild Geese and Enterprise was a brilliant polo game, and one of the fastest seen at the Park for some seasons. It was a cut-and-thrust match, played fast and tough without ever being dirty. Wild Geese started with a half-goal advantage on handicap, fielding Jamie Mackay, John Mulhern, Michael Herbst and Joe McGowan, and both Mulhern and McGowan scored a goal apiece. For McGowan, this was a dream start to his playing career in this, his first match.'

Polo is a costly sport, and I could not afford the time or finance to continue. A month after the Madhatters race, John Mulhern took me to Michael O'Toole's yard in the Curragh to see two horses: a three-year-old, already named Davy Lad, who was looked after by Paddy Carey, and a four-year-old, Arctic Heir, looked after by Johnny Sullivan. John Mulhern said: 'I cannot make up my mind between the two, so you will have to buy them both.' I was lucky: Jack Doyle, the bloodstock agent, who had played rugby for Ireland, sold Great Ben for me for close to the price I had paid for him, which enabled me to buy the two horses.

In February 1974, John Mulhern telephoned to say that Davy Lad would have his first outing at Fairyhouse in a two-mile bumper race two days later. I told John that Anne and I had already accepted an invitation to stay and hunt the next day with John and May Rohan at their home in Waterford. John Rohan was joint master and huntsman of the Waterford hounds. John Mulhern, without hesitation, said that Anne had to be at Fairyhouse to lead in her first winner. Anne and I arrived at John and May's house on Friday evening. The next morning, Anne left Waterford in plenty of time for Fairyhouse, and, as predicted by John, she led Davy Lad into the winners' enclosure before returning to Waterford for dinner.

The weather was atrocious that day, but still there was a good turnout at the hunt. We got back to the house soaked to the skin; John's brother, Ken Rohan, and his wife, Brenda, who had listened to the racing commentary on the radio, were able to tell us that Davy Lad took up the running half a mile out and went away to win by twelve lengths. We had a great evening: Tom and Elsie Morgan were there, and later, Harry De Bromhead, returning home from Fairyhouse, dropped in. Harry had ridden in the same bumper race, and was very impressed with Davy Lad. The next day, on our way home, we called on John Mulhern to thank him for picking out Davy Lad. John told us that Davy Lad was likely to run in the winners' bumper at Leopardstown the following Saturday.

John couldn't believe that I would be in France and would miss Davy Lad's second racecourse appearance; but I couldn't help it. We had arranged a skiing holiday with Brian and Catherine O'Halloran and their children, Rosalind, David, Jessica and Richard. Mick O'Toole phoned me in France to tell me how impressive Davy Lad was in winning at Leopardstown. He was backed from 100/1 to 8/1, to become second favourite for the Daily Express Triumph Hurdle at Cheltenham in 1974 – the richest hurdle race for four-year-olds. Attivo, owned by Peter O'Sullevan, winner on the flat and over hurdles, was far more experienced and was hot favourite at 7/4. It was highly unlikely that Davy Lad would take on Attivo at Cheltenham.

To avoid people continuing to back Davy Lad, Michael O'Toole contacted Tom McGinty, the racing correspondent with the *Irish Independent*, and the following statement was issued by Tom McGinty: 'Mrs Anne Marie McGowan, Davy Lad's owner, said yesterday: it was decided not to send Davy Lad to Cheltenham because of the uncertainty of the weather conditions. It could have meant unnecessary travel for my young horse. Davy Lad has a long career in front of him. No immediate plans have been made for his next run.'

Jim Beardsley, a chartered surveyor, was the largest shareholder of Beardsley Theobald, a firm of estate agents with twenty-three offices in the East Midlands in England. He was an experienced property professional with high personal impact, known for leadership. Ernest Ottewell introduced him to Ireland. He came to stay with us at least once every hunting season. Jim and I called to Dermot Weld's yard and he showed us a very smart four-year-old in training that one of his patrons was selling. We liked him, bought him and named the horse Oranmore. He came to hand very quickly and was doing good work on the gallops. Dermot Weld was delighted to ride him in a bumper at Ballinrobe in April because I was too busy on the building sites. Dermot said that Oranmore ran extremely well, and looked a possible winner with two furlongs to go, but was uncomfortable in the soft ground and finished second to Shining Flame, trained by Nick Rackard, the County Wexford hurler. Oranmore was rested until the second running of the Madhatters race, this time at Leopardstown. I rode a terrible race on him. I took a fair bit of criticism, and rightly so. One racegoer told O'Toole that I had thrown the race away; it was embarrassing.

Michael Fortune of the *Irish Press* forecast that Oranmore would win the bumper at Navan. The opposition at Navan was good; it included Ted Walsh riding the Seamus McGrath-trained Gay Borris, third at Naas, and the Edward O'Grady representative, Golden Express. Dermot Weld instructed me to keep with the leaders and wait until Ted Walsh made his move, and stay with him. This was no easy undertaking. Luckily, I carried out my orders to perfection, winning by half a length. Ted looked at me and said: 'Where the fuck did you come from?' I could now put the performance at Leopardstown behind me. After a deserved break, Oranmore won his maiden hurdle at Clonmel, ridden by Peter Russell.

My next racing involvement was with George Blackwell, a leading bloodstock agent: George bought yearlings for Tom Brennan, Bernie Cooke and myself, including Thrifty Trio, Amber Dawn and Mussorgsky. Thrifty Trio had her first outing at the Curragh as a two-year-old, finishing seventh. She won her next race at Navan with ears pricked. Thrifty Trio won six of her seven races in 1974. She won at Navan, the Curragh and Naas, and many times at the Phoenix Park, confirming that she was a top sprinter. I didn't think it was possible for anyone to get such a thrill as Bernie and Cathy Cooke and their two children, Michael and Caroline, got from watching and leading in Thrifty Trio.

As a four-year-old, Thrifty Trio would win at the Phoenix Park, and finished fourth in the King Stands stakes at Royal Ascot. Thrifty Trio was an extremely good-looking bay filly with an ideal racing temperament. She won two races in the USA before returning to Bryanstown Stud to become one of Bernie Cooke's foundation mares. Amber Dawn won a one-mile race as a three-year-old at Gowran Park, and was placed many times. Since Tom and Bernie did not consider her pedigree good enough for breeding, she was sold at a third of what she cost. Mussorgsky won a six-furlong race at the Phoenix Park.

Bernie Cooke, director of a building company that bought a stud farm in Leixlip for residential development, inherited the stud manager, Derek Kavanagh. Derek was a good find and managed the Cooke's Bryanstown Stud, bordering Moyglare and Dollanstown between Maynooth and Kilcock. Tom Brennan was also very lucky: he purchased Hilltown Stud in Clonee from Sir Cecil King Harman, just before land prices soared. Gerry McMullen had worked with Sir Cecil all his life, had immense knowledge of breeding and became a huge asset to Tom.

Like many other owner-breeders, Tom Brennan and Bernie Cooke find the breeding side of racing most interesting. They were lucky that the Irish National Stud acquired top-class stallions, whose services were available to Irish breeders on favourable terms. Even more important, the National Stud offered good advice to breeders, especially those starting off.

The 1974-75 Season

Our luck continued at Listowel. Arctic Heir, ridden by Frank Levy, won his maiden hurdle race by eight lengths; he was really impressive. The following day, Davy Lad won his second hurdle race, having previously won at Galway. He won three more hurdle races, the last at Naas in November, where he injured his back. Michael O'Toole was still confident that Davy Lad would be ready for Cheltenham in 1975 – and he was. We arrived at the Lygon Arms in Broadway, about nine miles from Cheltenham. Racing was cancelled the first day, and the races were rearranged to take place over the next two days, provided that the course was safe to race on. Jim Dreaper trained Lough Inagh to win the two-mile Champion Chase and Brown Lad to win the three-mile hurdle, both ridden by Tommy Carberry. Bannow Rambler won the two-mile novice hurdle.

Dessie Hughes, knowing that the conditions suited Davy Lad, was worried that the meeting might be cancelled altogether. Racing did go ahead, and Dessie Hughes gave Davy Lad a confident ride. Jumping the hurdles effortlessly, he joined the leaders at the top of the hill, took up the running and won like a favourite should, with Sunny Boy, owned by the Queen Mother, second. They got a great reception in the winners' enclosure, Davy Lad having been backed down to 5/2 favourite by the Irish visitors.

A month later, Davy Lad gave a wonderful display of gameness and ability in the Fingal Hurdle at Fairyhouse. Turning into the straight, with two flights of hurdles to jump, Michael O'Hehir said, 'The favourite would want to be jet-propelled to win from where he is.' But Dessie Hughes got him running, and he gave a magnificent jump at the last hurdle to take the lead. Michael O'Hehir said, 'Maybe he *is* jet-propelled.' Davy Lad won by four lengths.

Everybody involved in racing in this country and in England knew that Tom Nicholson, who trained his own horses in County Kilkenny, owned the two best young horses in the country: Parkhill and Artifice. I could only afford to buy Parkhill if I sold Arctic Heir. Michael O'Toole confirmed that he had formed a syndicate to buy Arctic Heir and that Dessie Hughes and himself were going to Tom Nicholson's yard to jump Parkhill over a few hurdles. The winnings of Davy Lad and the sale of Arctic Heir almost covered the cost of purchasing Parkhill, for £15,000. At that time, one could buy two houses in Kilnamanagh for £16,000. Kevin Prendergast and others joked and said, 'You chose the wrong horse', to which I replied, 'We will find out at Cheltenham next year.'

Parkhill

Parkhill won a maiden hurdle at Thurles, then the Delgany Hurdle at Leopardstown, and was very impressive in winning the Merrion Hurdle, at Leopardstown, three weeks before Cheltenham. This is how Tony Power described Parkhill's performance in winning the Merrion Hurdle, in the *Horse and Hound*: 'Several of the leading novice hurdlers contested the interesting Merrion Hurdle (2m) at Leopardstown, for which the dozen runners included four winners last time out. So impressive had been Parkhill when demolishing his rivals over the course and distance by a dozen lengths in January that he started at odds-on to complete his hat-trick. Each will be a worthy contender but there is no doubt that Parkhill is an exciting prospect, who Mick O'Toole has stated is one of the best horses he has trained and will be a hard nut to crack in the Sun Alliance, which he won for the same owner last year with Davy Lad. Parkhill is owned by Mrs J. B. McGowan and bred by County Meath Veterinary Surgeon, Miss Eileen Parkhill, after whom he is named. The five-year-old gelding is by Le Prince, a well-bred stayer by Prince Bio out of Atlantida, by Nimbus. Parkhill, an own-brother to Son and Heir, a year older, winner over fences in England, is out of Killossery Star, who comes from a noted speedy flat racing family.'

Dessie Hughes would have preferred a 'give' in the ground, but he was still extremely confident. Parkhill was up with the leaders at the start; on passing the stands with two miles left, he took the lead, led all the way and won easily. Dessie had every right to enjoy his success. Terry Biddlecombe, ex-Champion Jockey, said on BBC television, 'Parkhill will be a natural over fences, very strong, with an exceptional pedigree, could be another Arkle.' He really was impressive.

The target for the next season was the Handicap Hurdle at Leopardstown at Christmas. Parkhill was working well; he came second in a Handicap Hurdle in November, to become the raging favourite. Michael O'Toole telephoned, and told me to be at his yard the following morning. There was a bit of bad news: Parkhill had injured a leg and was unlikely to run. Joe O'Donnell, veterinary surgeon, said he should be rested for at least a year to allow time for the tendon to heal. We made the mistake of starting to train him after six months. This time the damage was done, and his career was ended.

The 1975-76 season was a good one for us, with Davy Lad winning his Novice Chase and Winners Chase, the Embassy Qualifier and a very good three-mile chase in Wetherby. Because the flight-times from Dublin to Leeds/Bradford required an over-night stay, John Mulhern arranged a private aircraft to take Mick O'Toole, Dessie Hughes, Richard Guernin, Margaret O'Toole, Anne and myself to Leeds Bradford. There was dense fog at Wetherby, but despite that, racing went ahead. Because visibility was so poor, there was no commentary until the horses came into view approaching the final fence. Here, Davy Lad challenged the favourite, Canchello, and pushed his brave head in front at the point where it mattered.

Arriving back at Dublin Airport a few hours later, the signal for the landing gear was not working properly. The pilot circled over the control tower and everything seemed to be in order, but he was told to continue circling until the fuel tank was almost empty, in case we had a 'belly landing'. Dublin Airport had ambulances and fire brigades on standby. We had sheet-white faces and worried expressions before a perfect landing. John Mulhern looked at me and said: 'The planners nearly got lucky.'

Chapter Eighteen

The Cheltenham Gold Cup 1977: A Dream

At the beginning of the 1977 season, Davy Lad's form was poor. He was easily beaten in the Thyestes Chase at Gowran Park in January by Bannow Rambler. A month later, Davy Lad was again beaten in the three-mile Leopardstown Handicap Chase, this time by a short head, by Bannow Rambler, but Davy Lad was finishing strong on ground that suited him, and giving seven pounds to the winner. Because the Gold Cup race was two furlongs further, we looked forward to Cheltenham with confidence.

Before the 1977 Cheltenham Festival meeting, we were in Meribal, France, with the Wrefords. One night while we were there, I had a dream. I was in a pub watching the Gold Cup with three horses jumping the second-last fence together. In the dream, Davy Lad jumped into the lead at the last fence, going on to win the race. It was so real and vivid that I wondered if this would be one of my dreams come true. We spent two weeks at home before arriving at the Lygon Arms, Broadway, for the Festival meeting. I could hardly believe that Tony Redmond had declared Strokemaster for the bumper race at Limerick on the same day as the Gold Cup, 17 March. I related my dream to Dessie Hughes and told him that I had made up my mind to take the first flight from Heathrow the next morning to ride Strokemaster in Limerick. Dessie said, 'I don't know about your dream, J.B., but Davy Lad will definitely be in the first three. We have him well prepared for this race, and he never felt as good.'

I took the hired car to get the flight from Heathrow, having accepted that David Johnson's driver would bring Anne to Heathrow Airport after racing. At Dublin Airport, Jim Gleeson said to me: 'You should have stayed where you were: there has been a downpour for the last twelve hours. Limerick racecourse will be a bog, if they race at all.' Jim and I arrived at the pub, a few steps from the racecourse, to watch the racing from Cheltenham. By the time it came to the big race, most of the publican's customers knew who I was.

I can still remember Peter O'Sullevan's commentary: 'Sommerville from Tied Cottage; Davy Lad in third is making the most significant progress; at the second-last in the Gold Cup there is little between them. Davy Lad is switched to the centre and at the last jumps into the lead, striding away from Tied Cottage and Sommerville. The one-two for Ireland, Dessie Hughes and Davy Lad from Tommy Carberry and Tied Cottage, and it is Davy Lad the winner.' I didn't see the presentation, as I had to get ready to ride in the bumper. Utter commotion in the jockey's room, and a voice was heard shouting: 'J.B. is here. He is not, don't be daft; he couldn't be. Davy Lad is just after winning the Gold Cup, J.B. is surely at Cheltenham.' I could only finish third, on ground that Strokemaster hated. Jim and I got back to Dublin Airport in time to collect Anne with the Cheltenham Gold Cup.

On the following evening in Tom and Nuala Brennan's house, we watched the recording of Anne, happy and beautiful, leading Davy Lad to the winners' enclosure and being presented with the Gold Cup by Marchioness D'Aulan and her husband, Marcus D'Aulan. Anne told us about her meeting with the Queen Mother. Immediately after the presentation, Lord Plummer took Anne by the arm and escorted her to the Royal Box. The Queen Mother clasped her hands and slowly said: 'I would love to win the Cheltenham Gold Cup.' Anne told the Queen Mother that her husband had left Cheltenham for Ireland that morning to ride in a race for amateurs in Limerick. The Queen Mother told Anne that she would love to visit Ireland, but that, sadly, it was not possible at that time. Lord Plummer walked Anne back to the owners' bar, where she introduced him to our friends.

My father's letter to Anne captures the atmosphere around Charlestown, County Mayo, my home-place, the day Davy Lad won the Gold Cup. A few months later, I told my father that he could not have seen me in the winners' enclosure because I watched the race in a pub in Limerick before riding in the bumper race. His response was: 'You daft eejit, well did you have him backed?' He was really baffled, and kept shaking his head, talking to himself in disbelief. He settled when Anne told him that the Gold Cup was ours for keeps.

Letter from Home

Egool
Kilmovee.

Dear Anne,

Thanks very much for the books, also paper and note.

It's sure nice to have the postman knock once in a while.

Yes I saw Davy Lad run. I was in Harrisons. It was crowded. There was hundreds backed on him, there's no Bookie in town now. So John takes the bets, he has an account with a bookie in Sligo, he phones them in. I saw one chap back him for £150, others £100, 50-30 nothing less. They were sweating for a while, he's lost, but all of a sudden he spread his wings then it was, what a horse.

I stayed out of sight. I got a great kick, hearing the talk after the race, who was the owner, was he so-and-so's son, he must have married into a rich family. I'd tell you a lot more when we meet. I saw you lead the horse in, and Joe came in behind you. I saw a stout fellow shake hands with him.

The drink began to flow then and I left. John asked me to stay, but I didn't want to get involved. He told me once if Davy Lad ran once a week he could soon retire. He had six of a staff for the day, God Bless.

Seosamh Mac Gabhann

Jonathan Powell, in his introduction to this book, outlines Davy Lad's subsequent career.

My First Point-to-Point Winner

I had finished second and third in point-to-points on Bilbo Baggins, trained by Tony Redmond. Pat Hogan was in the parade-ring at the Thurles point-to-point when I was second yet again on Bilbo Baggins. Pat said to me: 'You were beaten by a better horse, but you are getting better.' In the next breath, Pat asked me to ride one of his horses at the point-to-point in Bartlemy, near Fermoy, County Cork. Of course, I accepted. We left early with our house-guests, Roger and Roz Wreford, and our neighbour, George Crolly, an expert on point-to-point form. I changed and walked the sharp course. I noticed that Ted Walsh was riding another P. P. Hogan horse in the same race and I assumed he would be on the favourite. Pat Hogan came into the ring and said to me: 'Let those irons down. Who do you think you are, Lester Piggott?' He then said, 'This horse will jump from fence to fence, just relax and you will win.' Maurice Coleman, riding a tearaway, ignored the sharp bend and unintentionally nearly took me with him. On the third circuit, I was close enough to the leaders, jumping in fine style, and after a fantastic jump at the last, we won by two lengths. What a relief! It is just as well I didn't know my horse, Any Crack, was backed from 10/1 into even money. Any Crack went on to win eighteen point-to-points and hunter chases for P. P. Hogan and his joint owner, and gave me my first point-to-point winner.

In 1977, Madeleine, my sister-in-law, was dating Dr Peter Staunton, so we named one of our young horses 'Staunton'. I rode Staunton in a two-mile chase at Fairyhouse, and two weeks later, at Navan. He had improved so much from the Fairyhouse outing, that I was summoned before the stewards to view the video and explain why I wasn't able to ride a finish in the last two furlongs. Judge Frank Roe, one of the stewards, said: 'In future, if you are having trouble with your weight, get somebody else to ride the horse.' I received a severe caution and was told to be fit enough to ride a finish in future. We sold Staunton to Nick Henderson for a good profit.

Later, Tom Brennan and I joined Crawford Scott and Hugh Tunney in a syndicate to keep two flat-horses in training, with Dermot Weld, each season. Crawford Scott used to buy all the cattle for Mollaghans in County Longford, before going into business with Hugh Tunney. Hugh Tunney found a job in London in 1954 and got what was probably the luckiest break of his life: an introduction to George Londsdale, who had a large wholesale meat business. He gave Mr Tunney a cheque for £60,000 in advance to finance the purchase of six hundred cattle. Crawford, a very good judge, bought the cattle, and Tunney sold them to the English abattoirs. Gregory Shapiro, an agent, started buying cattle for the French market. After a few years, Crawford and Hugh had a dispute with Gregory over £60,000. Hugh heard that Gregory was staying in the Gresham Hotel. He got Crawford into the car and said: 'Let's go to Dublin, I'm going to throw Shapiro out of the hotel window', to which Crawford replied, 'Hugh, let's get the £60,000 first and then throw him out of the window.' They recovered the £60,000 over the years and continued in business, and remained good friends.

Hugh and Crawford, along with Gerry Tierney and Tim Henegan, bought a meat plant in Clones that became very successful, before Gerry went into banking. Hugh Tunney sold the business in 1993 for £10,000,000. The horses were an excuse for us to meet every month or two in the Gresham Hotel to talk a little about everything. We didn't have much success with the horses, but we had great fun. Crawford was a good storyteller, and told us good stories about the times when they were short of cash in the business.

Artistic Lad

Tim Gwyn Jones and I bought Artistic Lad after he finished second to The Arctic, ridden by Kevin Prendergast in a bumper in Down Royal. Within a month, I rode him to win a two-mile bumper at Downpatrick. Peter Russell thought this horse could not be beaten. Pat Flanagan and my friends, including Dermot Weld, backed him accordingly. Artistic Lad had considerable ability, and would settle in any part of a race. The summer of 1975 was very dry, and the good ground suited him. I rode him in a winners' bumper at Tralee.

Tom McCormack, writing in the *Irish Independent* on 19 July 1975, describes the race:

ARTISTIC LAD OFF LINE

An objection to Artistic Lad in the final Castlemaine Plate on the concluding day at Tralee yesterday was upheld following a stewards' inquiry and the race awarded to the mount of Mr Ted Walsh, Prince Fort, trained by Christy Kinane, giving him his second winner over the two days.

As the only surviving ticket on the jackpot pool was on Artistic Lad, this decision sent the pool of £603 forward to today's meeting at Thurles, which was the sole event to spoil what was otherwise a splendid fixture for the executives. Although the bookmakers were taking 5/2 about Artistic Lad keeping the race, there were many to disagree with this assessment. Kilcrow had made most of the running and was on the rail making the turn to the straight. He seemed to move out as Artistic Lad and Prince Fort challenged determinedly for the lead and scrimmaging certainly resulted between all three.

Coming out of the turn, Artistic Lad was closely pressed by Prince Fort and as they raced all out for the finish, Mr Joe McGowan, had cause to change his whip hand mid-way up the straight, no doubt doing what he could to keep his wandering mount off his close attendant, Prince Fort, which was still short half a length as he went by the post. Following the stewards' inquiry, a statement was issued, and included within it was a caution for Mr McGowan to keep a straight course in future.'

There was no interfering. The horses never touched and the Tralee racecourse did not have a camera patrol at that time. I was upset by the decision of the stewards. Two weeks later at Mallow, I rode Artistic Lad to challenge a very good-looking dark chestnut trained by Francis Flood and ridden by Gerry Newman, still an amateur at that stage. As he went for his whip inside the last furlong, his horse veered in front of mine. A stewards' enquiry was announced. The incident looked worse on the camera, so the stewards reversed the places. I got no satisfaction from being given this race.

Sale of St Clerans and Purchase of Dollanstown

When we began housebuilding on our land at Hartstown, we started looking for a suitable residential farm within thirty miles of Dublin. During this eventful period, Ken MacDonald heard that Captain Tim Rogers, who owned Airlie Stud and other farms near Maynooth, was in discussions either to buy or to advise on the sale of a rather special farm in his area. Captain Rogers told my good friend Conor Crowley that Mrs Plesch, the owner of Dollanstown Stud, was giving up breeding horses to race, and that the stud was for sale privately. Captain Rogers and Bob Griffin, the highly regarded vet from the Curragh, had been advising the owner for years on suitable stallions for her mares. Conor told Captain Rogers that we did not require any borrowings for the purchase of Dollanstown. Mrs Plesch lived at Avenue Foch in Paris and at Villa Leonina in Beaulieu-Sur-Mer, France, and only stayed at Dollanstown during the month of July each year. She said she would like to sell the stud, which came with 320 acres, to someone she thought could care for it, retaining the three full-time gardeners. Captain Rogers arranged for Mrs Plesch, the owner, to meet Conor and myself in early May. She was expecting a much older man but when Conor told her we had purchased St Clerans from John Huston and retained the staff, she relaxed and then asked me if I could afford to buy Dollanstown, to which I replied: 'I hope so, because it is the undiscovered house-and-gardens treasure in this country.' Conor arranged everything between solicitors, and the contracts were exchanged. Two weeks before completion, Mrs Plesch and her daughter, Bunny, invited Anne and myself for lunch.

Captain Rogers arranged to meet us at the Catholic Church in Maynooth, with instructions to be on time because Mrs Plesch insisted on the highest standards, and absolute punctuality. Dollanstown had a gentle presence: Gold Leaf on black painted iron gates with an old-style gate lodge on the right. This old-world cottage was occupied by Michael Gillick and his wife, a poultry instructress. She kept Rhode Island Reds caged in natural surroundings to fence off foxes. The grounds and avenue were manicured in a winding sweep. On the left side, as we drove towards the main house, was the Cedar Atlantica, followed by the Mammoth. Between these and other rare specimens was the tulip tree. All of these and so many more were allowed to behave just as nature wished, within the manicured, well-fed lawns.

We were welcomed by Madame Plesch's butler, who parked our cars in the first yard, since cars were not allowed to obstruct the views of the lawns and parkland from the large low windows in the drawing room and the dining room. Other guests included Conor and Pat Crowley, Bob and Eileen Griffin, Mr and Mrs Desmond Guinness from Leixlip and Eileen Plunkett from Luttrellstown. Madame Plesch had two Derby winners: Psidium, bred in Dollanstown, winning at 66/1; Major Dick Hern trained Henbit to win their second Derby in 1980.

Having completed the purchase, we moved to Dollanstown in June 1976. Christopher Berkeley, my brother-in-law, designed a most efficient central-heating system for the house. The first winter we lived in the kitchen beside the Aga cooker and Anne got dressed in the large hot press. We only had close friends to come and stay. We switched the dining room to the back drawing room to accommodate our three-pod dining-room table from St Clerans. What had been the dining room was now a study, with double doors opening to the west garden: a huge success. The garden created an unbelievable background to our first lunch party during Dublin Horse Show week, 1977. It was the first time most of our guests had seen Dollanstown. Mrs Berkeley, Anne's mother, was in tears with joy; she just could not believe the style, and such a setting, with the clear blue sky. 'Not even in Hollywood!' she said.

We were made very welcome at our new home at Dollanstown by families in the area whom we got to know through hunting and racing. Brigadier Bryan and Mary Fowler invited us for dinner at their home; we arrived at 8 PM sharp, unaware that dinner with the Fowlers was still black tie. Anne was dressed to suit the occasion and luckily I was in a charcoal suit, white shirt and tie. The Brigadier sat me in front of a mirror and helped me through the ten steps to tie a perfect black bow. Then he undid the bow and said to me: 'Join us when you have done it yourself.' We had a great evening; other guests included Anne, the Duchess of Westminster, owner of Arkle, and Simon Walford and his wife, Angela.

John Fowler, son of the Brigadier, rode 250 winners under rules and more than 200 point-to-point winners, including some good races at the Cheltenham Festival. He was tragically killed in an accident while cutting down a tree on their farm in Summerhill, County Meath, in December 2008. John was a great loss to his wife, Jennifer, his sons Harry and Charlie, to racing, and to the various committees he was involved with. John and his sister, Jessica (the trainer Jessica Harrington), were the first brother and sister to represent Ireland at the European Three Day Event Championships, in 1967. John was also a member of the Irish Three Day Event team at the 1968 Olympic Games.

Highway Patt and Thornacre

My dream was to ride at Cheltenham. With that in mind, I bought Highway Patt from P. P. Hogan. I knew the horse; I had ridden him in a point-to-point race. This horse was naturally fit and did not require a great deal of work. After his summer break, Noel McMenamin thought he was fit enough to run in the three-mile chase in Listowel, but we certainly did not think that he was ready to win at 33/1 – which caught us all by surprise. Noel dropped him off at Mick O'Toole's yard in the Curragh on the way home from Listowel.

I considered amateur riders in Ireland who didn't turn professional to be professional amateurs. At this time those amateurs included D. K. Weld, Ted Walsh, Colin Magnier, John Fowler, John Queely, Bob Townsend, Martin Brassil, Willie Mullins, Homer Scott and Harry De Bromhead. These were involved in racing every day. To keep fit, I cycled and ran most days and rode out two mornings a week. Michael O'Toole, Homer Scott and P. P. Hogan, and trainers and owners Jim and Pat Glesson, sometimes allowed me ride their horses in races, which helped me retain a level of fitness.

My hope of riding at Cheltenham ended at Leopardstown when I broke my wrist, having been brought down riding one of Pat Gleeson's horses. Niall Madden, still an amateur, was delighted to have the ride on Highway Patt at Cheltenham. Unfortunately, they came a cropper at the fifth fence. Highway Patt finished second to a very good horse, Diamond Edge, ridden by Peter Scudamore at the Cheltenham Christmas meeting. David Nicholson, known as 'the Duke', bought him as a Christmas present for one of his patrons at a price we couldn't refuse.

Anne and I became good friends with Eamonn Walsh and his wife Eileen when we were hunting with the Galway Blazers. Eamonn was a very sought-after senior counsel before becoming a High Court judge. At around the same time, he became joint master of the Galway Blazers. Eileen would have the jeep waiting near the Four Courts for their journey to Galway on Friday evenings for the hunt on Saturday.

Michael O'Toole spotted a young horse, Thornacre, winning in impressive style on his first appearance at the Limerick hunt point-to-point, in January 1982. Eamon Walsh took a half-share in Thornacre and was pleased when I rode him to win two point-to-points. I stupidly hit the front too soon in a three-mile chase at Navan, to be beaten half a length by Áth Cliath, ridden by Willie Mullins. Áth Cliath went on to win the Fox Hunters at Liverpool. I won two point-to-points on him. In November 1982, just two months after we had our annual trip to Burghley horse trials, Eamonn suffered a heart attack while hunting with the Blazers. This was a big shock for Eileen, their son Mark and daughter-in-law Hilary. Eamonn was a massive loss to all who knew him and to the Galway Blazers. We keep in touch with Mark, Hilary and their family.

Jim Beardsley, who had owned a half-share in Oranmore, purchased Eamonn's share in Thornacre. Jim decided that Thornacre should be trained by Michael Dickinson in Yorkshire, as this was more convenient for him than Nick Henderson's yard in Lambourn. This is what Peter O'Sullevan wrote in the *Daily Express* on Saturday 22 January 1983:

Earlier in the afternoon, Mick O'Toole will be interrupting breakfast in Barbados four hours behind GMT for a commentary via the transatlantic phone on Haydock's one o'clock. The Irish trainer's concern is for the progress of Thornacre and his owner jockey, Joe McGowan, in the Haig Whiskey Novices Qualifier. Mick, who trained Hartstown and Davy Lad to win in the McGowan colours at the Cheltenham festival, bought the new Michael Dickinson resident on the thirty-five-year-old rider's behalf. Joe and Thornacre have already teamed up successfully in a couple of Irish point-to-points but this assignment is far more significant and, with respect to this promising horse's handler, the pilot may represent as potent a danger as the opposition.

I was cruising with a furlong to go when Thornacre suddenly faded; he had burst a blood vessel. Charter Party, ridden by Peter Scudamore and trained by David Nicholson, won the race. After a long rest, Thornacre won two good hurdle races. He was favourite to win his first novice chase at Wetherby, but he over-jumped the regulation fence, took a crashing fall and had to be put down.

Chapter Nineteen

Hartstown: A Horse for the Future

George Rogers, whose honesty and experience I respected, phoned me from Goffs yearling sales in 1976 to say I had first refusal on a yearling he had just bought, costing 4,000 guineas. He said this horse had everything, including a very good pedigree. He could win the champion hurdle. He was right, until I messed it up. George prepared the two-year-old for me to show in hand at the RDS. We were second to a two-year-old shown by my friend, Tommy Brennan, who represented Ireland in both showjumping and eventing: a wonderful character. Noel McMenamin collected our horse and took him to Dollanstown, where he received special attention. Eighteen months later, Noel dropped him to Peter Russell's yard. Peter was training a small string of horses near the Curragh. He declared Hartstown for the two-mile 1979 Bumper for Easter Monday at Fairyhouse.

Hartstown looked great in the parade-ring. He gave me a copybook ride in mid-division of twenty-four runners. Turning into the straight, he took off with an astonishing turn of speed to finish second to a very good horse, Naïve Duke, trained by Edward O'Grady. The following season, I rode him in all his hurdle races, allowing him time to mature. At the start of the 1980-81 season, I rode Hartstown in the two-mile bumper in Down Royal, described in the *Irish Field* on 18 October 1980 by a Special Correspondent:

> Amateur rider Joe McGowan will hardly ride an easier winner than his own Rarity gelding, Hartstown, who scored a comfortable victory in the Bumper. Hartstown justified a nice gamble from 5/1 to 7/4, which resulted in the favourite, Videostar, drifting from odds-on to 2/1 and then into 6/4.

Joe settled this handsome gelding towards the back of the small field in the early stages as Fenaghy made the running ahead of Kilmore Prince, Videostar and Galway Maid. When they reappeared from behind the stables, Kilmore Prince had taken command in front of the improving Hartstown, Two Sovereigns and Kilmore Prince.

Before the straight, Hartstown went on and was chased by Two Sovereigns, the pair drawing away from Kilmore Prince and Videostar. Over two furlongs out, the winner was clear and only had to be steered home to win by a very easy eight lengths with Kilmore Prince third, another six lengths away.

The day after Down Royal, I was riding Rockingham, a horse owned by Bill Buller, in my first novice event at Borris in County Carlow. We crashed at the water-jump, leaving me with cracked ribs, less than three weeks before the first running of the amateur St Leger at the Curragh, run over the St Ledger distance, one mile and six furlongs.

Fred Kenny, the orthopaedic surgeon, gave me an injection late on the morning of the race to remove the discomfort. This was a hot contest, with all of the top amateurs riding. Readyup was clear favourite and Hartstown was 14/1. At the dip, before the bend into the long straight, I was cruising. Michael O'Hehir from RTÉ Radio, with two furlongs to go, said: 'They are not going to catch the leader, Hartstown, and his rider, Joe McGowan.'

He was backed in from 14/1 to 7/1. I told Ted O'Driscoll, Joe Duffy and anybody else who asked me what my chances were, that Hartstown would win. I could have won at Down Royal by a distance, and some punters had forgotten how Hartstown had quickened in the straight at Fairyhouse as a four-year-old. Tom Brennan, my business partner, owned a half-share in Hartstown. After the race, he had money coming out of every pocket, and he bought champagne for the rest of the afternoon, although Tom never touched alcohol.

There was no shortage of press coverage of our success.

Tony Power of the *Irish Press* wrote:

Owner rider Joe McGowan had the best success of his career as an amateur rider when winning the first division of the amateur riders' St Leger at the Curragh yesterday afternoon. Riding his own five-year-old, Hartstown, he beat the odds-on favourite, 'Readyup', to wreck the hopes of the Jackpot hunters.

Coming into the straight, the business cum sportsman kicked on with Hartstown, and, getting the first run on his opposition, had a clear lead at the furlong pole. From here, the Peter Russell-trained gelding was always a winner.

Hartstown, which comes from the same family as Farney Fox, was bought for Joe McGowan by George Rogers as a yearling for 4,000 guineas and was a rosette winner in the show ring at Ballsbridge before going racing. He is now likely to go hurdle racing.

The *Irish Times* were equally impressed. 'McGowan is no longer to be considered a playboy amateur rider, and his horse, Hartstown, an exciting National Hunt prospect, is a tribute to trainer Peter Russell. The favourite, Readyup, lost his place before the straight and was running on at the finish.'

Peter Russell was shy and said he would celebrate another time. I had great respect for Peter Russell and his parents from Limerick, but now, thirty-five years later, I still feel awful for transferring Hartstown to the more experienced yard of Michael O'Toole. In fairness, O'Toole did not put me under pressure, while Anne and Tom Brennan questioned my loyalty. I deprived Peter Russell of his first Cheltenham winner: Hartstown was such a good horse that a child could have trained him. It was not in Peter's nature to hold a grudge. The bottom line is about recognising that what I did was hurtful; I am truly sorry, Peter.

Hartstown, with Niall Madden, won the Hillcrest Hurdle at Leopardstown on a tight rein far more easily than the official verdict of twelve lengths. The bookies instantly made him 2/1 favourite for the Waterford Crystal Supreme Novice Hurdle at Cheltenham. This is Tom McGinty's description of the race in the *Irish Independent* on Wednesday 18 March 1981:

Niall Madden's triumph on Hartstown, the fifth consecutive Irish victory in the Waterford Crystal Supreme Novice Hurdle, was achieved dramatically, after all had seemed lost with three hurdles to jump. Crossed by another horse, Hartstown dropped back last of the sixteen runners but he made up the ground steadily and after Eddie Wee had led Pay Related, Fifty Dollars More and the Tsarevitch into the straight, Hartstown jumped the final flight in fourth place. From there it was plain sailing for this handsome six-year-old, who strode away to beat Fifty Dollars More by two and a half lengths. Another Story was a big disappointment. He never really figured with a chance – 'What a day he chose to run his first bad race', said his trainer, Dessie Hughes. Mick O'Toole has had five runners for Mr and Mrs McGowan at National Hunt meetings and Hartstown is their fourth winner – their previous successes included the Gold Cup with Davy Lad. George Rogers bought Hartstown as a yearling for the McGowans. They broke him themselves, and Mr McGowan rode him a winner last November in the Amateurs' St Leger before the horse joined the O'Toole string with Cheltenham in view.

Hartstown, with his powerful finishing burst up the Cheltenham hill, was installed as joint favourite to win the Champion Hurdle the following year. He would have to give fourteen pounds in a handicap to For Auction, the winner of the 1982 Champion Hurdle. I schooled Hartstown over three fences at home before and after his summer holiday. He was a natural and was ready to run in his first novice chase when Noel McMenamin dropped him at Michael O'Toole's yard. Michael arranged to work him with experienced horses after racing at Naas. He was impressive, as was another young horse, Simmonscourt.

Michael entered Hartstown in two races at Punchestown: a Maiden Novice Chase and a Conditions Chase against good winners and experienced horses from the previous season, including the favourite, Kilkilowen, winner over fences, trained by Jim Dreaper. I questioned Michael O'Toole as to why he decided to take on the experienced horses instead of running in the Novice Chase. It was a miserably wet day and Hartstown slipped into the first fence, nearly unseating Ted Walsh, and was left behind as the last horse by thirty to forty lengths. The horse should have been pulled up. Instead, he followed behind, jumping very well and turning into the straight with two fences to jump, he was in touch. Ted gathered him and made up a lot of ground, and got upsides with the leader and favourite approaching the last fence. Hartstown jumped it clean, but collapsed in a heap on landing, completely exhausted.

This was Hartstown's first run over fences in what was effectively a handicap for experienced chasers. This was not one of Michael O'Toole's better days, nor did Ted Walsh or myself shine either. Hartstown chipped a bone in his hock and, despite visits to the hospitals at the Curragh and Newmarket, he never fully recovered. I must confess that this race was a big disappointment to me. George Rogers was right: he had pleaded with me not to put Hartstown chasing. George firmly believed that Hartstown, the best horse we owned, could have won two or three champion hurdles if I hadn't gone chasing with him.

I had a half-share with Aidan O'Connell, bloodstock agent, in Ballysheehan, trained by John Joe Walsh in Doneraile, County Cork. He won a few races but didn't fully recover from a bad coughing virus. John Joe, his wife Celeste, and their two boys, Martin and Brendan, used to stay with us when they had a horse running at Leopardstown. I joined them at Goffs National Hunt sales in autumn 1982, when John Joe spotted a three-year-old gelding out of a good dam's pedigree by Golden Love. He needed time to mature, so I got him for £3,500. We named this horse Joseph Knibb. Peadar McCormack and his family lived in the bungalow at the back of Hollywood Rath, where he kept about six young horses on livery, including Joseph Knibb; his story will unfold later.

Around the same time, Simmonscourt, now a five-year-old by Deep Run that we had bought from Gaye O'Callaghan as a three-year-old, costing £5,000, was given time to mature. He was well prepared and Niall Madden had schooled him over fences at Navan, Fairyhouse, Leopardstown and Naas. Niall Madden rode him at Fairyhouse in a two-and-a-half-mile chase. His jumping was impeccable but between the last two fences he fell on the flat, having broken a fetlock; Niall heard the sickening crack as he collapsed. The racecourse veterinary surgeon, Mr Richard Teevan, put him down immediately. We all thought that Simmonscourt would be a Cheltenham horse – which made his loss all the more painful.

Anne and I had the reputation of being the luckiest owners under National Hunt rules in the 1970s. But luck was only part of the story; there was persistence, a degree of dedication, and extravagance, both financial and time-wise. I decided to cut back on my involvement in racing, but it happened in a way that I hadn't expected. An unfortunate series of injuries forced me to call it a day. Parkhill developed tendon trouble, and his career ended as a five-year-old. It was my own fault for not listening to George Rogers that we never saw Hartstown's true potential. Niall Madden said that he was the most impressive horse he had ever ridden. Thornacre, Simmonscourt and Rheinbolt were put down by the racecourse veterinary surgeons. My first three-day-event horse, Millhouse, injured his back on the journey to Holland and had to be put down. I cannot finish on racing in such a mood: despite the many 'downs', we retain fantastic memories of golden racing days.

Hilltown Stud

The breeding end of the bloodstock industry is not unlike the property industry: you have to take a long-term view and not get financially overstretched. Tom Brennan purchased Hilltown Stud on 150 acres near Clonee, County Dublin, from Sir Cecil King Harman in 1976. Sir Cecil lived in Rockingham House and Estate, Boyle, County Roscommon until 1957, when the house was destroyed by fire. Part of the estate is now Lough Key Forest Park and the remainder was divided up by the Land Commission. Joan, Sir Cecil's only surviving daughter, maintains a close interest in King House, Boyle, once owned by the family. Roscommon County Council fully restored the house, which is now open to the public as a museum and is the home of the Boyle Arts Festival.

Tom was unbelievably lucky: he inherited Gerry McMullin, a very knowledgeable man on breeding, having worked with Sir Cecil all his life. In fact, Sir Cecil, who lived nearby in Leixlip, County Kildare, continued to visit the farm at least once a month to inspect and discuss with Tom and Gerry what was happening and, in particular, which stallions the mares were visiting. Sir Cecil took a deep interest in the stud until he died in 1987.

Tom got off to a great start; at Newmarket Sales, Tom and Gerry bought a filly 'Bird of Dawning' out of training in foal for 14,000 guineas. A lot of buyers were put off because she was a twin. Bird of Dawning's first foal had to be withdrawn from the Newmarket Yearling Sales owing to a slight injury on the trip over. Tom and his family named the yearling 'Monongelia'; she was trained by Henry Cecil and won three races as a three-year-old before returning to Hilltown as a four-year-old to visit a good stallion. On Derby Day at the Curragh, Monongelia in foal, and trained by Jim Bolger, won a mile listed race. Tom sold Monongelia at Newmarket sales for 420,000 guineas.

Tom, Nuala, their children and grandchildren enjoy the excitement of racing and in particular Indiana Gal, trained by Pat Martin, who won over €200,000 before being sold to Japan. Indiana Gal has a very good pedigree, out of a mare by Dane Hill, and her sire was Intikhab. In Japan she has already bred a group-one winner, and Hilltown has some close relatives.

Chapter Twenty

No Longer a Gentleman Amateur

I always enjoyed a day out with Jim Glesson. Jim was looking for a young horse to point-to-point, so together we arrived at P. P. Hogan's yard at Bruff, County Limerick, early one morning in the spring of 1978. Sarah and Susan Hogan, Pat's two daughters, and Roger, his headmen, were returning to the stables after exercise. On the journey, Jim brought me up-to-date with all the gossip: he was still a regular at the Horseshoe Bar in the Shelbourne Hotel on St Stephen's Green. After breakfast, Susan and Roger trotted up a few horses that had already won point-to-points – which made them too expensive for us. Next, on to County Clare: it was easy to recognise Tom Costello's farm and the adjoining farms owned by his sons. They were all tidy, well maintained and with not a stone out of place in the walls. We looked at a lot of horses before Jim agreed to buy a four-year-old, subject to the vet's inspection.

A three-year-old caught my eye: Tom Costello's eldest son, John, said the horse had just recovered from a stone bruise. After tea and scones, John led out the three-year-old; he was a good-looking horse, and the best walker I had ever seen. He had a jumping pedigree; his dam had won seven races, including the Galway Plate. Then they took the three-year-old to the indoor riding school, allowing him to jump loose over coloured poles. He gave a breathtaking exhibition, jumping parallels, uprights and a gate, meeting them on short and long strides with ease. He never touched a pole and he enjoyed himself. My instinct told me not to haggle when Tom said the price was £10,000. I offered him £8,000 with a contingency for a further £1,000 when the horse won his first point-to-point or race.

On the way home, Jim said, 'That was a good deal', and added that he would like to take a half-share himself. I told Jim that this horse was for eventing and I would only race him as a last resort. We named the three-year-old 'Private Deal': he never raced, but became one of the best three-day-event cross-country horses in the world.

Introduction to Three-day Eventing

Badminton, near Bath in Somerset, and Burghley, Stamford, in Lincolnshire, are the only four-star, three-day events in the world. The first ever three-day event in England took place at the Duke of Beaufort's estate in April 1949, with six thousand visitors over the three days. In recent years, both events cater for up to 250,000 visitors over three days – the same as our National Ploughing Championships. Anne and myself really enjoyed our first trip to Burghley in September 1979. We stayed at Ketton Hall with David Johnson, four miles from Burghley. We had the most enjoyable week, and we attended Burghley every year for the next eleven years.

During those years, we made many new friends, including Dr Bob Silver and John Moore from New York, who owned Shutford Manor, in the very attractive village of Shutford. We stayed with Bob and John during the Cheltenham Festivals, from 1980 to 1984; they were wonderful hosts. David Johnson introduced us to Lady Audrey Hazell-Rigg, who lived at Cold Overton, a short distance from Burghley. When Audrey came into a room, her presence was overwhelming. She threw lots of parties. They were fun; there would often be twenty to thirty of us, and a real mixture too: Dukes, Archbishops . . . you never knew who was going to be there. My ambition to compete at Burghley was realised when I rode Private Deal there in 1988. In the following year I was honoured by being chosen to captain the Irish team at Burghley in the European three-day-event championships.

None of this would have happened without the guidance of my friend Iris Kellett and the encouragement of Van de Vater. Iris reminded me that I was getting on in years, but I told her that Bill Roycroft, the Australian, competed in his first Olympic Games at forty-five years of age, and went on to the 1964, 1968, 1972 and 1976 Olympics. He was the first competitor to ride three different horses at Badminton in 1965, and came fourth at the Aintree Grand National with one of his event horses. Iris reminded me that I hadn't come through the usual route, pony camp and juniors. She did say, however, that my experience jumping over fences and hurdles and competing at gymkhanas would be a considerable help.

Mary D'Arcy, coached by Iris, had passed all her British Horse Society examinations, including the ultimate: becoming a Fellow of the BHS. A Fellow is a trainer of horses and riders from grass-roots level to the very top. Mary D'Arcy agreed to make her Irish base at Dollanstown, where we had the best facilities: indoor and outdoor arenas, cross-country fences, a full set of showjumping poles, and an all-weather gallop.

In 1979, Diane Willson put me on the Punchestown Three Day Event Committee. I listened carefully to the Chairman, Hon. Director, Col. W. B. Mullins (Bill), and the other very experienced committee members: Mr Bill Buller, who had represented Ireland; Captain Ian Dudgeon, who also represented Ireland; Miss Iris Kellett, international rider; Mr Hugh McIlveen, architect and organiser; Bill McLernon, amateur jockey, who rode for Ireland; Brian MacSharry, broadcaster; Baron de Robeck, whose estate adjoined Punchestown; Captain Tommy Ryan, ex-army, an organiser and a true gentleman; Mr Thady Ryan, M.F.H., well-known huntsman of the Black and Tans, before emigrating to New Zealand; and Mrs Jackie Samuel, who was making a brave attempt to promote carriage-driving in Ireland.

Rockingham

I had ridden Rockingham in two novice competitions before my first three-day event at Punchestown in the National competition, in May 1980. Our dressage score was poor. The next day, he took off two strides before the regulation fence on the steeplechase course and landed the other side. I'll never forget it: the best jump ever. The cross-country at Punchestown is a galloping course that suits the free-moving, long-striding horse. I rode him in a snaffle. Hugh Suffern, veterinary surgeon, and a competent three-day eventer, had ridden Rockingham in a curb chain bit. I was lucky to have a big, thick hedge to slow him down before the water complex. The next obstacles in the middle of a big field were interconnecting fences, where precision was necessary. We approached it at speed, taking one long stride, instead of two, between A and B, and he picked up to jump the third solid rails. Ted Walsh said: 'I think that McGowan is on a death-wish.' We completed the cross-country in nine minutes and ten seconds; the time allowed was ten minutes. On the third day, I rode him in a curb chain in the showjumping. We had a clear round, finishing on our dressage score and moving up to eighth place.

Mary D'Arcy had the technique, understanding and patience to bring on young horses – a great art. We travelled up and down the country during the eventing season, from April to October, for the next six years, to get the horses upgraded to advanced class, taking in trials at Tinahely, County Wicklow; Ballindenis, County Cork; Craigantlet, Belfast; Ballinlough, County Meath; Milverton, Swords, County Dublin; Longhurst, Dunmanway, Belfast; Borris, County Carlow; Ardsallagh, County Tipperary; Greenmount, County Limerick; Rademon, County Down; and Rosemount and Grey Abbey in Northern Ireland.

The next year, 1981, I finished second in the National three-day event at Punchestown on Millhouse, after a middling dressage, and going clear in the cross-country and the showjumping. Jean Mitchell, one of our selectors, told me to compete at the three-day event in Boekelo, Holland. It was very exciting travelling with the other Irish competitors: Yvonne Monaghan, Gerry Synott, Gillian Kyle, Melanie O'Brien, Captain David Foster, Claire Ryan. Mary, and Nancy Twomey, had done everything they could have done to make this a successful trip. Unfortunately, Millhouse damaged his back on the journey. One vet said he should be walked and rested; another vet advised complete rest. On the return journey, the pain got worse, and when we arrived home, Millhouse had to be put down.

Drinks at Dollanstown

Diane Willson invited the overseas riders to Dollanstown for drinks in 1981. The competitors included Ian Stark, Rodney Powell, both winners at Badminton, Eddy Stibbe, Karen Straker and her mother Elaine, Anne Taylor, Andrew Nicholson, Robert Lemieux, Helen Ogden and Rachael Bayliss, Judy Bradwell, Mike and Angela Lucker, Lucinda Prior Palmer, who won Badminton six times, and her husband, David Green, Nicola McIrvine, also a Badminton winner, who later married Sebastian Coe, Maureen Piggott and Lorna Clarke, who was usually first on the GB team – a wonderful competitor. It was a great introduction for us. They were very careful and disciplined, took little alcohol and did not hang about. This occasion only made me more determined to get a grip on the dressage and to find the right horse to compete at this level. These competitors were a great help to me when I moved to England.

Hollywood Rath

When we moved to Hollywood Rath, we asked Bill McLernon, who built the cross-country fences at Punchestown, to design and build a novice and advanced cross-country course at Hollywood Rath. The timber used had to be pressure-creosoted. Many of the fences were confined to the hedges and woodlands, to avoid having fences in the middle of the field. The first two or three fences had to be straightforward; the more difficult fences should have alternative routes. The first event took place in October 1981. Pam Stokes moved in for a week to help with secretarial work. The weather was good. We had a reception for all who helped so generously with their time: the dressage judges, the commentators Ernest McMillen, Robert McCarthy and the late Peter Young, the timekeepers, the fence stewards, the scoresheet collectors on their ponies and, especially, Joe Whitaker and his sound-system.

The following article by Jim Norton appeared in the *Irish Independent* on Saturday 25 October 1986:

Hollywood Rath trials attract a big entry. The increasing popularity of Eventing was never better demonstrated than at the highly successful Hollywood Rath two-day trials which attracted over 120 horses from all over the country. The Open Championship, the main event of the trials, was won by the County Wicklow rider, Johnny Kyle, who was riding the Grey Duke, a gelding which Kyle has been riding with considerable success over the past eighteen months and which is owned by Pam Horan from Tinahely. In second place, was North of Ireland rider, Ian Olding, who was riding Willie, which he owns himself. In third place was Feathers, owned and ridden by Deirdre Keane, who comes from Skerries.

The Intermediate event was very well supported with over fifty starting. It was won by Water Colour ridden by Mairead Curran, one of the country's top riders; Aidan Keogh was second on Spruce Lad. Young Keogh is a son of Mr and Mrs Michael Keogh from Spruce Lodge, Kilternan. His father is an official at the Turf Club and his mother, Joan, owns one of the most successful riding centres in the country, Spruce Lodge, hence the name of the horse. Patricia Lawlor from Kilkenny was third on Desert Fern. There were two novice events, one of which went to a nice young horse, Peacekeeper, ridden by Ralph Conway, with Jane Jeffers second. Neilis O'Donoghue from Cork was third on Marcus, another young animal, which may yet replace the good eventer, which was sold some time ago to America.

The hostess of the day, Anne Marie McGowan, won the other novice with her Arbitration, which was ridden by her husband, Joe. He beat Little Vic, the mount of Paddy Byrne, and Bracklyn, which was ridden by well-known international rider, Gerry Synnott, from County Wexford.

The Junior competition brought out a nice lot of young riders and the winner was Ken Mahon, who is attached to the Con Power stable at Summerhill. He was riding a horse owned by showjumping owner and Dublin businessman Conor Crowley, and he beat young Patricia O'Loughlin from Shankill, who was riding Elegant Prince. In third place was Barna, owned by Diane Connolly and ridden by Sarah Connolly. In spite of the long spell of dry weather, the going at Hollywood Rath was much better than most people had anticipated, as the rain had put back a bit of give in the going, something which was appreciated by both horses and riders.

Rademon, Crossgar, County Down

My favourite horse trials in Ireland were at Rademon, Crossgar, County Down, between Hillsborough and Downpatrick. The setting was Commander Ossie King's six-hundred-acre estate, with the river flowing through it, as wild garlic scented the accompanying paths through the woodland. Mr Ernest McMillen of Sumner McMillen sponsored the event. Ernest and his wife, Alma, had often stayed with us at St Clerans when hunting with the Galway Blazers. They invited us to meet and have lunch with Ossie King and his wife, Patsy, in their magnificent home. Ossie King founded Smith Griffin estate agents in Belfast and Dublin. The name was changed to Osborne King and Megran and later amalgamated with an old firm, Hamilton and Hamilton, to become Hamilton Osborne King. It is now called Savills.

Ossie King was the first important property man to appreciate that, sooner or later, the institutions would not continue providing finance on a straight loan basis but would want part of the action. He was one of the first to put syndicates and banks together, adding a completely new dimension to the shape of the property industry. Patsy King, his charming wife, had been lady-in-waiting to the Queen. Rademon was efficiently run and was the pipe-opener before Punchestown. The cross-country course was regarded by many to be more technical than Punchestown; the variety of fences required careful riding, particularly some of the turns and approaches. The going was usually good, but it proved to be almost impossible to get within the time allowed. Private Deal and myself won the Advanced in 1986. In April 1987, we were placed in two very prestigious trials in England at Brigstock Kettering and Belton Park, Grantham, with Private Deal and Stage Payment.

Chapter Twenty One

England Becomes My Second Home

In 1987-88 I sold Hollywood Rath and moved to England, which became our second home for the next ten years. George Dowling, our farm manager, remained with Hollywood Rath. Noeleen Geraghty moved to a better job at the Curragh, which was more convenient to her home. Noel McMenamin got a good position with one of the Arab stud farms, Peadar McCormick and his family returned to their own home at Clane, and Mary D'Arcy was spending more of her time teaching and training in Texas. Mary D'Arcy arranged that our horses would be stabled at Somerford Park farm in Cheshire under the supervision of Rachel Bayliss. In April 1988 we left Hollywood Rath, myself driving the lorry, with Private Deal, Staged Payment, Arbitration, and of course Nancy, who had looked after Private Deal for six years since he arrived as a three-year-old. In England, my first one-day event was the advanced at Durham Castle. Private Deal jumped every fence with yards to spare. This outing set me up for the British Olympic selection trials at Hooker Hall. Grania Willis wrote in the *Irish Horse World* on 13 August 1988:

JOE HITS FORM IN HOLKER

Joe McGowan and Private Deal put up their best ever performance to finish 10th in the British Olympic selection trial at the Holker Hall horse trials in Cumbria last weekend.

After a spectacularly good dressage for a mark of forty-four that kept him in contention, the ten-year-old Paddy's Stream gelding excelled himself across country but, with Joe riding to orders from chairman of selectors Van de Vater, picked up twenty time penalties.

However, he was in good company as Ian Stark's Olympic selection Sir Wattie, who won one of the divisions, collected fourteen time faults, and Stark's other winner, the ex-Ginny Leng ride Murphy Himself, incurred fifteen.

With one fence down in the showjumping, Joe and Private Deal finished 10th overall, a great morale-booster before the pair embark on the Scottish championships at the end of the month, with the final goal for the season being the four-star CCI at Burghley in September.

After the Olympic trials at Holker Hall, the Irish selectors gave me a choice of competing at the Olympics in Seoul or Burghley. I choose Burghley because Anne, our children and Mrs Berkeley and all our friends would be there and not in Seoul. I had being planning this for years. Private Deal and I were ready. Rachel Bayliss had worked hard on our dressage. Timothy Randall, a veterinary student, had his good horse, Legs Eleven, also stabled with Rachel Bayliss. We arrived two days before the dressage to become familiar with the surroundings. We took the horses round the park and gave them a short gallop in the space provided. The next morning we had coffee with the director of the trials, Bill Henson, and Captain Mark Phillips, cross-country course designer.

At the briefing, Captain Mark Phillips outlined a few fences to which we should pay particular attention, where it was unwise to attempt the direct route if our horses were not experienced. But it was for the competitors to make their own individual assessment. After the briefing, we were piled into trailers and Land Rovers and were taken on a tour of phase A, roads and tracks, the Steeplechase Course, and phase C, the second roads and tracks. After a sandwich, Timothy and I walked the cross-country course with Rachel. I walked the course three more times, giving extra attention to the difficult fences, and instantly made up my mind not to take the direct route at the Coffin fence, but to take the alternative route. Thursday mid-morning, came the dressage test: nerves do come into it. If the horse or rider is inclined to be tense, it will reflect on the marks one gets. I was relieved, but a little disappointed, when our dressage score left us in fortieth position out of eighty-seven competitors. Anne had arranged a party for the Irish contingent, together with the people who had been so helpful and good to us. I stayed with David Johnson at Ketton, four miles away, to get my sleep.

Some experienced competitors, such as Richard Meade, Rachel Bayliss, Richard Walker, Lorna Clarke and Captain David Foster, gave me advice on how to compete at this level. A competitor should walk the cross-country course alone so that he concentrates on the route he has decided to take and be certain of the alternatives at each fence. I never changed the route I had planned. I just made sure I was on the right line so that I would jump the fence at the point where I wanted to. I lined up that point with some object in the distance. The way one fence is jumped has a bearing on how the next fence is jumped. Big narrow corners never appealed to me; I always took the alternative. I was able to achieve the rhythm and regularity of speed, avoiding checking or shortening the stride in front of fences.

The first roads and tracks, and the steeplechase course, were straightforward and the second roads and tracks didn't take a bother out of my horse. After a ten-minute compulsory stop, we set off on the cross-country course. The first two fences were very straightforward and I was just as relaxed jumping the bigger obstacles, never losing concentration. We were held up because of a bad accident. I had to keep Private Deal walking for thirty minutes before we were allowed to continue. We completed the cross country within the time allowed, which showed his bravery and jumping ability.

The accident occurred at obstacle twenty-seven, which delayed us: Mark Davies took the direct route at this fence, and his horse hit the solid upright and did a somersault, and his full weight fell on Mark, who unfortunately wasn't thrown far enough away. Mark was taken by helicopter to hospital, where he died shortly afterwards. It was devastating for his family and everybody involved in eventing. The following morning, Sunday, Private Deal passed the compulsory vets' inspection, striding out. He was just calm with his steady temperament, clearing the showjumping course, which was long and demanding. We moved up from fortieth after the dressage to finish seventh. If only Private Deal and myself could have improved our dressage, we would have no equal. We were now looking forward to the European Championships at Burghley, the following September, 1989.

It was a magical three months for Catherine and Joseph and their grandmother, Mrs Berkeley: they attended pony camp at Burghley and Peterborough. Catherine formed a great friendship with Caroline Rowley, only child of Peter and Terez. The Rowley family included Catherine in all their travels in Europe. In fact, Catherine divided her time between Hambledon Hall and Quarry House. I took a two-year lease on Quarry House at Barnack in 1987. Barnack is a handsome stone village, two miles from Stamford, one of the finest stone towns in England. Behind Quarry House on the way to the Village Green there was an area called 'Hills and Holes', which was a child's dream. We were introduced to many parishioners by attending the Catholic 6 PM Mass every Saturday evening at the Protestant church at Bainton. The priest from Peterborough made this a social outing with a few prayers thrown in.

Joseph Knibb

To add to the excitement of that summer, Joseph Knibb, our last racehorse, won two races on consecutive days at the Galway Festival, trained by Tommy Carberry and ridden by Conor O'Dwyer. Catherine was especially pleased, as she had led Joseph Knibb to the enclosure after he won the feature race at Kilbeggan in May 1988. She would have loved to be in Galway, as would all of us. My brother Gerry and his pals had a big flutter. They still talk about it.

On Saturday 4 June 1988, the *Irish Field* reported:

Skipping what looked to be an easier assignment, at Down Royal earlier in the day for the featured Michael Moore Car Sales Novice Chase, Joseph Knibb justified trainer Tommy Carberry's decision with a good win from the favourite Rosenaire and Monksville. Jumping with precision Joseph Knibb made the running, keeping wide . . . and reaching the last jump in front ran on to win by three lengths and eight lengths in the colours of Mrs Joe McGowan.

Joe McGowan had some compensation for his disappointment at having to withdraw his Punchestown runner Private Deal after the first phase of the event, when his Joseph Knibb won the novice Steeplechase at Kilbeggan this week. Joe's winner was led in by his six-year-old daughter Catherine, who was following in her mother's footsteps as Ann-Marie had done the honours in the past for Joe's Cheltenham winners, Davy lad, Parkhill and Hartstown.

European Championships

Rachel Bayliss, herself a European champion, experienced and practical, persuaded me not to compete at Badminton in May 1989, because three months later was the more important European Championships. I agreed to leave Badminton until 1990. Private Deal was in great form at one-day events in preparation for the European champion-ships. Thirlestone Castle in Scotland, twenty-five miles south of Edinburgh, was the last outing before the European Championships at Burghley. I was delighted when Tommy Brennan came to supervise and report to his other selectors on who, he felt, should be selected for the Irish team. This was my fourth consecutive year competing there. Rachel Bayliss, Nancy Twomey, Anne and myself were guests of the farming Tweedie family, Douglas and Senga, and their two children, Charles and Louise. Private Deal went clear within the time allowed in the cross-country and clear in the show-jumping. Tommy Brennan said, 'Make sure you keep that horse sound: you are on the team for Burghley in three weeks' time.'

Tommy Brennan won more than seventy international competitions and eleven hundred national classes. Captain Con Power, who represented Ireland at home and abroad, best described Tommy Brennan's career: 'He was a dedicated competitor who was a pathfinder for Irish riders, both at home and abroad. He was a winner on so many different horses and in different disciplines – showjumping, eventing, racing. He would like to have raced but, just like myself, his legs grew too long. He was always a mentor and someone who was very generous with help for younger riders like myself coming along behind him. His advice was wise and helpful. I remember one time he told me that many of his classes were won over the first three fences. "That way you always have something in hand over the rest," he said. I have to say that it was very sound advice and it helped me win a number of classes down the years.'

Rachel Bayliss, Christopher Walker and Timothy Randell arrived with Private Deal on Monday. Now is a good time for me to thank the Walker family from Cheshire for taking Private Deal in their luxury horsebox to many one-day events up and down England and Scotland over the years. Tommy Brennan and the other Irish competitors arrived the following day, Tuesday. Private Deal was alert and in full command. Anne and her mother, Mrs Berkley, Catherine and Joseph were even more excited when Tommy made me captain. I will never forget the worry of that week.

This is one of the many letters to Anne, describing the excitement of the week:

Dear Dear A.M.

The days with you at Exton and Burghley were so brilliant as well as glorious that they will never ever be forgotten by me.

You were so wonderful, A.M., to cope, with us all, and not only cope, with a smile, but to be a constantly gracious and concerned hostess, even taking the time in all the hectic rush to show me the land and the beauty of the place.

How can I ever thank you, for there are not enough suitable words. However, please know that all my thank you's come from the heart.

How immensely proud you must be of Joe's fantastic achievements, especially when one remembers that he gets little time to school and practise, unlike the other riders. I am sure that he and P.D. will end up with that elusive Gold.

Please do overlook this very latent letter, but there was no way way I could first scribble a note in a rush after having had *such* a magical time.

Again, many many thank you's to you both, as well as much love.

Maggee

As Dermot Collins wrote in the *Irish Horse* in October 1989:

McGowan Magic Earns Team Bronze for Ireland

The hordes of enthusiastic Irish supporters who made their annual pilgrimage to the Burghley Remy Martin Horse Trials were well rewarded when the Irish team won a bronze medal, but it was the inspired performance of Joe McGowan and Private Deal which was the main talking point. Ireland's representatives, Joe McGowan, Eric Horgan, Olivia Holohan, Melanie Duff and Kieron Ryan, and ten other teams, from Belgium, France, West Germany, Italy, Poland, Spain, the Netherlands, Russia and of course Great Britain, took part, with Austria, Sweden and Switzerland sending individual competitors.

Ireland's Chef d'Équipe, Tommy Brennan, commented that the course was beautifully built and presented, and although it was very 'strong' there were options on all the fences. 'If riders wanted to go for the honours they could. This was a very well-balanced course and the proof is in the fact that there were no serious mishaps!'

After the first day of dressage, Olivia Holohan and Rusticus for Ireland had 68.2 penalties, while Melanie Duff and Rathlin Roe had 66.2. Friday saw the second day of dressage, with Eric Horgan and Homer, Joe McGowan and Private Deal to compete for the team, and Kieron Ryan and Pickpocket to compete as individuals. Eric collected 72.8 penalties, Joe 65.8 and Kieron 74.0. So at the end of the dressage phase, the German team were leading, with Great Britain a very close second and Ireland in seventh position.

The pressure was now on Eric Horgan and Joe McGowan. Eric and Homer completed the course with just one mishap at the Trout Hatchery when Homer surprised Eric with an exuberant response to some mild coaxing in the water, stumbled on the way out and had no chance of jumping the first part of the combination (fence 14). Eric wisely opted for the longer route and was soon on his way again.

Mark Philips had predicted that Joe McGowan would be one of the few riders to complete the course inside the time and his prediction was ably fulfilled as Joe and Private Deal pulled out all the stops to come up with a brilliant performance. There were only two nail-biting moments for the Irish supporters, once at Centaurs Leap and again at the Remy Martin selection when Private Deal, still running on strongly, almost missed his turn. However, he was soon back into his stride and galloped through the finish in fine style in 12 minutes, 52 seconds, overtaking the Russian, Boris Vailey, on the run in. After the speed and endurance phase the teams position had Great Britain in the lead with 157.6 penalties, France second with 235.4, Holland third with 300.8 and Ireland fourth with 340.6.

On Sunday morning you could feel the tension as the horses were presented to the Ground Jury for the final inspection. The horses were presented in team order, which meant that the trio of Irish horses were presented one after the other. They looked superb and passed without any discussion. It is always reassuring to see the Ground Jury nod assent to each other when the horse is halfway back down the trot-up area. This they did for all the Irish horses. Congratulations to all concerned, but more especially to Hugh Suffern, our vet.

This is the writeup in Angela Phelan's 'Weekender File' in the *Irish Independent* on 16 September 1989:

> The showjumping took its usual toll with only five clear rounds out of the thirty-five jumped. Olivia and Rusticus had one fence down to give them a total of 166 for 25th place, Eric and Homer had three fences down and 25 time penalties to give them a final score of 129.05 for 20th place overall. Joe and Private Deal had already moved up one place because of the elimination of Rodney Powell and with only 2.25 time penalties to add to their score after a beautifully ridden round they moved up three more places to finish 5th overall on a score of 68.05 penalties.

Chapter Twenty Two

'On Your Mark'

While Princess Anne's estranged husband Mark Phillips was the centre of attention at the European Three Day Championship at Burghley last weekend, the Irish team with Joe McGowan in particular were also making their presence felt.

Of the six who finished Saturday's course which was designed by Phillips, without either jumping or time faults, five were British, with McGowan on Private Deal producing the goods for Ireland.

Overall, Ireland finished third to Great Britain and Holland while McGowan was fifth in the individual stakes.

Quite a large Irish contingent travelled to Burghley to encourage the Irish team.

Conor and Pat Crowley, Prince Az and Princess Bo Guirey, the Hon. Patrick Connolly Carew, the Hon. Audrey Hazel Rigg, Catherine O'Halloran, wife of Dublin architect Brian, Brenda Rohan, wife of property supremo Ken, Paul and Maris Hamilford (Steinberg), Hugh and Marie Mac Dermot, Captain David Foster and his wife Denise, Van De Vater, Stephen Miley, Pat and Yvonne Monaghan and McGowan's wife Anne Marie were just some of the Irish crowd who cheered the team which included Eric Horgan, Melanie Duff, Olivia Hoolihan as well as McGowan.

Princess Di was on hand at trophy time and while her peck on the cheek for the beleaguered Foggy Phillips was the one shot the paparazzi were looking for, instead they had to settle for HRH bemedalling all the winners.

Fintan and Maureen Gunne flew in to support me just for the cross-country. Stephen Miley was very good to bring George Dowling with him. George was our farm manager when we owned Hollywood Rath. At the reception in the sponsored Remy Martin marquee for drinks and photographs, George made a beeline for Mark Phillips, only to be intercepted by a security guard. George said to Mark: 'I am Joe McGowan's farm manager.' Mark said to the security guard: 'I want to talk to this man.' George continued: 'Captain, I believe you are a big tillage man with no cattle; a few charolais in the fields around that big house of yours would look well.' George cherished the photograph taken with the Captain and walked part of the cross-country course with the Captain at Punchestown in 1991.

That was an unforgettable year: captain of the Irish three-day-event team, and Private Deal at his brilliant best. Catherine had trips to London with Caroline Rowley and her parents, Peter and Terez, visiting museums, playing tennis at Hurlingham and taking in a few days at Wimbledon. Catherine, Caroline Rowley and Joseph had great fun at the well-organised two-week pony camp in Burghley, supervised by parents, grandparents and teenagers. Those two weeks were pure joy for Mrs Berkeley, their grandmother. In December of that year, to crown everything, our daughter, Christine was born – a momentous happening in our lives.

Private Deal had his deserved holiday out in the paddocks every day for a few hours. Nancy Toomey began working him on the bridlepaths around Somerford Park farm in Cheshire after Christmas 1989, and I started back on my bicycle around Exton Hall in Rutland. Private Deal's near foreleg was sore from a growth beside the tendon – called a splint – before the World Equestrian Games trial at Milton Keynes. I just took Private Deal slowly on the cross-country, but that evening and the next morning he was really lame.

The following is from the *Irish Field*, on Saturday 4 August 1990:

Joe McGowan may have missed his chance of competing in the World Equestrian Games when he was forced to withdraw Private Deal, but he wasn't going to forsake his planned trip to Stockholm just because he wasn't riding.

On arrival at the Games, Joe immediately offered his services to *chef d'équipe* Commandant Ronnie MacMahon and was equally promptly deputed to scoop up any erring Irish riders at the first water complex. A swift break for lunch in the McGowan camp nearly resulted in disaster, however, as Anne-Marie put her foot in a hole coming out of the tent, injuring herself quite severely. But Joe didn't wait around to take his wife to hospital for an x-ray, instead he left five-year-old son Joseph in charge, while he dashed off to take up his post at the water. And not a moment too soon as Polly Holohan appeared over the horizon seconds later, clinging to Rusticus' ears as he hurtled down the steep descent into the water after a massive leap over the sandbags at the top. But Polly barely had time to get wet before she was swept back up into the saddle by the gallant Joe, who was probably quite pleased to be taking an unscheduled dip on such a hot day. Meanwhile, back at the local hospital, and Anne-Marie was dozing off while waiting to be x-rayed, much to the horror of young Joseph, who broke his arm at the beginning of July and is still wearing a support bandage. 'Mum, Mum,' he said, shaking his mother anxiously, 'don't fall asleep or they'll think it's me they're supposed to look at and not you.' The x-ray was eventually carried out on the right limb and a broken metatarsal bone was diagnosed in Anne-Marie's foot. She appeared at the following morning's horse inspection with both legs bandaged and sporting a pair of crutches.

Nancy spent months pressure-bandaging, icing and cold-hosing to reduce the swelling on Private Deal's leg. We rested him for six months until the end of January 1991, before we started preparing him for the European championship in Punchestown in May 1991. We travelled to Iris Kellett's farm near Punchestown to do some fast work on Private Deal on the all-weather gallops at the Curragh to avoid the firm ground in England. Unfortunately, I was forced again to withdraw: it was very embarrassing. Private Deal had the splint removed at the veterinary hospital, in the Curragh, County Kildare. I thought things over and realised that my dream of competing at Badminton was over. It was now time to concentrate on my young family. I telephoned Van de Vater four months after the operation to let him know that there was a good chance of Private Deal remaining sound, but only if he was nurtured along, before competing up to intermediate level only. His leg would not stand up to preparing him to compete at the top level. I could trust Van, who understood and appreciated what Private Deal was capable of achieving in the future. Van takes up the last competitive years of Private Deal as follows:

> It is twenty-six years since Joe rang me and said he could no longer continue riding competitively owing to pressure of business. He kindly offered Private Deal to me to lightly compete with. I was thrilled with his generosity and immediately collected the horse. We began getting him fit, and after several months competed lightly, locally. What a spectacular horse he was to ride, brave and speedy, professionally schooled over years of work with Joe and Mary D'Arcy. I had ridden a great number of good horses over the years, but Private Deal, with his power, movement, athleticism and speed, was a sensation to ride. I was utterly delighted with him. We went to Boekelo in Holland, and were third in team competition and were placed many times at home. Regrettably, he developed a heart condition in his later years, and died in his box at Ardsallagh, and is buried there. Joe developed such a great partnership with him; they both were ultimate athletes, possessing great balance and lightness, and were such a pleasure to watch.

> This Rainer Maria Rilke poem brings this part of my story to an end.

> I live my life in widening rings
> I live my life in widening rings
> which spread over earth and sky.
> I may not ever complete the last one,

but that is what I will try.
I circle around God, the primordial tower,
and I circle ten thousand years long;
and I still don't know if I'm a falcon, a storm,
or an unfinished song.

Part 4
The Planning Tribunal: The Theatre of Ice

EMPTY SEATS

The Tribunal of Inquiry into certain planning matters and payments
Opened at the Print Works theatre in November ninety-seven.
The play weighed moral values against social justice.
Faceless outsiders offered reward for a plot, dead or alive.
Shady influences. Bungalows at the crossroads.

Actors and understudies probing the history of all your aunts,
Elliptical comments deliberately leaked and timed
Attracted sell-out audiences to the state-funded production.
Oddities out to defend their version of public morality.
Measured matinées, disenchanted public.

Strong tea at the nearby café helped formulate headlines,
Witnesses and performers with their version of events.
Today's newspapers, tomorrow's fish and chips.
I did not take the opinion badly.
Let it be.

Some actors returned to the Law Library, their true career.
Flat, uninspired, indigestible soundbites,
Long-winded infelicities, the play came a cropper.
Wandering eternally on the scenic route,
Taking the country for a theatrical ride.

J. B. McGowan

Chapter Twenty Three

'Some of the Allegations Are Frivolous'

A notice appeared in two Irish daily newspapers in 1995, offering a £10,000 reward to anybody who could provide information leading to the conviction of persons involved in corruption on planning matters and zoning of land for residential development in the Republic of Ireland. Donnelly, Neary, Donnelly, Solicitors, from Newry, County Down, placed the advertisements on behalf of unnamed clients. These notices attracted a lot of media attention and public comment in the newspapers and in Dáil Éireann. The *Sunday Business Post* published an article by journalist Frank Connolly, under the headline, 'FIANNA FÁIL POLITICIAN PAID OFF BY DEVELOPERS'. It was alleged that a serving Fianna Fáil TD had been accused of receiving payments from property developers in Dublin in return for helping get land rezoned for housing.

By the middle of 1997, a few newspapers had named Ray Burke, alleging that he was one of the politicians who had allegedly received large financial contributions from a well-known property company, on the understanding that Mr Burke might be able to assist in certain planning matters. Both Mr Burke and the developer denied these allegations and claimed that these payments were political donations. Public statements by Mr Burke followed, before he came to a decision to resign from the position of Minister for Foreign Affairs and from Dáil Éireann on 7 October 1997. That same day, a parliamentary debate was taking place in Dáil Éireann on a motion to set up the Tribunal of Inquiry into Planning Matters.

There was some unease, even prior to the creation of the Tribunal, as these extracts from the Parliamentary Debate on the Bill setting up the Planning Tribunal show. Alan Dukes, in opposition, agreed with the Minister for the Environment, Deputy Noel Dempsey, when he said he hoped that Messrs Donnelly, Neary and Donnelly,

Solicitors, would make available to the Tribunal what information they had at their disposal. He said: 'I very much share that hope, it is most important that they do so.'

Mr Dukes, who was even then a wise old fox, added that the letter sent by that firm of solicitors to Deputy John Bruton and other Members of the House, dated 30 September 1997, contained some rather curious phrases. Speaking of fifty-two allegations concerning planning and rezoning around the country, but particularly in Dublin, they said the following:

> Some of these allegations are frivolous and most do not lead me to believe that criminal proceedings would be likely to ensue.

They went on to say:
some of them seem, prima facie, to give cause for concern. Six of these have been forwarded to the Gardai, but more warrant proper investigation.

Mr Dukes warned: 'This is the opinion of some person with a typical lawyerly indecipherable signature, writing on behalf of Donnelly, Neary and Donnelly. I do not know who that person may be, he or she may well be a very eminent solicitor, but it is not his or her business to decide what, in our jurisdiction, amounts to improper or illegal conduct and what does not. It is not the business of that person to decide which allegation is frivolous and which is not. That is the job of the Director of Public Prosecutions. It is not the business of that person to say that some of these allegations, prima facie, give cause for concern and that some do not. That is the business we propose to hand to a Tribunal properly established under the legislation of this State. Six of these allegations have been forwarded to the Garda and that is a very public-spirited thing for Donnelly, Neary and Donnelly to do. However, it is not their business to decide what is put to the Garda and what is not.'

A wary Mr Dukes added: 'While Donnelly, Neary and Donnelly and the people they represent, those who came together some time ago to offer a reward of up to £10,000 for information, may have been well-intentioned in doing what they did, they have taken a wrong road in getting results.' He gave several reasons for this view, noting: 'They have allowed Donnelly, Neary and Donnelly to take unto themselves the functions we expect the Garda, the Director of the Public Prosecutions and the Chief State Solicitor to carry out. Secondly, they have gathered information and made allegations in a way which leaves the rest of us in the dark as to their substance, the motivation of those who made them, and their readiness to provide the information our legal system and the British would require to substantiate a charge brought before a duly constituted court of law.'

Mr Dukes added: 'I do not criticise these people for their views and concerns; it is just that they have chosen a route which is fundamentally flawed. Given that we are going to the trouble of establishing this Tribunal, they should make available to the Tribunal all their information, regardless of whether or not they think it is frivolous, so it can be handled by a body properly constituted to do so.'

Noel Dempsey, the then Minister for the Environment, said: 'From the contributions which have been made, no one disagrees that there is a need for a judicial investigation to get to the bottom of the allegations, rumours and innuendoes which have beset the planning system and have scant regard for the good name and reputation of those who serve on public authorities, whether as elected members or officers. If people are guilty of impropriety, I hope this will be established and they will have to face the consequences of their actions. If, on the other hand, people who have been fingered are innocent, it is even more important that their good name is restored, that they are vindicated and that the allegations and innuendoes are refuted. As is clear from the Programme for Government, it is a major ambition of mine during my term as Minister to improve the operation of the planning system. The process has commenced.'

Mr Dempsey thanked Deputy Dukes and continued: 'One of the clearest demands from all sides of this House is that Donnelly, Neary and Donnelly Solicitors, their clients and all their complainants would put before the Tribunal, at the outset, the facts and evidence they have in their possession. That is the one clear message to emerge from this matter. It will greatly facilitate the Tribunal in its deliberations and remove the need for much preliminary work which might otherwise have to be done. With no sense of acrimony, I say to those solicitors that they now have what they desired, namely, a judicial inquiry into the planning process in Dublin. I expect they will do their utmost to co-operate with that inquiry and make available to it all the evidence in their possession.'

Mr Dempsey continued: 'I refer to a comment relating to councillors lining people's pockets by rezoning land, etc. In fairness to councillors, they have a job to do and they sometimes work under enormous pressure. They have a duty to become involved in and take responsibility for the planning process and development plans. It is unfair to characterise them doing their duty as doing it for the sole reason of lining people's pockets. It is the responsibility of this House to ensure that, if people are making money from decisions relating to rezoning, etc., a regime is to be put in place to deal with such matters and collect suitable taxes from those involved. I have referred this matter to officials in my Department and the review group in order that consideration might be given to the provision of services in respect of rezoned land. I thank Members for their contributions and, assuming that the motion is passed, I wish the Tribunal well in its work.'

The Murphy Gogarty Module

The witnesses to the Murphy Gogarty Module attended the Tribunal before ourselves (Brennan and McGowan). Their experiences set the tone for what was to follow. James Gogarty was the star witness. His cosseted position was safeguarded by an opening statement where barristers were warned to go easy on this old, frail gentleman. In this regard, he was facilitated by the performance of the Chairman, Fergus Flood, which resembled a hunt master who had forgotten to bring his horn to the chase.

The essence of any Tribunal – and the reason why Tribunals secure such great powers – is that it is supposed to consist of a disinterested search for truth. That is why they are allowed be their own judge, jury and executioner. The Planning Tribunal utterly failed to understand this, particularly in their cavalier dealings with James Gogarty.

The Tribunal was satisfied that, in the course of giving his evidence, Mr Gogarty was truthful when recounting the facts, and that the beliefs held by him were bona fide. The Tribunal did not believe that Mr Gogarty's credibility as a witness was successfully challenged by those disputing his account of events, or by his evidence as a whole.

Mr Gogarty negotiated an option agreement for Mr Michael Bailey, the builder, to purchase all the Murphy land that Joseph Murphy Senior had been acquiring in different locations in North County Dublin from the late 1950s onwards. This agreement was conditional on Mr Bailey being successful in getting the land zoned for residential development. Mr Ray Burke told the Tribunal that he actually opposed rezoning some of this land in 1993, and had led a delegation to the then Minister of the Environment urging him to reject certain zoning applications and to follow the plan prepared by the planners of Dublin County Council.

Mr Gogarty worked closely with the Murphy family for many years, becoming a consultant to their companies. Mr Gogarty was unhappy with his pension arrangement until he successfully negotiated a pension which Joseph Murphy, Junior, felt to be overgenerous. Mr Gogarty appeared very bitter and made it absolutely clear that he hated Joseph Murphy, Junior with the Murphy family: this was eventually settled in a rather awkward context.

Mr Gogarty made exceedingly nasty allegations against his former employers. His outbursts and his choice of words attracted the sort of attention more normally associated with *The X Factor*. Mr Gogarty imagined lines such as: 'Will we get a receipt, will we fuck' to put an end to tough questioning. Generally it worked. At the beginning, everyone was having too much fun at the Tribunal to question its methodology, but just like Topsy, it continued to grow and grow.

Chapter Twenty Four

Measure for Measure: The War of the Barristers

Of course Tom Brennan and I, because of our long connection with Mr Ray Burke and his father, Mr Paddy Burke, were summoned to appear as witnesses. Tom and I gave preliminary evidence lasting a few hours at the Tribunal. I was expected to recollect certain things from almost forty years previously. I answered the questions without any advance warning and made some errors. After a difficult first day, our solicitor, John Walsh of Miley & Miley, needed clarification on a number of issues: he requested Tom and me to meet him in his office the next morning at 9 AM. At that meeting, he emphasised that all the relevant information and documentation in our possession should be made available to the Tribunal. He further stated that if we were unable to recollect any particular detail, we should say so. Dealing with John Walsh, our solicitor, was a daunting task in itself. He was demanding and precise. Martin Hayden, our senior counsel, had that invaluable quality of telling you tough truths to your face. Stephen Miley could read my thoughts. Miley & Miley made every effort to assist the Tribunal – which the Chairman appreciated.

I wasn't at all worried, however: all the land we purchased through those years had planning permission or was zoned for residential development. The exceptions were my own farm, 145 acres in Clonsilla, and 89 acres, known as 'Aiken's land', in Sandyford. My farm was part of 920 acres in the Clonsilla/Mulhuddart area which was zoned for residential in 1971. Aiken's land and another 650 acres in the Murphystown region in Sandyford were zoned residential in 1980. Both of these zonings happened in the normal way without influence on our part. It is not very challenging; you don't have to be a genius to identify future development land. Finance was the crucial element – that, and being in a position to act quickly. Dan Miley, our solicitor, often said, 'Owning land is a good idea provided you live long enough and have no borrowings.'

Twelve months later, Tom Brennan spent five weeks in the witness box and made attempts to travel overseas in an effort to aid the Tribunal. I attended during those five weeks and was in the witness box myself for a further four weeks, two weeks before the summer recess and two weeks after the one-month summer recess. The Tribunal attracted attention, both because of its approach and because of its subject-matter. The exaggerated material, together with whispers and leaks from the Tribunal and from the public-relations people who were employed by some of the witnesses, seemed deliberately designed to grab headlines and soundbites for radio and television. I felt that the Chairman sometimes allowed proceedings to drift down a slippery slope.

The Planning Tribunal was my 'Theatre of Ice'. The theatre is the most exciting profession in the world. It is also a very dangerous and treacherous one. My 'Theatre of Ice' opened in a large building, approached through an entrance from Dublin Castle, a short distance from the Olympia Theatre. In 1997, I likened the Tribunal to one of Shakespeare's comedy plays, *Measure for Measure*, and in many ways it was. The unresolved conclusion to *Measure for Measure* is one of the reasons it is often identified as an unruly play where 'Some rise by sin, some by virtue fall' (Act II, Scene I). I stated clearly at the Tribunal that I often asked Mr Burke for his opinion, which I respected. There was nothing inappropriate in me finding out if there were any future government policies that might affect our industry.

Early each morning, I would set out from Donnybrook, with the least possible baggage, to a café in Dame Street, near Dublin Castle, discovering the world along the way. I was smartly turned out each day. On my first day as a witness to the Tribunal of Inquiry into Planning Matters and Payments, I arrived at the narrow entrance to the depressing building in the grounds of Dublin Castle. Inside the old print works, I studied the military-style layout. The chair for the witness was positioned with the Chairman and his entourage to the left. The Tribunal team faced the witness, with the press directly behind. On the right, plain folding chairs were arranged facing towards the Chairman for the gallery, with the toilets a long journey away at the far end of this huge, neglected room. The morning sessions started between 10 and 10.30 AM, lasting two hours or more, then a break for lunch, returning at 2.15 PM and continuing until 4 PM or later. The gallery was packed with a collection of oddities, stimulated by press stories, which were out to defend their own version, imagined or real, of public morality. The play (Tribunal) became an industry with little hope of it coming to an end, as it had access to an unlimited budget.

Sitting in the chair on the opening day, I was on tenterhooks, but once I had apologised to the Chairman and to the Tribunal for not remembering certain details from long ago, I settled down, despite moans from the gallery and the odd burst of laughter behind me.

The Tribunal's legal team had a backroom staff to support, prompt and brief them. I felt sometimes that the questions were timed in such a way as to grab the news at one o'clock. Pat Hanratty, senior counsel for the Tribunal, would interrupt his line of questioning to Tom Brennan at about 11.45 AM to ask him what progress was being made in getting the documents from the Isle of Man. The Chairman would then say: 'Well, then, Mr Brennan, we may have to go to the High Court to deal with this matter.' This implied that the witness was facing a few days in prison. Just in time for the one o'clock news, the headline 'MR TOM BRENNAN MAY HAVE TO GO TO PRISON' would certainly grab the attention of the public. The Tribunal had taken a previous witness to the High Court for not producing certain documents, and he had to spend five days in prison. That is what could happen if you had to go to the High Court for not producing documents. Tom had been so anxious to help the Tribunal that he had chartered a plane to fly to the Isle of Man, but, due to dense fog, the plane had to beat a hasty retreat as it began to run out of fuel. Luckily, the documents arrived a few days later; that avoided further headlines.

The Tribunal had a team of researchers who went through every aspect of our business lives, every planning permission granted to our companies, and the zoning of my farm in Clonsilla and Aiken's land in Sandyford. They knew that Ray Burke and George Redmond were not involved in any way in those decisions. Yet I took the view that questions were being put in a manner designed to vilify our reputations and credibility. The Tribunal Barristers knew where the questions were leading, while I was expected to remember and answer those questions instantly. This was a great disadvantage for me. There was even one occasion when a question was put to me which was clearly outside the Tribunal's terms of reference. My Barrister immediately protested but he, in effect, was told by the Honourable Chairman to shut up.

The mood of the Tribunal was not improved by our unwillingness to yield to whatever it was they wanted; in truth, it was often unclear if they themselves knew what that was. They seemed to desire some general confession of imagined sins. Whatever it was that they desired, they took long enough about getting to it. It seemed, at times, that they were on a 'fishing expedition'.

As the days went by, the Tribunal grew more and more ill-tempered, and started scraping the bottom of the barrel. I have explained in Part Two that the affidavit I had prepared in three days contained mistakes, but no lies. The rushed affidavit that was settled long ago, and had nothing whatsoever to do with the Planning Tribunal, led to the most dramatic confrontation of my life. Much to the surprise of all who know me, the Tribunal attempted to portray me as a serial liar. There again, unlike Mr Gogarty, it appeared that our credibility was fair game.

Builders have always attracted a degree of distaste from certain quarters, such as barristers and some journalists. The hope of those arbiters of morality was that, at last, builders and developers would be brought to heel. I remember when Stephen Miley, a witness at the Tribunal, made two attempts to tell the Tribunal about some of our achievements. On the second attempt, the Tribunal told him not to continue, that this was outside the terms of reference of the Tribunal. All Stephen wanted to say was, 'Take Kilnamanagh as an example; Brennan and McGowan completed 1,650 houses on 230 acres in five years. At least one hundred of those purchasers came off the housing list. Brennan and McGowan were involved in building and selling 7,000 houses in the Dublin area over twenty-five years. Some purchasers of these houses never dreamt they could own their own home.'

One day, as Tom and I were walking up Aungier Street after leaving the Tribunal, we met a couple who had bought one of our townhouses at the Laurels in Terenure, in 1968. They recognised us and immediately said: 'How upsetting all this Tribunal thing must be for you and your families!' One of them remarked: 'My house is now worth twenty times what we paid for it thirty-four years ago.'

The Affidavit

On my last day as a witness before the summer recess, the Tribunal brought up the affidavit I had signed in 1985 in the legal dispute with Allied Irish Finance, Read and McNabb, and Brennan and McGowan – even though this dispute had being settled almost two decades earlier, and was considered to be outside the Tribunal's terms of reference.

Here are some of the exchanges between Counsel for the Tribunal and myself as reported in the *Irish Times*. The report began by noting: 'The builder, Mr Joe McGowan, has admitted lying in an affidavit he swore during court proceedings in 1985.' It continued:

> Working through the affidavit, Ms Dillon pointed to numerous statements which she said were incorrect: Mr McGowan wrongly swore that he had not moved money out of the jurisdiction; that he did not have money in the Channel Islands; that he was not the owner of Canio Ltd; and that he had not failed to disclose his beneficial interest in any company.
>
> He also misled the President of the High Court in relation to the identity of lands at Sandyford which were purchased by Canio. Ms Dillon pointed out that £606,000 had been transmitted to Mr McGowan's company in Jersey, Gasche Investments, in the preceding years.
>
> Mr McGowan said the affidavit was not accurate.
>
> Mr Justice Flood said he did not accept that 'not accurate' was an acceptable excuse for anything which was sworn as 'the full truth' before the court.
>
> 'Is it your normal habit to lie with impunity?' Ms Dillon asked.
>
> Mr McGowan said it wasn't. This was an isolated occurrence.
>
> Mr Justice Flood said under no circumstances could a lie be excused. There were no exceptions to the truth in a solemn, sworn document.
>
> 'This illustrates a lifetime of lying. When you are cornered, you lie,' she said.
>
> 'This is but a written illustration of the way you conducted your business. When expediency demanded it, you will lie with impunity,' Ms Dillon said. 'Why should any person accept that anything that comes out of your mouth is the truth?'
>
> 'I can't answer that,' Mr McGowan replied.
>
> The witness denied lying to the Tribunal. 'I came here originally not having sufficient resources and I told it exactly as it happened.'

As Ms Dillon listed another inaccuracy in Mr McGowan's affidavit, she asked: 'How many lies is that?'

'Certainly more than the number of apologies I made yesterday,' he replied.

Cheap and Nasty Soundbites

There was no coughing, no shuffling, just incredible stillness, even from the reduced number in the gallery. So what does it feel like when an interview goes off the rails? I remained calm, and remembered that our legal team had advised us to 'Answer the questions, if you are able to. Don't elaborate, just grin and bear it.' It was an uncomfortable feeling until Martin Hayden and John Walsh tapped me on my shoulder and said, 'A controlled interview.' I regarded Ms Dillon's approach to be sneaky, bad-mannered, off-the-rails and outside the terms of reference of the Tribunal.

On the evening of that gruelling session, I paid a quick visit to Mrs Berkeley, my mother-in-law, in the nursing home, to reassure her that everything was fine and not to be worrying. Later I dined in a Ballsbridge restaurant with my wife and children, who had been a tower of strength throughout these difficult months. I assured them that the purpose of resurrecting this affidavit had been a deliberate act designed to destroy my credibility. On that same evening, my son, Joseph, said to me that one of his friends in Blackrock College, who was genuinely concerned, had asked him: 'Will you be able to come here next year if your Dad is sent to prison?'

The next morning, I left Dublin to work and help with a little project between Ballaghaderreen and Boyle. Gerry, my brother, received a phone call before eight that morning from a pal saying: 'I've just been talking to your brother, Joe, in his wellies at Cooneys, the builders' providers, and he was on the RTÉ televised nine o'clock news last night. Just who do they think they are up there in Dublin trying to bring a good man down?' Gerry wasn't a bit worried once I told him that we didn't get, or didn't ask for, any favours, as a result of our substantial political donations; he enjoyed the banter with his neighbours and friends at the cattle marts.

I spent the month of August helping Johnny Loftus and John Dolan extend the house where Anne and her family spent every summer with their Grandmother Casey – the house that Peter and Madeline now own. At the same time, Colin Galavan cleverly designed a distinct home, hidden away, and with uninterrupted views from every window on part of the land I purchased adjoining Casey's farm. Noel Hill, the renowned concertina musician, and a loyal friend, gave Anne and myself a signed hardback copy of his friend, John O'Donohue's, *Anam Cara*. That August I read the two hundred and seventy-eight pages of *Anam Cara* slowly for the umpteenth time: my Bible. The Face and the Second Innocence on page sixty-eight best describes the character and mood of the Tribunal:

Your face is the icon of your life. In the human face a life looks out at the world and also looks in on itself. It is frightening to behold a face in which bitterness and resentment have lodged. When a person's life has been bleak, much of its negativity can remain unhealed. Since it is left un-transfigured, the bleakness lodges in the face. The face, instead of being a warm presence, has hardened to become a mask. One of the oldest words for person is the Greek word prosópon; and prosópon originally meant the mask that actors wore in a Greek chorus. When bitterness, anger or resentment is left un-transfigured, the face becomes a mask. Yet one also encounters the opposite, namely, the beautiful presence of an old face which is deeply lined and inscribed by time and experience, but has retained a lovely innocence. Even though life may have moved wearily and painfully through such a person, they have still managed not to let it corrode their soul. In such a face a lovely luminosity shines out into the world. It casts a tender light that radiates a sense of holiness and wholesomeness. The face always reveals who you are, and what life has done to you.

After the Summer Recess

The first day back at the Tribunal after the summer recess, I arrived at the café in Dame Street to meet Tom Brennan and our legal team. Contrary to the predictions of one or two journalists, the Tribunal resumed in a calm atmosphere. Nothing particularly new or surprising seemed to emerge – which made me think that Patricia Dillon herself may have had second thoughts when she saw some of the bold headlines, especially 'LIFETIME OF LIES' a month previously. In the middle of my last week as a witness, my mother died.

She had a big country funeral: all our neighbours, relatives and friends from many parts of the country came to express their sympathy. Also in attendance were Ray Burke, Stephen Miley, Kevin Molloy, Pat and Jim Gleeson, Bernie Cooke, Jack Foley, Frank Finnegan, John O'Mahony, the Stauntons and the Brennan family, Michael, Cathal and Seamus Cannon, Owen Kirk, Aidan McAvinue, Antoin McGowan, Jim Caralon, Noel Hill. Father Cawley, one of my teachers at Coláiste Padraic, who was now parish priest in Charlestown, said the Mass. He asked Pa, Gerry and myself if we wanted to say a few words. I just asked him to say how grateful we were to our mother 'for teaching us how to work'. One thing I must acknowledge is the support of my neighbours in Charlestown; they even commented on how well I looked in the photos. I was one of their own.

My mother's last letters to Anne and me showed signs of confusion: she had dementia for the last three years of her life. It was a pity. She was always on the go. She would cycle into town every first Friday of the month for Mass. The first Fridays, as they were called, were a major devotion in rural Ireland at that time. My mother was what I would call 'a reaching-out person' who was always there to help when help was needed. I never feel that she is gone; even now, if I have an awkward decision to make, I visit her grave to ask her to pray for me. She was a wise, wise woman. I just loved her. I will always appreciate Gerry, his three children, my brother Pa, and our neighbours for their love and support during my mother's last years. A few weeks after her funeral, Anthony Kenny, a very good friend of mine, and like myself, a Patrick Kavanagh fan, sent me this poem that Kavanagh wrote the week his mother died:

You will have the road gate open, the front door ajar
The kettle boiling and a table set
By the window looking out at the sycamores –
And your loving heart lying in wait

For me coming up among the poplar trees.
You'll know my breathing and my walk
And it will be a summer evening on those roads,
Lonely with leaves of thought.

We will be choked with the grief of things growing,
The silence of dark-green air
Life too rich – the nettles, docks and thistles
All answering the prodigal's prayer.

You will know I am coming though I send no word,
For you were lover who could tell
A man's thoughts – my thoughts – though I hid them –
Through you I knew Woman and did not fear her spell.

The Tribunal expressed its sympathy for the loss of my mother, and that effectively was the end of me as a witness. The mood had changed. When a show is going well, people feel like going to it as often as possible. When a show is starting to become a flop, it is very hard to hang around the lobby looking cheerful. When the audience began to fall off, the show could only be helped by creating soundbites for radio and television. But it rarely got the balanced reviews it sometimes deserved. As the ratings began to collapse in a sigh of decline, Mr Patrick Hanratty, a Senior Counsel for the Tribunal, decided to leave the cast, so that he could get on with his true career in the Law Library. The rest of the cast remained, and were perfect for the parts they played.

The Tribunal refused to pay all or even part of the huge costs to the Murphy family and their companies which had been incurred over several years. It did not believe their evidence and also found that they were guilty of hindering and obstructing the work of the Tribunal. The Murphy family were unhappy, and appealed to the High Court for their costs. The High Court (Record Number 2004/4910P) in November 2004 found in favour of the Tribunal not to award them their costs. The Murphy family appealed this decision to the Supreme Court.

The Tribunal concluded that our payments to Mr Burke in the Isle of Man and Jersey were made with the intention of securing some, as yet unidentified, benefit. As no legitimate explanation in its view had been provided for the substantial payments, it was the opinion of the Tribunal that those payments were made in circumstances which gave rise to a reasonable inference that the purpose of making those payments was improper.

We spent many months of our time, and incurred great costs to our legal team, participating in the work of the Tribunal. The Tribunal also refused to pay our costs; in order to save time and costs, our legal team decided – a decision agreed with by the Tribunal – to await the decision of the appeal to the Supreme Court by the Murphys.

The Supreme Court on April 2010 unanimously overturned the findings by the former Chairman, Mr Justice Fergus Flood, that Joseph Murphy Junior and Frank Reynolds had obstructed and hindered its inquiries. The Supreme Court ruled that these findings had been made outside the Tribunal's terms of reference. It was unlawful, and couldn't form the basis for refusing their costs. As a result of the Supreme Court decision, the Murphys were awarded their legal costs in full. A year later, we received our costs in full. In my opinion, it is a pity that the findings of the Supreme Court received very little media attention.

Defendants and Respondents

The judgement of Mr Justice Fennelly, delivered on 21 April 2010 (thirty-six pages), the judgement of Mr Justice Hardiman, delivered on the same day (seventy-four pages), and Justice Denham's judgement (thirty-six pages) are comprehensive and straightforward. I would feel uncomfortable selecting excerpts from the 142 pages; this report can be purchased from the Government Publication Office, and it's worth it.

Here are a few excerpts of the submission on behalf of Messrs Brennan and McGowan from our legal team to the Sole Member, the Right Honourable Mr Justice Fergus M. Flood.

On day 271, our Counsel sought clarification as to whether the lines of inquiry and questioning were actually permitted within the terms of reference of the Tribunal. On that date, the Sole Member indicated that if we waited, Counsel for the Tribunal would make it clear that the line of questioning relating to our business would become clear, and that it did fall within the Terms of Reference. The exact words of the Sole Member were:

> I think you will find it does come within the Terms of Reference as to how this whole transaction was carried out. If you wish to renew your application to a later point in time when the matter has been developed, you are welcome to do so . . . I don't propose to enter into any discussion with it at the moment until the matter has been clarified by Counsel. He's just beginning to open what I believe to be a relatively complicated exercise, [and] he will demonstrate what is the object of his explanations in a few moments.

This comment on the part of the Sole Member clearly suggests that the Sole Member had absolute knowledge of the approach that the Tribunal lawyers were going to take. In such circumstances, it would appear that this was a clear pre-determination on the part of the Sole Member, and showed that he had participated in the presentation of a pre-determined position. No clarification or attempt to deal with our concern was made, and in such circumstances this amounted at best to an appearance of unfair procedure, and pre-determination at worst. It appears that the Sole Member was aware of what questions the Tribunal lawyers were going to ask, the answers they were seeking, and the conclusions they were hoping to draw, before he had heard all the evidence. On another occasion, on day 271, the Sole Member said: 'I really do object to interruptions like that. You will have an opportunity of clarifying these matters in due course, and I must – now, I will not tolerate it. You are interfering with the conduct of this examination.' On day 294, our Counsel was told, 'Please do not interrupt.' It is my opinion that the approach taken by the Tribunal was one of preventing objective inquiry, so as to confine the issues and direction of the inquiry to a pre-ordained and pre-determined course. This was also the view of our legal team. In their submission, they noted the following:

113. The extent of the Tribunal's powers is clearly defined. It does not permit of the Tribunal and the Sole Member to embark upon an Inquiry into matters outside of the Terms of Reference. In the context of such Inquiry as is in fact carried out, it must be done in a fashion that balances the Constitutional entitlements and procedural entitlements of all parties and an inquisitorial inquiry. A fundamental and significant aspect of such rights is the right to privacy and the right not to have matters opened in a public forum relating to matters that the Tribunal knew or ought to have known were outside the Terms of Reference and knew or ought to have known did not form part of a legitimate line of Inquiry in the context of the Terms of Reference. The case law to date and the conduct of the Tribunals to date, have in large part, been predicated upon the striking of such a balance in a fair and equitable manner resulting from private session Inquiry excluding from contemplation and consideration and publication matters clearly outside the Terms of Reference. For ulterior motives in the instant case, despite offering to attend private session, the Tribunal refused to inquire in a private fashion of the witnesses insisting at all times for the public Inquiry and investigation. Had this basic entitlement on the part of Messrs Brennan and McGowan been adhered to, the vast amount of time expended by the Tribunal on matters that were neither relevant, significant nor within the Terms of Reference would have been avoided. Like a mantra, Counsel for the Tribunal repeated that this was not an Inquiry into the business affairs of Messrs Brennan and McGowan but merely an Inquiry into the money trail as to how the payments were made to Mr Burke. When one examines the transcripts, the inquiries go far beyond this. Objections were ignored and disregarded. The pressure sought to be put on Messrs Brennan and McGowan by reason of the public format in which the Tribunal advanced the Inquiry, it is submitted, is of itself ultra-vires the powers of the Tribunal.

114. The issue does not rest there however. Messrs Brennan and McGowan were called as witnesses by the Tribunal. They were at all times the witnesses of the Tribunal and at no stage was there any alteration of that status identified either to them or their legal advisers and as such no adverse findings can be made as against them.

115. The Tribunal made great play of discrepancies in recollection. However, the reality is that spanning a period of thirty years relating to a limited number of transactions in what has been described variously as long careers in building development, it is neither realistic nor fair to join issue with a witness over recollection of complicated transactions thirty years later which, as has been acknowledged by Mr Owens, were always his structures.

116. Separately, as identified herein, the extent of the Tribunal's entitlement is to inquire in the context of the matters set out in the Terms of Reference. Despite five weeks in the witness box on the part of Mr Brennan and four weeks on the part of Mr McGowan, regardless of any period of time that Mr Burke may have spent in the witness box, nowhere has any event been identified, alleged or put to the witnesses as suggestive of any conduct sought to be influenced in the manner and fashion as defined by the Terms of Reference. In the early stages Counsel for the Tribunal sought to suggest that the planning situation in relation to the lands at Sandyford was an issue. That this was done in itself was and is inexcusable in the context of the actual facts that must have been known to the Tribunal at the time and in circumstances whereby it was at all times clearly and well known that Mr Burke did not even participate in any vote on re-zoning. Add to that the unchallenged evidence of Mr Brennan to the effect that the site and area was always within the contemplation of anybody with experience as a likely area for planning, the allegation is even more surprising. Despite all of the questions put to Messrs Brennan and McGowan, nowhere was there any question put that would come within even the remotest or broadest interpretation of the Terms of Reference. The extent of the Tribunal's suggestion to both Mr Brennan and Mr McGowan without forewarning or notification within the context of their obligations so to do as to any alteration or change of status, is to suggest that it was strange that the payment be made where it was made. The Terms of Reference are not predicated upon the Inquiry based upon geographical location of such payments nor could it ever be the basis of any finding. Before such finding could be made in any event, the Tribunal must identify and offer all parties an opportunity to answer what it is supposed to have been for or achieved.

117. If the Sole Member makes findings on the basis of the evidence to date as coming anywhere within the Terms of Reference, such findings would be Orwellian in the extreme as in essence they would be findings based upon no evidence; based upon evidence that was at all times corralled and steered towards predetermined conclusions; obtained in breach of any fair procedures and in breach of both the provisions of the 1921 Act as amended and the Constitution. In essence such findings would at best and at their highest be unsubstantiated assumptions based upon a desire on the part of the Tribunal to justify itself.

An Irishman's Diary

I remember being introduced to Joseph Murphy Senior in the 1970s by Michael Fitzsimons, Solicitor; I found him soft-spoken, generous, loyal and trustworthy. He is best described in 'An Irishman's Diary' by Wesley Boyd (the *Irish Times*, 14 August 2000):

Joe Murphy, big builder, big man, and latter-day Flood Tribunal witness, who died in Guernsey recently, was probably the last of the Irish emigrants who found gold in the streets of London. Long before the word entrepreneur entered into the textbooks of the schools of management, he and others saw and took the opportunities in a Britain laid waste by war and crying out for reconstruction. Like Joe, they were rough-hewn men, mainly from the western seaboard, who started out with nothing more than a shovel and a hunger to succeed. They worked hard and long and the success they yearned for was conceived and nurtured in their own toil and sweat.

They were at the height of their glory in the early 1960s before financial advisers, off-shore tax havens and labyrinthine family trusts occupied their minds. They could have dined in Claridge's and bought the finest champagne without causing a ripple in their bank accounts, but they were most comfortable in each other's company.

Causeway Contract

Tales were told of tenders won and lost. There was no bravado, no boastfulness. One night Joe recounted how he had won a huge contract for a causeway to an island off the coast of Northumberland. 'They were all in for it,' he said. 'All the big boys, Taylor Woodrow, McAlpines, McLaughlin and Harvey. . . . They spent fortunes on the tenders. They had geologists, deep-sea divers, civil engineers, aerial photographers, the whole bloody lot, employed. I drove up on my own one day and walked the land and watched how the tides were running. I put in a tender that sunk them all. And I'll make good money out of it as well.

The night porter was indulgent, and well rewarded with generous tips. He confided in me that he had bought a farm of land in his native Tipperary.

'I'm stocking it with cattle,' he said. 'Every heifer I buy I name it after one of the builders. It's only right. They're paying for them after all.' And he would reel off the litany of names as the herd grew.

One night, a stranger ventured into the territory of the fridge. He was young, well-spoken and personable. He was, he told us, working in management consultancy, a field of activity new to the company. After listening to the tales of contracts won and lost, of work on motorways running behind time, of rows with local authorities and other problems of the day, he ventured to suggest that the builders should consider modernising their business practices.'

Chapter Twenty Five

The Theatre of Ice Meets Its Own Nemesis

I believe that history will show that the Tribunal was the watchdog with no teeth, which got lost. Many people blamed the media for its sorry end. In fact, it was all rather more complicated. Carol Coulter, Legal Affairs Correspondent with the *Irish Times*, said: 'Media coverage is only one of the factors that can inhibit a successful prosecution. Allegations can be aired at tribunals, and a tribunal may even make a finding that such allegations are true, but this does not amount to a basis for a prosecution. A report from a tribunal can be sent to the DPP; but this does not mean the DPP can then prosecute on that basis. Mr Hamilton, the DPP, said that nothing in a tribunal report in itself proves anything. There is a statutory provision that any admissions people make cannot be used in a prosecution. People can be compelled to give evidence to a Tribunal, including admitting to a criminal offence, but the deal is that that can't be used against them. People have been accused by tribunals of obstructing their work, and this seems to be a clear basis for a prosecution. Not necessarily so, according to the DPP. The tribunal chairman can say he does not believe one version of events, as against another version, but in a trial I have to put up all the versions and ask the jury to believe the version believed by the tribunal chairman, he said. Where something like concealing bank accounts is concerned [it] is easier. But there is a different burden of proof in a criminal case. A tribunal can hear two versions and prefer one over the other without any corroboration. But the bar in a criminal trial is beyond "reasonable doubt", a lot higher. People often want prosecutions in order to air suspicions, said Mr Hamilton, but I can't do that. There is a two-stage test – is there credible evidence that a judge could send to a jury? And could a jury, properly directed, convict?' Ironically, it was the Tribunal itself which was to be finally tried and convicted, two decades after its birth.

Statement from the High Court, 3 March 2017

The judgement was damning. In an Order made by Mr Justice Noonan in the High Court on 3 March 2017, it was directed that the serious findings, including corruption, against Joseph Murphy, Junior and the late Joseph Murphy, Senior were unjustified and must now be quashed. The silence of our political class was even more damning. Our timorous politicians allowed this circus to continue, regardless of costs. This court decision represented some change for a Tribunal that was once a case of 'house full' every day. Today, it is a case of 'house private, no flowers please'.

I met Frank Reynolds, a man of great ability and charm, for the first time recently. We had a long lunch at the RDS; he gave me a copy of the statement issued by the High Court, and a copy of Mr Joseph Murphy's statement.

The following is the Statement from the High Court on 3 March 2017.

1. 'The Tribunal of Inquiry into Certain Planning Matters and Payments was established by Ministerial Order on the 4th November 1997 on foot of a resolution by Dáil Éireann. The Tribunal initially comprised a Sole Member, Mr Justice Fergus Flood, who retired in 2003.

2. The first Module of the Tribunal's hearings concerned an allegation that the Applicant in these proceedings, Joseph Murphy, and his late father, also Joseph Murphy, together with other persons and companies associated with the Murphy interests, were party to the making of a corrupt payment to Mr Ray Burke, TD. Subsequent Modules concerned an allegation that the same parties were involved in the making of a corrupt payment to Mr George Redmond, the former Assistant City and County Manager for Dublin.

3. Mr James Gogarty, a former senior executive in Joseph Murphy Structural Engineering Limited, was on many matters the only witness against the Murphy interests. In the circumstances, any adverse finding against Mr Murphy or his late father in relation to the alleged payment to Mr Burke or Mr Redmond rested on the basis of an issue of credibility between Mr Gogarty and the Murphy interests, including, in particular, Mr Murphy. In order to deal effectively with the question of Mr Gogarty's credibility, it was therefore essential as a matter of constitutional justice and fairness of procedures that the Murphy interests were in a position to conduct an effective and comprehensive cross-examination of Mr Gogarty.

4. In the context of Mr Murphy's ability to cross-examine Mr Gogarty, the Tribunal acknowledges that a number of statements taken during the private investigative phase of the Tribunal's activities were either not disclosed or disclosed in redacted form in the course of the Tribunal's public inquiries in the period 1999-2001 in relation to matters which were subsequently the subject matter of findings in the Tribunal's 2002 Second and Third Interim Reports.

5. Some of the material not disclosed to the Murphy interest was obtained by Mr Murphy in proceedings instituted by him against the Tribunal. The Supreme Court described the relevance of the material as 'obvious'. More recently, in February 2016 the Tribunal furnished to Mr Murphy further material which had not previously been made available. On the basis of the decision of the Supreme Court in O'Callaghan v. Mahon (2008) 2 I.R. 514, the Tribunal acknowledges that some of this material also was obviously relevant to the matters before the Tribunal and ought to have been disclosed to the Murphy interests.

6. The Tribunal acknowledges that the second and third interim Reports contained findings which were made in circumstances which breached the constitutional rights of the Murphy interest to fair procedures in that statements relevant to the evidence of Mr Gogarty which ought to have been provided were not.

7. The Tribunal acknowledges that the adverse findings in respect of Mr Murphy, his father and the Murphy interest which the Tribunal acknowledges to have been unlawful, received enormous publicity which has been extremely damaging to them. The Tribunal acknowledges that its unwarranted findings have had a profound effect upon Mr Murphy, have severely damaged his reputation over a period of many years and have caused him great personal distress. The Tribunal acknowledges that Mr Murphy's sole motivation in bringing these proceedings has been to vindicate his good name and that of the Murphy interests.

8. Prior to the institution of these proceedings the Tribunal, in February 2015, sought Submissions from the Applicant in relation to those findings in the Second and Third Interim Reports which referred to Mr Murphy, his late father and the Murphy interest. Detailed written submissions were received from the Applicant, and having regard to those submissions, the Tribunal proceeded to remove the relevant passages and findings from the Second and Third Interim Reports. It did so by removing the original versions of those Reports from its website, and replacing them with the versions of the Reports which excluded such passages and findings. The revised versions of the reports were furnished to the Clerk of the Dail. This was also done prior to the institution of these proceedings.

9. In the circumstances outlined above, the Tribunal consents to Orders being made in these proceedings in the following terms:

   (i) An order of certiorari quashing the findings relating to the Applicant, his late father and the Murphy interest contained in the Second and Third Interim Reports of the Tribunal of Inquiry into Certain Planning Matters and Payments and more particularly described in the schedule hereto which the Respondents agree are invalid;

   (ii) The costs of the within proceedings, same to be taxed in default of agreement.

10. In addition, the Tribunal agrees to pay Mr Murphy not only the costs incurred by him in connection with these proceedings, but also all the costs incurred by him in the examination of material previously supplied by the Tribunal and an investigation of the extent of the quashing orders that ought to be made. All costs are payable on a party and party basis. The Tribunal will forward a copy of the Order of this Honourable Court together with a copy of this statement to the Clerk of the Dáil with a request that he take all reasonable steps to bring these documents to the attention of the Members of both Houses of the Oireachtas and that they be placed in the library of Dáil Éireann for permanent reference.'

Joseph Murphy's Statement

Mr Joseph Murphy made the following statement on 3 March 2017:

1. The Order made yesterday by Mr Justice Noonan in High Court, and the statement read out to him, are a complete and formal vindication of me, personally, my late father, Joseph Murphy, and other persons and parties associated with our business enterprises in Ireland. By its making of this statement in open court, the Flood Tribunal (as it was at the relevant time) fully and formally acknowledges that all of its findings, including the most serious findings of corruption, were unjustified, must now be quashed and, insofar as possible, removed from the public record of the Houses of the Oireachtas.

2. The Flood Tribunal now publicly acknowledges that during the two/three years of what it describes as the 'Gogarty Module', it withheld information which was critically relevant to the credibility of the late Joseph Gogarty, who was the principal and only accuser of and witness to these alleged acts of corruption. It took multiple High Court and Supreme Court actions to coerce the Tribunal into revealing the existence of this critical information and that would never have happened were it not for the persistence of the late Mr Owen O'Callaghan and myself and the fact that we were in the fortunate position of being able to finance these actions. Ultimately, of course, the high costs of these actions were an addition to the enormous public expenditure associated with the operation of this Tribunal.

3. Bearing in mind the contents of this suppressed material, it is indeed remarkable that it was withheld; it must have been clear at all times to the Tribunal that it was entirely relevant to the issue of Mr Gogarty's credibility and the reliability of the accusations which he had made against me, my father and associated persons. Among the twenty or so persons who were the targets of Mr Gogarty's vitriolic and false accusations in this suppressed information were a Taoiseach, a Minister for Justice, a Judge of the Supreme Court and many other people of greater and lesser prominence in public life.

4. The Supreme Court itself described the relevance of all of this material as 'obvious'. In this context, it should be recalled that the then Chairman of the

Tribunal, Mr Fergus Flood, SC, was a sitting Judge of the High Court with many years' experience in trying and deciding cases and, before that, had long experience as a Junior and Senior Counsel. Additionally, he had, during the entire course of the Tribunal business, the advice and assistance of a large team of experienced counsel and solicitors. The collective decision to suppress this relevant information was and is inexplicable and has given rise to many dire consequences.

5. In tandem with the suppression of this relevant material, Mr Gogarty was cosseted by the Tribunal to an extraordinary degree. For instance, he was privileged by a private visit to his home by the Chairman of the Tribunal, by frequent personal contact by Counsel for the Tribunal, and was afforded Garda protection 'around the clock' at his home and transport by Garda car with an armed escort. All of this 'security' was provided by the Gardai at the direct insistence of the Tribunal and against the advice of the relevant Garda experts that Mr Gogarty was under no threat whatsoever and that such protection was entirely unnecessary.

6. This extraordinary behaviour extended beyond shielding Mr Gogarty from cross-examination on many matters which would have undermined and, indeed, entirely destroyed his credibility. For instance, the Tribunal permitted him and encouraged him to say in evidence many things which were quite irrelevant to the matters the Tribunal was enquiring into but which were grievously offensive to me and to my late father and which were all false and obviously motivated by great bitterness. Quite some time before the Tribunal was established Mr Gogarty spoke about 'hounding them . . . right, left and centre' and 'throwing the book at them' in relation to my family. He confirmed this intent directly to me when he said: 'I will destroy you.' This was no idle threat, as subsequent events proved.

7. Great material and financial loss were inflicted on many of our business interests. Most obvious was the destruction of Joseph Murphy Structural Engineering Ltd, a well-established and thriving company in the Irish construction industry which had employed at least one hundred people. Most painful and grievous of all was the reputational damage inflicted on me and my late father and other persons associated with us. This was vile, extensive and lasting; it permeated into every aspect of our personal and business lives and even some sixteen years later its poison still lingers on.

8. As we have now finally reached the end game of this sorry saga, it is worth recalling the words of the late Justice Hardiman in his judgement in the Supreme Court in 2010 in a case which I, together with my associates, brought against the Tribunal: 'There is sometimes a tendency to be a little suspicious of persons who take legal proceedings against Tribunals of Inquiry on the basis that this itself is an act of obstruction. I do not agree with this. It is salutary to remember that the concealed materials would never have come to light in this case had the appellants not taken the proceedings. It is chilling to reflect that a poorer person, treated in the same fashion by the Tribunal, could not have afforded to seek this vindication.'

In another reference, Mr Justice Hardiman also stated: 'in the well-known miscarriage of justice referred to as that of the "Guildford Four", the investigating police officers were actually in possession of evidence providing an alibi for one of the Four. But they had so become convinced of their guilt that they decided the alibi could not be reliable and concealed it.'

9. It has taken many years, great persistence and expenditure of much energy and money to reach this point of final vindication. None of this would have been necessary had the Tribunal, in my case, adhered to the elementary principles of constitutional and natural justice.

10. Finally, for the record, I now publicly state that I have never in my life met with Mr Ray Burke and met, only casually, with the late Mr George Redmond for the first time at the Tribunal hearings.

The newspapers carried flattering photographs, and comprehensive but fair reporting, if only people took time to read them, instead of glancing at the headlines. I considered the newspaper coverage of the Tribunal balanced: Paul Cullen and John Drennan were most impressive. Of course, the irrepressible Miriam Lord kept us in a constant state of expectation. In addition, there was the occasional well-thought-out contribution from John Waters. Charlie Bird was fair in his reporting. The Tribunal was the big story for journalists, until the public became bored with it, and angry at the costs. I cannot overstate the gratitude I continue to feel to so many for their support in such difficult circumstances.

With hindsight, it is clear that I was unprepared for my introduction to the Tribunal. I made mistakes; this provided the Tribunal with ammunition to fire at me for four weeks, but not to bury me. I finish Part Four, my 'Theatre of Ice', with two verses from Rod McKuen's poem 'Pushing the Clouds Away':

I've been going a long time now
Along the way I've learned some things
You have to make the good times yourself
Take the little times and make them into big times

And save the times that are all right
For the ones that aren't so good
I've never been able
To push the clouds away by myself.

Chapter Twenty Six

The Phantom Cup

One day, as the Tribunal circus continued, I selected the Planning Tribunal rugby team to play the Moriarty Tribunal rugby team for the Phantom Cup. I have selected the players most suited to each position.

1. Loose-head prop	John Drennan	Journalist
2. Hooker	Judge Flood (Honourable)	The Sole Member
3. Tight-head prop	John Gallagher	Tribunal SC
4. Second row	Brian O'Halloran	Witness
5. Second row	Paul Cullen	Journalist
6. Blind-side flanker	Tom Brennan	Witness
7. Open-side flanker	Joe McGowan	Witness
8. Number 8	Martin Hayden	SC for Brennan & McGowan
9. Scrum-half	George Redmond	Witness
10. Fly-half	Stephen Miley	Solicitor Brennan & McGowan
11. Left wing	Patricia Dillon	Tribunal Senior Counsel
12. Inside centre	Des O'Neill	Tribunal Senior Counsel
13. Outside centre	Pat Hanratty	Tribunal Senior Counsel
14. Right wing	Ray Burke	Witness
15. Full back	John Walsh	Solicitor for Brennan & McGowan

1. John Drennan: a good scrummager, tackled and hit the rucks and mauls. He put the opposition loose-head under pressure.
2. Judge Flood: like all rugby players these days, the hooker has to be able to handle the ball and scrummage. He carried enormous responsibility with honesty. Sometimes, his Home Counties accent agitated the referee.
3. John Gallagher: had some good moments. To be a prop you have got to enjoy the position: it's not everyone's cup of tea, putting your head where it hurts.
4. Brian O'Halloran: fit, strong and athletic. He was quick off the mark and powerful. The most competitive, cutthroat person you would ever meet.
5. Paul Cullen: brilliant in the lineout and set-pieces. Set high standards and always looked for improvement.
6. Tom Brennan: blind-side flanker, made sure the opposition didn't get over the advantage line. He refused to buckle under pressure.
7. Joe McGowan: there is a real art to open-side play; it is such an important role. At the heart of a brilliant career, he was never frightened by the sight of the All Black jerseys lining up in front of him.
8. Martin Hayden: invaluable and inspirational, an incredible brain. Number 8 has such an important role: to release the wingers, the fly-half and full-back. He had great awareness of creating space.
9. George Redmond: a strong mind. A scrum-half needs to be able to deliver the ball, whether that is over the head or through the legs. He had a broad range of skills; the kind of man who breaks biscuits in two and saves the other half until later.
10. Stephen Miley: following in the footsteps of his father, Dan, he was the general, running the game, bossing his forwards. His kicking from hand was superb; playing the best rugby of his life.
11. Patricia Dillon: she is a modern winger, with pace and commitment. She is practising her grubber-kicking to improve her chances of scoring more tries. She loves scoring tries.
12. Des O'Neill: reads the game well, seems to be always in the right place. O'Neill can put wide passes in, he can put short passes in, or take the ball into contact and pass the ball out of the tackle.
13. Pat Hanratty: gifted in all aspects, subtle, and could burst through the opponents' line of defence; was greatly missed when he returned to play his rugby in New Zealand.
14. Ray Burke: wingers must have a big work ethic in the modern game. It can be a lonely position. You have to go looking for the ball and pop up in all sorts of positions instead of waiting for the ball to come to you. If you miss a scoring opportunity, you know the crowd are going to be baying for you.
15. John Walsh: the last line of defence, awesome under the high ball, his counter-attacking is brilliant and decisive; essential to any team.

The Planning Tribunal team won the toss, so the game was played at Old Belvedere and not Clontarf. Old Belvedere was considered a home venue for the Tribunal Team. The gale-force conditions made it a game of two halves. The Planning Team had no pattern to their play in the opening quarter and allowed the Moriarty Tribunal to score a soft try under the posts, to leave the score at half-time, Moriarty Tribunal 19, Planning Tribunal 0.

In my imaginary game, Miriam Lord (journalist), the Planning Tribunal's coach, is a superb tactician. At half-time she was furious, and told us the importance of team-work. She said, 'You have to believe you can win.' She made some tactical changes in the second half and, with the advantage of the strong wind, the Planning Team pinned the opposition in their own half.

Towards the end of the first half, Flood had to leave the pitch, to be replaced by Justice Alan Mahon (Tribunal Chairman). His throwing is the best I have seen. He controlled the game very well.

John Finnegan (Witness), with his dancing feet, bewildering changes of direction, and boldness when it came to taking chances, took over at scrum-half in the last quarter.

Michael Cush (Senior Counsel to Murphys), with Olympic speed and hard, straight running, had a huge impact when Hanratty got injured early in the second half.

Michael Fitzsimons (Solicitor to Murphy) had that extra yard and was able to exploit space; replaced Ray Burke.

Vincent Shannon (Solicitor to Ray Burke): an Old Belvederean, didn't get much time to show his pace when he came on.

With ten minutes remaining, Brian O'Halloran pinched the line-out ball when they were inside our twenty-two, passed to John Finnegan, to Michael Cush, a player with style and elegant touch, who broke two tackles before passing to Michael Fitzsimons, who did a side-step and released the ball to John Walsh, who scored under the post. Stephen Miley converted, to level the match at nineteen points each.

Moriarty Tribunal 19, Planning Tribunal 19.

The referee, Alain Rolland, allowed the game to flow.

I look ahead to what is set to be a fascinating replay in 2047. This replay will take place on neutral grounds – or Purgatory. The late Honourable Justice Adrian Hardiman will be asked to referee the replay.

Part 5
Life Goes On

Chapter Twenty Seven

Parkinsons

Throughout the spring, summer and early autumn of 2006, while building our house in Dublin, I started to slow down. Naturally, I was worried, but kept it to myself. It was a kind of gentle tiredness. Sometimes, my left hand would begin to shake a little. I'd stop in the middle of the day to find a spot to rest my back for twenty minutes or so, and then I'd go back to work. One day, a year later, Dr Peter Staunton and myself were tidying up the stone walls in the fields surrounding his house near Ballaghaderreen. As we went along, one of us on either side of the wall, I couldn't help thinking of Robert Frost's poem, 'Mending Wall'. The previous month, Anne had given me a present of a collection of Robert Frost's poems.

> We keep the wall between us as we go.
> To each the boulders that have fallen to each.
> And some are loaves and some so nearly balls
> We have to use a spell to make them balance:
> "Stay where you are until our backs are turned!"

I remember helping my father repair the dry stone walls in the 'Road Field' at home in Tavneena. When he would come on a completely round stone, out of sheer annoyance he would put a face on himself and growl: 'Another hoor of a round one.'

When Peter and I were having supper after our wall-repairing exertions, my left hand began to shake; the shaking continued for much longer than it had done on previous occasions. Peter told me to drop into his surgery when I got back to Dublin. I told him that, as far back as 2002, my left leg would occasionally drag for two or three strides. He told me that this was the beginning of Parkinsons, and he arranged that I should have x-rays in the Blackrock Clinic. He also said: 'You will have to pace yourself, you are not thirty any more.' Dr Laura McNaughton, whom I had not seen for many years, was looking after me in the Blackrock Clinic. Laura, her brother Alfie, and their first cousin Malcolm McNaughton were part of the fashionable Dublin set in the 1960s. We used to attend hunt balls during the Dublin Horse Show.

When the neurologist, Dr Brian Murray, saw my x-rays, he confirmed Peter Staunton's diagnosis. He prescribed medication, and told me that my lifestyle should not change a lot at this stage. The arrival of Parkinsons was a bit of a shock. Still, for a time, life went on as before. I continued cycling with the Willow Wheelers until my dreadful experience at Zermatt a year later. In February 2008, we joined friends in Zermatt, Switzerland, for ten days' skiing. For the first three or four days, I took it easy on blue, red and black runs, but no off-piste skiing. The conditions were perfect.

On the fifth day, I got the biggest fright of my life. Tim Gwyn Jones and I arranged to meet his son, Dominic, Vincent Shields from Galway, and Charles Bazely at a café on the Italian side of the Alps for lunch at 12.30 PM. The others had gone on ahead of us. Tim got lost. We were skiing all over the place, arriving at the café two hours late. I was exhausted, my left hand trembling. That hadn't happened for months. Twenty minutes later, after some food, we began our return journey. When we got to the Swiss side of the Alps, I unfortunately insisted that the others go on, as I was taking my time. My head got lighter and lighter, before I collapsed in a heap, my body completely drained. I really thought it was the end. I said a Hail Mary and asked for a few more years to get my affairs in order. Passing skiers took my skis off, while others carried me to the ski-lift and gave me glasses of water. I made it back to the chalet. Anne gave me two Disprins, and we went to the medical centre around the corner. A young doctor immediately checked my blood pressure. It was sky-high, out of control. I was kept for two nights in this ultramodern care centre. This was no ordinary incident. I was a shadow of myself for six months.

Seán Boylan

On returning to Dublin, my friend from the Willow Wheelers Cycling Club, Professor Declan Sugrue, heart specialist in the Mater Hospital, gave me a thorough examination; it was a relief that everything was clear. Other good friends from the Ward Union stag hunt days, Charles Smyth and his wife, Lizzie, from Kells, County Meath, arranged to meet Anne and myself for lunch locally. That morning, Charles collected me at 11 AM; he told me that he had arranged an appointment for me with the herbalist Seán Boylan. Neither Seán nor I could remember where we had met before. The Mayo-Meath All-Ireland Final replay was the first item for discussion before we got on to Parkinsons. Seán told us that his father had Parkinsons for thirty years and lived to be almost ninety. His father only took the prescribed medicine but his secret was 'to rest before he got tired'. He always had a nap in the middle of the day; this advice has been a huge help to me.

A More Fulfilling Life

With the onerous planning conditions, there was no profit in housebuilding in the 1980s. Rather than giving away our residential land, we stopped building. This was a worrying period until we cleared our loans and got rid of our personal guarantees. Life had changed in other ways too: shortly after moving to Hollywood Rath, our lives were transformed by the arrival of our beautiful daughter, Catherine Mary Elizabeth, at the beginning of 1982; our son, Joseph, in 1985; and our daughter Christine in 1989. They enjoyed a wonderful time growing up. They were involved in every aspect of farm life; I spent more time looking after Joseph around the machinery than helping Bill McLernon and Noel McMenamin alter and prepare the cross-country fences for the autumn events at Hollywood Rath; Catherine helped Pam Stokes and Mary D'Arcy, her godmother, with the entries and enquiries, and presenting the prizes.

Catherine was certainly a precocious child. I was competing at Doddington Park in Wiltshire in 1990. It was getting near the time for Private Deal and myself in the show-jumping phase. I could not believe my eyes when I found Catherine marking the names of the horses in jumping order. 'Oh', she said, 'Holly has left me in charge while she takes her coffee break. There are two before you Dad, and good luck.' She was nine years old.

Joseph began walking at nine months, and a month later he ran everywhere. One morning Joseph went missing; he was two and a half years old. Anne thought he was with me in the yard, and I thought he was in the house. We searched the house, the stables, the shed and the horse lorry. Total panic, until George Dowling, the farm manager, arrived with his son, George Junior, and noticed that the dogs were also missing. At this stage, the fear had left Anne and myself in a daze. We started in the fields and checked the ditches, which had a good depth of water from the downpour during the night. Anne spotted Joseph in the third field, a long way from the house. She screamed with delight; there he was sitting beside Sheeba, our labrador, with Spick and Span, our two Jack Russsells, at one of the cross-country fences. Joseph, sobbing, told us he was looking for 'nabbits' (rabbits).

Anne thoroughly enjoyed spending much of her time ferrying our children to junior school, swimming, athletics, tennis, rugby and music, and to parties and entertaining their friends. I was at their beck and call when I gave up my equestrian life. Joseph started Junior Infants at Willow Park, Booterstown, in 1990. He was involved in everything. Saturday morning was a spectacle, in unimaginable surroundings, with the parents and families watching their boys on the ten rugby pitches at Willow Park – some parents hoping to see their children play for Ireland someday. The motto of Blackrock College is *Fides* et *robur* ('Faith and strength'). I believe the college provides an education that is balanced for all levels, offering a choice of sport and other activities. Catherine, now twelve years, and Christine, five, loved the Saturday-morning rugby at Willow Park and mini-rugby at Old Belvedere on Sunday mornings.

Anne was hoping that one of our children would continue our involvement with ponies and horses. Joseph and Catherine enjoyed pony camp in Burghley every summer, until rugby and other activities took over. This left Christine; Anne took her to Brennanstown Riding School either Saturday or Sunday morning from her fifth birthday onwards. Jane and Brian Bloomer's daughter, Louise, had outgrown her pony, Safety Pin. I was delighted when Anne told me that Christine would compete in the Lead Rein class on Safety Pin. Her first outing was at Fethard, County Tipperary. Magee Ogden-White and Van de Vager organised a party in Magee's home, Kiltinan Castle. We were all pleased when Christine finished in fourth place in the Lead Rein. Safety Pin and Christine finished second at Goff's, County Kildare, and this qualified them for the Pony Championship at the RDS. Great excitement for everybody. After walking and trotting, and a chat with the judge, she was promoted from sixth to third; the judge asked her did she ride her pony every day. I said, 'Most days.' 'Dad', she said, 'it is not my pony, and I only ride it when I am not playing tennis.' The judge laughed, and said, 'I don't want to start a row between father and daughter.'

Old Belvedere Rugby Club had about one hundred boys and girls between the ages of six and fourteen registered when Catherine and Joseph joined the mini-rugby in 1990. The professional approach to all matters involving the mini-rugby through the years has been responsible for its growth and success. I was on the committee with Dorothy Collins, Sammy Lyons, Ollie Campbell and others who started the mini-rugby festival, which attracted three hundred boys and girls from Leinster clubs. Fintan Gunne, may he rest in peace, and myself sponsored the medals; each child received a medal for taking part. In 2018, Old Belvedere has almost four hundred boys and girls registered with the club. The mini-rugby festival has to take place over two days because of the numbers competing: 1400 boys and girls took part in 2016. From playing mini-rugby in Old Belvedere, supporting Joseph on the sideline at Willow Park, and her love for Old Belvedere, Catherine could easily be a rugby correspondent, with her knowledge of the game. Catherine actually met her husband, Barry Murphy, 'a Lunster' (a Louth man supporting Munster), playing tag rugby at Old Belvedere.

Joseph and I joined the Willow Wheelers Cycling Club in 1995, when he was ten years old. Blackrock College and Willow Park share the Willow Wheelers Cycling Club, founded in 1989 by Christy McDaid. Every Easter we spent a week cycling either in Clare or Donegal. I remember, in particular, one of the trips to Clare when I refereed the soccer match between Willow Park boys, and the boys and girls of the local national school in Liscannor. This was the first time Willow Park boys lost! They did not speak to me for the rest of the week, and they said I was the worst referee ever. It was a fantastic week; the sun shone every day.

The Willow Wheelers cycle between thirty and sixty miles every Sunday to locations around Dublin, regardless of the weather. The Wheelers raise €150,000 for charity each year on a one-hundred-mile cycle from Blackrock College to Trim, on to Kinnegad and back to the college. I miss the fun, laughter and lunchtime discussions with other enthusiastic parents, Mike McDonnell, Des Cummins, Willie O'Grady, Justin McKenna, Dr Ciaran Bent, Professor Declan Sugrue, Richard Kelly, Michael Crichton and Jim Donovan. Friendships formed then, continue.

During the 'marble' season, which lasted five or six weeks before Christmas, Anne or I would drop Joseph to Willow Park early. I couldn't really grasp the rules; I had to get used to terms such as 'run away', 'a game for keeps', or 'killed', or 'you have to throw that marble three times'. Joseph was dedicated, and very sharp, and he loved having the biggest and best marbles. If he lost one of his better ones to Brian O'Farrell, he was in bad mood until he won it back. But those marble games – winning and losing – helped prepare him for life.

Catherine, our eldest daughter, started Suzuki violin with Magsi Goor when she was two years old. The three children attended the School of Music for piano, encouraged by their aunt, Madeline Staunton. Madeline has been in the RTÉ National Symphony Orchestra most of her adult life. Anne, who had been a member of the Dublin Symphony Orchestra, transferred her allegiance to Irish traditional music when Joseph and Christine took classes on the tin whistle from Ciarán McCabe at Comhaltas Ceoltóirí Éireann in Monkstown. Christine was fortunate to continue with the enthusiastic Mikie Smyth, All-Ireland champion countless times with the tin whistle. Another flute player who influenced Christine's musical style was Sarah Jane Woods. Catherine attended Liam de Brúin's fiddle classes in Monkstown. Catherine and Christine attended Antóin MacGabhann's fiddle classes in Ashbourne, County Meath. Antóin and his family are well-known musicians, playing all over the world. Christine won three All-Irelands: tin whistle, flute, and fiddle playing in a trio with Bláthnaid McCabe and Muireann Bird.

Catherine McGorman, renowned flute player and gifted producer, with the support of her husband Tom and daughter Jane, brought together Na Mothúcháin (the Emotions) to win the All-Ireland Gael Linn Siamsa championship for under-eighteens in two consecutive years. The music evolved, pure and natural, from the enjoyment and laughter at rehearsals. The winning group was described by Michael Rooney, one of the judges, as 'unbelievable for their age'. The group of young musicians comprised Ruairí McGorman, guitar and fiddle; Fergus McGorman, flute, whistle and saxophone; Christine McGowan, fiddle, flute and tin whistle; Bláthnaid Nic Cába, concertina; Darach Mac Mathúna (fourteen years old), séan nós singer and accordion; Aimée Courtney Farrell, bodhrán world champion.

Over eighty artists and young musicians from Ashbourne featured on a double CD to raise money for the Mater Hospital Cancer Research Fund. This unique production, *Lámh ar Lámh*, ('Many Hands'), was produced by Antóin MacGabhann with the support of Padráic MacMathúna, Noirín Ní Ghrádaigh and many others.

Of course, I haven't failed to tell my children about my own musical performances with the Coláiste Padraig Fife and Drum Band. I do not think they were over-impressed. Anne, myself and our family have not missed a Fleadh Cheoil since we were in Ballina in 1977. When I think of Irish music, I think of Labhrás Ó Murchú, Director General of Ceoltoiri Comhaltas Ceoltóirí Éireann, and his wife Úna: together, they have formed the backbone of Comhaltas Ceoltóirí Éireann for more than fifty years. I have discovered in Úna a great goodness of heart and a great imagination; Labhrás has exceptional qualities – determination and dedication – and is an excellent speaker; comfortable at all levels; irreplaceable.

First Official St Patrick's Day, London 2002

Over the years, Anne presented many Comhaltas Ceoltóirí Éireann concerts in Britain. She met men and women who had left Ireland and made their homes in England – in particular, John and Joan Burke, now deceased, who were completely committed to Comhaltas Ceoltóirí Éireann in England. John and Joan invited Anne and Christine to join them and other members of the London Comhaltas Ceoltóirí Éireann on to the stage at Trafalgar Square for the first official Saint Patrick's Day parade in London in 2002. This was an invitation they will always cherish. It was a historic and heart-warming occasion for the Irish to march into Trafalgar Square, where Irish people had been banned from meetings and gatherings in the past. On that St Patrick's morning, we went to 10 AM Mass in the Oratory in Fulham Road. The parade set off at 1 PM from Westminster Cathedral. The Lord Major of London, Ken Livingstone, greeted the crowd at Trafalgar Square. He said: 'We are today recognising the contribution that millions of Irish have made to this city. They have helped to build it, to nurse the sick in it, to educate their children in it.' The square was transformed with crafts, stalls and dancing. The event was a phenomenal success, attracting over one hundred thousand to celebrate being Irish with pride.

There are many stories of the Irish who built up successful businesses in England, especially in the construction industry: the Murphys and the McNicholases in London, the Gallaghers in the Midlands, and Joe Kennedy in Manchester. Joe left Doocastle, County Mayo, in 1953 at the tender age of sixteen. His companies now employ nearly one thousand people. These were hard, clever men in a tough business that took few prisoners. Along the way, some Irish did not make the good times, and drowned their sorrows in alcohol. On that last memorable St Patrick's Day, walking along in the crowd I found myself talking to an elderly man who seemed out of breath. 'Ah,' he said, 'I didn't give up those cigarettes soon enough.' He had worked in the buildings for over forty years. A relative had brought him to the parade and had arranged to meet him at the Harp pub in Chandos Place off Trafalgar Square to take him home. He was dressed in a white shirt and brown tie and a smart tweed jacket. I walked slowly with him to the pub. He had a pint of Guinness and he bought me a coke. He hadn't been home to County Sligo for five years, but he said he would like to be buried there. 'Ah', he said, 'sure I squandered my money.' As I left, I put two twenties in his pocket. This was a proud day for the Irish, the well-off and the not so well-off – a day Anne, Christine and I will never forget; joy tinged with sadness.

Anne, also at this time, became involved in the Sligo traditional music at the Coleman Heritage Centre in Gurteen, County Sligo. She was attracted to that distinctive Sligo style: it has flair, with a smooth, rich tone and an infectious lift. Anne went on tour to North America with Killavil session group, which included Colm O'Donnell and his daughter, Siobhán, Michael Hurley and his daughter, Mairéad, John McHugh and his wife, Maria Lynn, Colette Gaffney, Declan Payne and Donal Hernon. Speaking about Irish music sessions, which are so famous across the world, Declan Payne says: 'Half the enjoyment is playing the music, the other half is the people you meet.' Colm O'Donnell, the presenter, also notes, though, that talk is not everything and that often 'There might not be a word spoken: the communication is in the music.'

Connemara Community Radio

On St Patrick's Day 2007, our Christine, Tara Breen, Seán and Gearóid Keane represented Comhaltas Ceoltóiri Éireann for the first time in China. Anne presented the concerts and recited one of W. B. Yeats's last poems, 'Under Ben Bulben'. A member of the Irish Diplomatic Corps in Shanghai suggested to Anne that she should contact Kathleen Faherty in Connemara Community Radio. Kathleen has a one-hour radio programme, *The West Wind Blows*, which is broadcast every Sunday evening. It consists of poetry, music, song and storytelling.

Anne and I arrived at Letterfrack to meet Kathleen. She has a relaxed voice – the female version of Peter O'Sullevan, the racing commentator with the golden voice. We met Bridie Cashin, the producer of the programme, and Gráinne O'Malley, always smiling, who likes to have everything organised. The next morning, Anne recorded poems for the programme, including 'The Owl and The Pussycat' – a poem that appeals to the child in all of us. She also recorded 'Train Ride' by Ruth Stone; 'Where Water Comes Together with Other Water', by Raymond Carver; 'Inniskeen Road' and 'Shancoduff', both by Patrick Kavanagh, and 'Rusty Coat', by Samuel S. McCurry. Anne also recorded Richard Murphy's 'The Cleggan Disaster'.

Chapter Twenty Eight

Art and Construction: Creating a New Life in Poetry and Song

The Wind began to play, like country fiddlers
In a crowded room, with nail boots stamping
On a stone floor, raising white ashes
The sea became a dance.

Richard Murphy was born in the west of Ireland in 1927 lived in Sri Lanka. His major works as a poet include 'The Battle of Aughrim', 'High Islands', 'The Price of Stone', and 'Cleggan Disaster'. In 1927, twenty-five fishermen from the local area of Cleggan bay in County Galway were drowned during a great gale. The storm arose without warning while they were fishing for mackerel in the bay. The nearby village of Rossadilisk lost sixteen men; nine men from Inishbofin, and twenty men from County Mayo were lost.

Kathleen Faherty, after listening to my 'home' recording of Kavanagh's poem 'In Memory of My Mother', encouraged me to record other poems for *The West Wind Blows*. This was a turning point for me. I began reading more and more by poets such as Rainer Maria Rilke, Edgar Allan Poe, Dylan Thomas, T. S. Eliot, Rod McKuen, Derek Mahon and Galway Kinnell. Page after page, I find myself laughing, crying, wondering, remembering, reliving and wishing. The poems I read for *The West Wind Blows* include 'Pushing the Clouds Away' by Rod McKuen; 'The Open Road' by Walt Whitman; 'The Chinese Restaurant at Portrush' by Derek Mahon, accompanied by the music 'The Immigrant', by Joanne Madden and Cherish the Ladies; 'Going Blind' by Rainer Maria Rilke; 'In Memoriam Francis Ledwidge' by Seamus Heaney; 'The Tree

Speaks' by Cathal O'Searcaigh; 'In Praise of Walking' by Thomas A. Clarke; 'The Way Through the Woods' by Kipling; 'June' by Francis Ledwidge; and 'The Road Between Here and There' by Galway Kinnell.

I have mentioned earlier that Patrick Kavanagh – the fiftieth anniversary of whose death occurred in November 2017 – is one of my favourite poets. I find myself returning to his poems again and again. With my roots in rural Mayo, and having lived for years in the city, I can connect with both the 'rural Kavanagh' and the 'city Kavanagh' of the Canal Bank:

> O commemorate me where there is water,
> Canal water, preferably, so stilly
> Greeny at the heart of summer.

And then there is Paul Durcan of the hypnotic voice. As we say in Mayo: 'You'd stand barefoot in the snow listening to him.' Paul, of course, has many links with Mayo – my own county. His poetry is witty, incisive and, most important of all, accessible.

Paul was to play a special role when Anne organised a lunch party for me in September 2011. As I talked to friends at the gathering, the poet himself strolled in. After a few introductions, Anne took the microphone and firmly told the guests to switch off their mobile phones, and if they wanted to whisper to go to the pergola garden. He started with 'Surely My God Is Kavanagh', before reciting the poem 'Rosie Joyce'. In this poem, the poet is driving from Mayo to Dublin for the expected birth of his granddaughter. On that Sunday, as Durcan held us spellbound, there wasn't a cough or a murmur outside, apart from the odd nod, as he continued for well over an hour. The poet's happy mood is reflected in nature itself, as if nature is celebrating the birth of a baby. The sun comes out to herald the baby's arrival; nature is putting on a visual display for the baby. The blue and white of the sky is like China and the gorse bushes in the fields are like tartan rugs. I know of no other poet who can capture the beauty of rural landscape in Maytime, as Durcan does in 'Rosie Joyce':

> Down at the Sound the first rhododendrons.
> Purpling the golden camps of whins;
> The first hawthorns powdering white the mainland:
>
> The first yellow irises flagging roadside streams;
> Quills of bog-cotton skimming the bogs;
> Burrishoole cemetery shin-deep in forget-me-nots;
>
> The first sea pinks speckling the seashore;
> Cliffs of London Pride, groves of bluebell,
> First fuchsia Queen Anne's Lace, primrose.

Now that our children are working and my business life is less hectic, Anne and I have more time to indulge in our love of music and poetry. We have jointly prepared a double

CD where poetry and music complement each other to appeal to that Intimate Space, that quiet place within, where poetry, music and song work to stir memory, awaken emotion, give insight, or, in some mysterious spiritual way, feed the soul. I am grateful to Alan Stanford, the late Susan Fitzgerald, Anne, and Catherine, our daughter, for reading the various poems with such feeling – not forgetting Gerard Grogan and Mark Duffy from Beacon Studies, who did the mix so well. The double CD will be released for charity when we get permission from the Performing Rights Society. The work involved in preparing this CD makes me appreciate what Kathleen Faherty and Bridie Cashin achieve in producing a one-hour programme every Sunday: better than perfect.

Talking about poetry, there is a brilliant young English poet, Kate Tempest, the rapper poet. I am a huge, huge fan. Kate graduated in English Literature from Goldsmith's College in London. She is one of five children. Growing up in south-east London, she was influenced by seeing her father attending night school to qualify as a solicitor when she was eight years old. She made a scathing attack on the state of society, directly accusing Prime Minister Teresa May of 'dividing the people'.

Music

Music, like poetry, seems to unlock and express emotions in a way that prose just doesn't. We did not have much time to listen to music as children growing up in Mayo. Only the odd house had a gramophone. We didn't have one. We did have a battery radio, but that was used sparingly in order to save the battery for the news. The world of music opened up with the arrival of the showbands. Bridie Gallagher, the girl from Donegal, had a huge hit with 'The Boys from the County Armagh'. Brendan Bowyer and the Royal Showband came later and then, most sensational of all, came the Beatles, the biggest pop band the world had ever seen, with hits such as 'My Sweet Lord', 'Penny Lane', 'Hey Jude', 'Lady Madonna' and 'Eleanor Rigby'.

One memory I will always cherish is hearing Bob Dylan in Dublin in 1964. He was one of my idols, and I was delighted when he was awarded the Nobel Prize for Literature some fifty years later, in 2016. There are those, of course, who question why a musical artist like Bob Dylan should be given an award for literature. Those people just can't understand poetry.

I enjoy all music, including film soundtracks, in particular 'I Will Always Love You' from *The Bodyguard*, 'Mrs Robinson' from *The Graduate*, 'The Way We Were' from *The Way We Were*, 'My Heart Will Go On' from *Titanic*, 'As Time Goes By' from *Casablanca* and 'The Streets of Philadelphia' from *Philadelphia*. *Crocodile Dundee* became the highest-grossing film in 1986. The clothes designed by Norma Moriceau for Sue in both *Crocodile Dundee* and its sequel were exquisite. Other artists I admire are Kris Kristofferson, Mark Knopfler (especially his arrangement of 'Raglan Road' with Liam O'Flynn), Seán Keane, Donal Lunny and other traditional Irish artists. I still love country and western: Dolly Parton, Emmylou Harris and Linda Ronstadt. Bobby Gentry made up the story of Billie Joe McAllister jumping off the Tallahatchie Bridge in 1967. It replaced the Beatles at number one. Amy

Winehouse did a duet with Tony Bennett, 'Body and Soul'; Burt Bacharach and Cilla Black did another wonderful duet, 'This Guy's in Love with You'; these are among my favourite duets. I also like Bill Withers singing 'Grandma's Hands'. Noah and the Whale is my latest favourite group.

There are two CDs I never tire of listening to: *Farewell to Evening Dances* by Colm O'Donnell and *The Best of Dolores Keane*. Dolores Keane is still captivating her audiences after all those years.

Colm O'Donnell, singer, gifted musician, music composer and researcher, is a farmer and sheepdog trainer in County Sligo. Colm's flute and whistle playing is lively, bouncy and varied. He has charmed audiences at home and abroad. A recent composition, 'Horses and Plough', describes a rural way of life that is no more:

And up at the headlands,
Every once in a while,
I rested my horses,
All steaming with toil,
With the sleeve of my shirt,
Swept the sweat off my brow.
As I gazed on the work of my horses and plough
And in the evening, as the sun sank low
With my hurley and ball, to the sports field I'd go,
To win an All-Ireland we all made a vow.

The 1951 All-Ireland

I was seven years old when Mayo won the All-Ireland in 1950. I was well able to read, and I devoured pages and pages in the *Western People* about the great Mayo team. Somehow, though, I have a much clearer memory of the atmosphere surrounding Mayo's victory in 1951. On that memorable Sunday, all the locals, young and old, gathered at 'Tom the Shop' to hear Michael O'Hehir's commentary; I was there with my father. Tom the Shop made sure that the radio battery was well charged for the occasion.

I'll never forget Michael O'Hehir's voice as he described 'the men of the west wearing the all white of Connaught and the men of Meath in the green of Leinster' as they paraded behind the Artane Boys' Band. Then came the playing of the National Anthem, the throw-in, and the game was on.

We were delighted at half-time when Mayo led by two goals and three points to Meath's eight points. And what a cheer went up at Tom the Shop's when the final whistle sounded and Mayo had won by two goals and nine points to nine points. The heroes of that Mayo team were Paddy Prendergast at full-back, the great full-forward Tom Langan, Eamon Mongey, the 'flying doctor', Pádraic Carney, the team captain, Seán Flanagan, Seán Mulderrig and Joe Staunton, the chemist from Louisburg. What a debt the people of rural Ireland owe to the great Michael O'Hehir, who brought the magic of Croke Park into the remotest villages. And racing folk who listened to his commentary on his section of the Aintree Grand National in 1967 will never forget how he was able to identify Foinavon as he emerged from the mayhem of horses at the fence after Becher's Brook, second time round, to win the Grand National at 100/1.

Michael O'Hehir played an important part in promoting the games of football and hurling. I had the pleasure of getting to know him and his family at race meetings. In October 1980, I told Michael and his son, Tony, that I expected to ride the winner of the first running of the Amateur St Leger at the Curragh on my exceptional horse, Hartstown, and we did win; he was backed down from 14/1 to 8/1.

I must also acknowledge other gifted commentators, such as Mícheál Ó Muircheartaigh, who could make listeners feel that they were actually at the game he was describing. His colourful snippets on the players are best described by Paul Durcan in 'Greetings to Our Friends from Brazil':

> We send greetings to you all from Djakarta down to Crossmolina
> And the ball goes to Kenneth Mortimer having a great game for Mayo
> He has a brother doing research work on the Porcupine Bank
> But now it goes to Killian Burns of Kerry
> The best accordion-playing cornerback in football today.
> We hope you're on the astra if you're in outer space.
> On my watch it says two minutes and fifty-three seconds left but
> We haven't had time to send greetings to our friends in Brazil
> Proinnsias O Murchú and Rugierio da Costa e Silva.

Brough Scott MBE is one of the best-know figures in racing and sport in recent decades. As a journalist, he has covered Wimbledon, the Open, the Olympics, the football World Cup and a rugby Lions tours; he has written several books and is involved in considerable charity work. I remember, when Brough stayed with us at Hartstown House in 1975 and 1976, the amount of work he put into preparing to commentate on three races for ITV on Derby Day at the Curragh. He is a perfectionist, and great company. Our daughter, Catherine, and her husband, Dr Barry Murphy, County Louth hurler, threatened not to discuss sport with me in the future, unless I name my favourites in most sports; this doesn't leave me much of a choice.

Croquet

But first I must write a few words on croquet, a sport that has become popular worldwide. Anne and I took family membership at Carrickmines Croquet and Lawn Tennis Club in 2005, two years before moving to within a five-minute drive of the club. The club has ten outdoor and three indoor tennis courts, and four croquet lawns of international standard, which become eight tennis grass lawns for the big tennis tournaments. The Irish croquet teams and individuals compete at the top level; the majority of these young and not-so-young players hail from the Carrickmines club.

Mark McInerney became the first non-Egyptian player to win the world golf croquet championship in 2011. Simon Williams, a European champion, has been Irish

Open champion several times, most recently in 2017. Evan Newell reached the semi-finals on a few occasions. Fred Rogerson was one of the founding fathers of the World Croquet Federation in 1986 and was president for two years. The WCF now oversees tournaments in twenty-five countries. Fred still plays good croquet when he is not sailing. Patsy Fitzgerald from County Meath is on the Irish teams for both golf and associated croquet when he is available. Andrew Johnson, from a farming background in County Wicklow, has been the Irish Open Champion for the last three years, came third in the last world championships, and is preparing for the next world cup championship in 2019. Ed Cunningham was reared on the lawns; his father, Joe, a champion of the past, regarded croquet as a combination of chess, snooker and war. Only the top players in the world are invited to play in the President's Cup. Ed won this cup when it was played in the UK, in 2000.

Ireland is fortunate to have some promising young players, including Danny Johnson, runner-up to Andrew Johnson in the Irish Open last year, Kieran Murphy, Jack Clingham, Liam O'Broin from Cork, James Carroll from Tipperary, and the Martin boys John Francis, Joseph, Matthew and Christopher from Kells, County Meath. We also have Mark Stephens, Robert O'Donghue and Jack Gleeson from County Dublin. Anne has been bitten by the croquet bug; she spends considerable time practising, and won the Newell Candlestick Trophy and the handicap doubles at Strokestown Park, County Roscommon, with Michael O'Shaughnessy. Among the stalwarts at Carrickmines are Ann Woulfe Flanagan, Mary Dobbin, Patricia Keavey, John McCauley, Padraic Thornton, former captain of croquet, and Dr Richard Assaf. Ed Cunningham, my croquet mentor, helped bring my game to a higher level, when we won the prestigious Coronation Bowls in 2009, in the Irish Open Handicap Doubles. The Irish Open Championship has attracted more overseas players every year, including David Bent and Howard Sosin from Florida. The croquet committee asked me to become captain of croquet at the club in 2009, for three years, a positon I took very seriously.

Now, as President of the Croquet Association of Ireland, and with the support of Dr Richard Assaf, Chairman of the CAI, and the dedicated support of Simon Williams, we are hoping to double the three hundred members of the association. Simon has worked with Fingal County Council and Anne Brophy to promote croquet in one of the best settings imaginable, Newbridge House, Donabate, County Dublin. We have had four croquet festivals at Strokestown Park, County Roscommon, and we are working on other venues. 'Croquet has the advantage over other games that more or less anyone can play anyone else, regardless of sex or age, or you can practise for as long as you want on your own,' as A. E. Gill puts it in *Croquet: The Complete Guide*. The tennis at Carrickmines Croquet & Lawn Tennis Club gets better and bigger every year. This progression is driven by the club's professional tennis coach, Pat Crowe, with the help of the tennis committees. The junior championships attracts more entries than any other tennis tournament in the country. Each year we get more and more juniors from abroad, competing for ranking points. Bowling is thriving at the club, and is played by members of all ages – in serious and not-so-serious matches.

The following is from the Swinford Amenity Park Newsletter, by Philip Durcan:

Following initial telephone conversations and a meeting with members of the Carrickmines Croquet and Lawn Tennis Club, The Swinford Amenity Park kindly hosted Croquet demonstrations on Sunday June 28, 2015. This was attended by the chairman of the Croquet Association of Ireland, Simon Williams, and Joe and Anne McGowan and a mixed-age profile of local people. Joe and Simon also presented Swinford with two starter sets of croquet equipment, for which we are very grateful. It was a very successful morning which has evoked much interest across the community from both young and not so young.

Joe McGowan is a native of our neighbouring town, Charlestown, and he, like some of the attendees at the croquet demonstrations and many others in the area, first played croquet while attending school in Swinford in the 1960s. The common link between all these people is that the interest fostered in them by the priests and nuns all those years ago, has remained with them to this day. So much so, that many in our community feel that it is time to bring croquet back for all the community to avail of. To this end, the Swinford Amenity Park has provided us with our first lawn, located at the road side of their training pitch, together with the use of their facility for a cup of tea and chat as required.

Chapter Twenty Nine

My Favourite Players

My Favourite Rugby Players

There was no rugby around Charlestown or the surrounding area when I was growing up. It was all Gaelic football. In fact, I was twenty-three years of age when I saw my first rugby game. It was in January 1967 at Lansdowne Road: Ireland were playing Australia. I was instantly hooked, and have been a rugby fanatic ever since. Two great rugby occasions stand out for me, not for the standard of play, nor because Ireland won, but for sheer emotion and atmosphere.

In 1972, the Scottish rugby team failed to travel to Dublin to play Ireland in the Five Nations, because of the tensions in the North of Ireland. The Scottish Rugby Union made the decision without consulting the Scottish players, who were upset when the game was called off. Pages and pages were written in all the Irish papers about how furious and ashamed the Scottish people living in Ireland were. Wales, to everyone's surprise, decided not to come to Ireland either.

Fair play to the English RFU, they made the decision to send a team to play Ireland the following January. The English Union left it to each individual player to decide whether to come or not. Running out on to the pitch, they received a standing ovation that lasted for five minutes. Everybody at the game said it was an unbelievable feeling. Ireland won. At the dinner that night, John Pullin, a farmer, stood up to make the captain's speech, and said: 'We might not be the greatest team in the world but at least we turned up.' Sport was the winner.

The most memorable rugby occasion for me was the Ireland v. England game played at Croke Park on 27 February 2007. 'Today is about so much more than a game

189

of rugby,' explained John Inverdale of the BBC. The preparation by the Department of Foreign Affairs, the British Foreign Office and the BBC was meticulous. Two or three weeks after the game, John Inverdale received an anonymous letter from a person who, he assumed, had been involved in the Republican movement during the recent troubles. The letter said there was a part of him that wanted the day to be a disaster and part of him that wanted it to be a huge day of reconciliation. He said that on the morning of the game he was very confused about how he wanted the day to pan out off the field. Then he said, 'I just want you to know the BBC team did an amazing job in getting the atmosphere and the ambience of the day absolutely right, and this will be one of the most unusual congratulatory letters you will ever receive. I want your team to know that they did the occasion proud.'

The reception after the playing of 'God Save the Queen' was particularly moving, when the English captain, Martin Corry, acknowledged the respect shown. John Hayes wiped his tears away at the most powerful rendition of 'Amhrán na bhFiann' by the Combined Garda Síochána and Army Bands. Ireland won the game; the real winner was the GAA and the Irish people.

Rugby may have changed over the past fifteen years but the basic skills of the out-half remain the same: running the game, and linking between the backs and forwards. Ollie Campbell scored forty-six points, including all twenty-one points against Scotland, in the Five Nations Championships when Ireland won the Triple Crown in 1982. Ollie Campbell still devotes much of his time to rugby and the IRFU Charitable Trust.

Willie John McBride went on five Lions tours. As captain on the tour to South Africa, he told his players not to retaliate individually on receiving rough treatment, but on his signal all fifteen Lions would 'take on' their nearest opponent, not only to show the South Africans that they were not going to back down, but also to reduce the risk of a sending-off, as the referee was highly unlikely to dismiss an entire team. Willie John was consistent, and a great leader.

Paul O'Connell is an all-round sportsman. Luckily, he decided to concentrate on rugby when he was sixteen years and was selected for the Irish schools side. He was influenced by Frankie Sheehan, Mick Galwey and, particularly, the late Anthony Foley. Paul inspired players all around him.

Fergus Slattery represented Ireland over fifteen seasons and is rated one of the greatest open-side flankers of his time. He played his schools rugby for Blackrock College and, at the age of twenty-two, was selected for the Lions squad to tour New Zealand. Two of his achievements were Ireland's unbeaten tour to Australia, and his captaincy of Ireland to win the Triple Crown in 1982.

John Muldoon, capped for Ireland, has been the backbone of rugby in Connaught for what appears like a hundred years! He shows great respect for the referee. He said to me in Lough Cutra Castle recently: 'the referee is always right, even when he is wrong'. John is a loyal and perfect gentleman.

Many 'overseas' players, such as Jim Staples, John O'Driscoll and Feidhlim McLoughlin, played for Ireland, but Simon Geoghegan was my favourite. He played for Ireland during the bleakest of periods for Irish rugby: 1991-96. Catherine, Joseph and I were in Twickenham for the Ireland-England game when Simon Geoghegan scored a superb try and won the match. Defensively, he was solid, and he had speed, with a sidestep, when he got the ball – which wasn't often enough. C. J. Stander, born and brought up in South Africa, has become an invaluable, and inspirational, player for Munster and Ireland. He is the rugby player I would most enjoy having lunch with.

Gaelic Footballers

The legendary Mick O'Connell comes first. Mick was recently interviewed by Gerry O'Sullivan on Kerry Radio. He said: 'For me, anyway, it was always ball first, man second. To try and negate the other player was not my style. Winning the game was not triumph and losing the game was not disaster. It was winning and losing games that was all part of sport. There is no such thing as one player being better than the next, because football is all about style of play. When I see people talking about Kerry being beaten and the disastrous results, there is no such thing in the game of sport. Win or lose, you take your win or your beating in your stride. Any day if I caught a few good balls and kicked a few good balls, that was success.' Mick O'Connell was the most stylish footballer I have ever watched.

Bernard Brogan has the most fantastic skill and awareness in Gaelic football today. He is probably the most difficult forward any opponent has to mark.

Lee Keegan, half-back for Mayo, after losing the 2016 All-Ireland final, sent the following message in an open letter to the *Mayo News*: 'Sadness and regret fill me. We lost, but I had the honour and privilege of running into battle with legends that I will respect for life. Dublin GAA is a supreme outfit and deservedly All-Ireland winners.'

James Nallen's preferred positon was half-back; he played in five All-Ireland finals for Mayo, and won two All-Stars. Now he devotes his spare time and energy to his club, Crossmolina.

Colm McManamon, tall and strong, a real athlete, played centre-forward for Mayo. He was always in the right position and was the best distributor of the ball I have ever watched. He puts his spare time into his club, Burrishoola. I put Colm in joint fifth position with another Mayo footballer, Tom Parsons, the midfielder from Charlestown Sarsfields; he was inspired by John Casey, Aidan Higgins and David Tiernan – my pal Malachy's son. Tom would like to invite Al Pacino to dinner and get him to recite the *Any Given Sunday* speech.

My Favourite Hurlers

Of all the hurlers I have watched over the years, Joe Cooney is the best. The farmer from Bullaun, outside Loughrea, is the unassuming gentleman of hurling. He was Galway's shining light in the 1980s and 1990s.

Joe Canning, another Galway hurler, is pure magic to watch. I rate him as one of the very best. I admire his accuracy: he scores from seemingly impossible angles, and seems to know instinctively where the goalposts are.

Jimmy Barry Murphy was one of Cork's greatest hurlers and footballers; he is probably the GAA's greatest dual player ever – even greater than Jack Lynch himself. I watched him play, and listening to his interviews, he comes across as an absolute gentleman.

People will argue till kingdom come as to whether Christy Ring or D. J. Carey was the best hurler of all time. I never saw Christy Ring in action, so I opt for D. J. My friend, and GAA guru, Frank Finnegan, said that he would break into Croke Park to see D. J. play, at his peak.

Lar Corbett was one of Tipperary's best hurlers. Who can forget his goal-scoring spree as he put paid to Kilkenny's five-in-a-row dream? I like to see the All-Ireland titles go round.

Soccer Players

There have been many world-class players on Irish soccer teams throughout the years: Packie Bonner; Denis Irwin, a full-back for Ireland and a player who had a twenty-year career with Manchester United; John Aldridge, who scored 330 League goals, the sixth-highest total in the history of English football. John told Jack Charlton that Ray Houghton, born in Glasgow, was longing to play for Ireland; the three of them – John Aldridge, Ray Houghton and Jack Charlton – helped put Irish football on the world stage. Roy Keane was a no-nonsense, outspoken leader; George Best, the greatest football genius of all time, played for Northern Ireland and Manchester United. There are two players I would most like to have lunch with: Eric Cantona and Paul McGrath. I loved Cantona's swagger. Paul McGrath was one of Ireland's greatest defenders. He was just heroic, despite all his injures. I especially admire Paul's generosity in the way he acknowledges Jack Charlton's understanding of his alcohol problem. Paul McGrath is a beautiful person.

My Favourite Golfers

When I was growing up in Mayo, golf was only played by the elite; I can remember that solicitors, doctors, dentists, vets, a few merchants and, sometimes, the parish priest were members of the golf club. Between Tooreen and Ballyhaunis was the nine-hole Ballyhaunis Golf Club, which was very basic. The maintenance of the fairways was carried out by grazing sheep.

The first time I held a golf club in my hand was at Edmondstown Golf Course, in July 1964, with Tom Brennan. For the next three years, I played golf with Tom and his friends about twice a month on different courses, including Woodbrook, Portmarnock, The Grange and, my favourite, Edmondstown, with its wide fairways, which were ideal for my often erratic drives. I didn't join a golf club, but enjoyed the game until the horses took over my life.

*

Jack Nicklaus was responsible for popularising golf, especially on television. Pádraig Harrington went from being a good golfer to winning three majors. Nick Faldo was ranked at number one in the world at one stage, and was very consistent. Tom Watson has been one of the leading players in the world for thirty years, from the 1970s until recently; he is recognised as golf's ambassador.

My outright favourite is Seve Ballesteros; he played a leading role in helping the European Ryder Cup team to five wins, both as a player and captain. He won the world matchplay championship five times. Ballesteros died of brain cancer in May 2011, aged fifty-four: a big loss to the game.

My Favourite Tennis Players

Among my tennis greats are Rod Laver, the Australian, who played professional tennis for twenty years; John McEnroe, now an entertaining analyst on television; Tim Henman, with his clean-cut image; Stefi Graff, with her amazing footwork; and the remarkable Martina Navratilova. I pass over all these and name my daughter, Christine, as my favourite tennis player; and as a doting parent, why not?

Jennifer O'Brien, Christine's first coach, gave her time to develop her natural talent and style at Donnybrook Lawn Tennis Club. Later, she was coached by Stephen O'Shea and Eoin Casey. Mary Beardsley watched Christine and Niamh Coveney win the Irish under-fourteens doubles at Fitzwilliam Lawn Tennis Club in 2002. Mary arranged that her friend and neighbour, Tony Pickard, and his wife, Jeanette, would come to Dublin for a golfing weekend and at the same time help to make a plan for Christine's tennis.

Tony Pickard is best known as the coach and manager of Stefan Edberg, a former world number one. Tony arranged for Christine to attend a course with his friend, Martin Smith, a tennis technician in Norwich. Anne and Christine joined Martin Smith and some of his other pupils at the junior tournaments in Germany, in July 2003 and July 2004. This was serious stuff, opening their eyes to the professional approach of the juniors, especially the boys and girls from Eastern Europe. As things turned out, however, Christine did not pursue a career in tennis. The demands, including giving up school, leaving home and moving abroad full-time, were too great; and after all this, there would be no guarantees of success, as very few make the grade. Christine still plays tennis to a high level.

The Greatest Athletes

Mohammed Ali (Cassius Clay) was an Olympic gold-medal winner before becoming the world heavyweight boxing champion. Floyd Patterson said: 'It's very hard to hit a moving target, and Ali moved all the time, with such grace, three minutes of every round for fifteen rounds. He never stopped. It was extraordinary.'

Ali had a profound and lasting influence on boxing and was considered the best in the history of the sport. He was articulate in interviews, especially with Michael Parkinson and later with Cathal O'Shannon. He was entertaining inside and outside the ring. After retiring, he was diagnosed with Parkinsons. Ali said: 'Maybe my Parkinsons is God's way of reminding me what is important. It slowed me down and caused me to listen rather than talk.' Ali said he was 'the greatest'. In my view, he was the greatest athlete of all time. We'll never see his like again. While my life, to a certain extent, has also been restricted by Parkinsons, it has also shown me what is important in life.

Sir Steve Redgrave won five consecutive gold medals at the Olympic games and nine world rowing championship golds. He is regarded as one of Britain's greatest ever Olympians. After retiring, Redgrave completed his third London marathon, raising £1.8 million for charity.

Usain Bolt, a Jamaican, is the fastest person ever timed; he is the first man to hold both the 100-metres and 200-metres world records. Usain Bolt is known as a down-to-earth person; he has brought life to track and field.

I was thirteen years old when Ronnie Delany won a gold medal for Ireland at the Melbourne Olympics, in 1956. Only now do I fully appreciate this incredible middle-distance runner's achievement. Ronnie Delany was fancied but not favourite. His mind and body were conditioned as never before, and he knew that Jumbo Elliott, his Villanova coach, believed in him. Delany made his break at the last bend, passed the favourite, John Landy, and won convincingly. I admire him to this day.

Sonia O'Sullivan still holds the world record at 2000 metres, set in 1994. She was like Nijinsky, with a dramatic turn of speed, which helped her win a gold medal at the 1995 World Championships and a silver medal at the 2000 Olympic Games. Her consistent performances through the years encouraged more athletes into track and field.

Tony O'Reilly played for Ireland at the age of just eighteen. He celebrated his nineteenth birthday during the British and Irish Lions' four-month-long tour to South Africa in 1955. Tony played fifteen games, including the four Tests against South Africa, scoring sixteen tries. On the 1959 Lions Tour he played twenty-three games, including two Tests against Australia and four Tests against New Zealand, scoring twenty-two tries. His total of thirty-eight tries for the Lions on two tours remains a record. As Cliff Morgan put it: 'Tony O'Reilly was fast, a fine reader of the game, and a brilliant finisher.

My Favourite Showjumpers

I have to acknowledge what the Irish Army Equitation School has done for showjumpers in this country since its inception in 1926. The Army Equitation School continued to provide most of the Irish showjumpers until the 1960s. Those army riders included Ned Campion, Gerry Mullens, Brian McSweeney, Con Power, John Ledingham, Ulick McEaddy and Gerry O'Gorman. I have already mentioned Jed O'Dwyer and Dan Corry.

*

David Broome was the most natural showjumper, with a career that spanned thirty years. His good horses retained a freshness and desire to compete for many years, all thanks to David's relaxed style. I once saw David's father at the RDS giving him a few nudges to wake him up for the second round in the Aga Khan competition as he lay asleep on a bale of hay. He was the only rider to win the men's individual championship three times, the King George V Gold Cup six times and the British National Championships six times.

Eddie Macken came to Iris Kellett at Mespil Road intending to stay for six months – and stayed for six years. Iris recognised Eddie's talent at a very young age. Eddie Macken had it all: he looked the part and was one of the best international riders, winning Hickstead four years in a row. He remains deeply grateful to Iris Kellett for all her guidance and for providing him with some good horses to ride. Iris herself was a champion, winning the British Ladies National title in 1947.

John Ledingham was on five winning Aga Khan teams, won the Hickstead Derby three times, and competed in sixty-three Nations Cups for Ireland.

In my own sport, Captain David Foster was just forty-three years old when a horse fell on him at an event ten miles from his own home, in 1998. Sadly, he died in the ambulance. He was a huge loss to his wife, Denise, and their three children, Lucy, Jessica and Nick. Captain Foster was one of the most popular and talented international three-day-event riders. He represented Ireland in three Olympics, won the three-day event in Punchestown, and won the team gold in the European Championships at Burghley. David's widow, Denise, is undoubtedly the most honest, hard-working person in bloodstock we know. She now trains about twenty horses on her farm at Enfield, County Meath, which has very good facilities. Each horse gets individual attention, and she is beginning to turn out good winners, including the winner of the Ladies Derby at the Curragh recently. Evan Newell, one of Ireland's leading croquet player, is a patron.

My Five Favourite Racehorse Trainers

It is very easy to select the greatest racehorse trainer of all time: Vincent O'Brien. At first, he trained steeplechasers and hurdlers, winning the Grand National three times, the Gold Cup four times, the Champion Hurdle seven times, and numerous other races at Cheltenham. Then he turned to flat-racing. He had the incredible gift of picking world-class horses, especially at the Kentucky sales in the USA, and then training them to win countless classics. He won the Prix de l'Arc de Triomphe with Ballymoss (in 1958) and with Alleged twice (in 1978 and 1979). Alleged was bought as a yearling for Robert Sangster by my friend P. P. Hogan, who trained Any Crack, my first point-to-point winner, in 1977 at Bartlemy, County Cork. Vincent O'Brien is a legend of racing.

I have to include my friend Michael O'Toole, who trained four winners for us at Cheltenham and was a very successful trainer on the flat and over jumps. He was skilful in producing a horse at his peak for an important race. He was the best of company at all times, win or lose.

Dermot Weld trained winners on the flat and over the jumps, and was the first non-Australian to train the winner of the Melbourne Cup. He always surrounded himself with an excellent staff and is now hungrier than ever to train winners.

Jessica Harrington is an outstanding trainer both over jumps and on the flat. In her day, she was a brilliant cross-country rider, finishing third at Badminton on a middling horse, Amoy.

Jim Bolger began training a few horses at Castleknock before renting in Lohunda Park, Clonsilla, and then moving to County Carlow. He is now recognised as one of racing's greats, training and breeding classic winners. Jim has created a state-of-the-art facility. He now breeds the vast majority of the horses he trains: a remarkable achievement, considering that he started from scratch.

My Favourite Jockeys

Lester Piggott, known as the 'Long Fellow', has won the Derby nine times. As he approached eighty, he was asked if he considered himself to be the greatest jockey ever. He replied: 'You hope you are, but how can you tell?' He was a man of few words.

Frank Berry has been Irish champion jump jockey several times, and was extremely popular. He now has the busiest job in the bloodstock industry: managing J. P. McManus's racing empire. Frank Berry's instinct is not to divulge the tiniest bit of information.

John Francome was the most stylish jump jockey, with the best hands of all time, according to my friend, the late John Mulhern. Francome was the third most successful jump jockey. He is now a TV presenter and author: his books have featured on the bestseller lists. He is very witty and never short of an answer.

Dessie Hughes was a true friend, a brilliant jockey and horseman, dedicated and loyal, honest and sincere. He achieved success at the Cheltenham Festival on horses trained by Mick O'Toole and others. Only Dessie Hughes would have won the Gold Cup on Davy Lad: he knew the horse so well, and had great perseverance. He rode Monksfield to a famous victory over Sea Pigeon in the Champion Hurdle. He was Mick O'Toole's right-hand man for sixteen years before becoming a trainer himself. His training career was cut short by illness; he died in November 2014.

At the funeral mass, Dessie's grandson David read a letter which Dessie had written to his mother fifty-six years previously, when he was apprenticed at fifteen years of age to Mr O'Grady, in Tipperary. There was laughter in the church when Dessie's letter recalled a simpler life: an egg for breakfast, his 6.30 AM start, and the comment that 'we get a good dinner'. He concluded his letter by reassuring his mother: 'And they are Catholics.' I never saw Michael O'Toole cry as much as he did at Dessie's funeral. Dessie is survived by his wife, Eileen, who was always with him, their daughter, Sandra, and son, Richard, a highly successful flat-jockey in England.

Tommy Carberry, the most gifted horseman I have ever seen, has won all the top races many times. Tommy came up the hill at Cheltenham on Tied Cottage to win the Gold Cup in 1980, having been second to Davy Lad in 1977. At that time, the Jockey Club had no alternative but to disqualify Tied Cottage after a prohibited substance had been detected in the horse's post-race urine. Tommy won the Cheltenham Gold Cup in 1970, 1971 and 1975. He rode L'Escargot to win the Grand National, and trained Bobby Joe, which his son, Paul, rode to win the Grand National. Tommy died after a long illness, in July 2017. At the funeral, in Ratoath, County Meath, there were as many people outside the church as inside, on one of the sunniest days of the year. I will never forget the homily of Father Brendan Ludlow. When the coffin was being lowered into the grave,

Anne, my wife, played the Foxhunters Chase on the violin. (The hounds in full cry: music that, once heard, can never be forgotten.) He had a wonderful life with his family.

The Single Most Important Event in My Lifetime

I was recently chatting with a friend, John O'Doherty, and was telling him how this book was coming along. Out of the blue, he asked me what I regard as the most significant event in Ireland in my lifetime. That set me thinking: Queen Elizabeth II and her husband Prince Philip, Duke of Edinburgh, made a state visit to the Republic of Ireland in May 2011 at the invitation of the President of Ireland, Mary McAleese. The Downing Street Declaration was signed on 15 September 1993; Monsignor Horan's single-minded drive developed an international airport near Knock; Dr Patrick Hillery guided Ireland's entry into the European Economic Community, in 1973. Dr Hillery's favourite saying was: 'You can achieve a lot in life if you don't mind who takes the credit.' This encapsulates both his achievements and his modesty.

These events were, of course, very important, but in my view the greatest event in Ireland in my lifetime was Donogh O'Malley's introduction of free secondary education in 1967. This would transform Irish society. Before 1967, less than half of primary-school children went on to secondary school. In certain areas, less than 10 percent of primary-school children went on to secondary school. This was very much the case where I grew up: I was only the third pupil from the whole of Tawyinah to attend secondary school, and I had to cycle ten miles each way, six days a week. The school fees in the late 1950s and 1960s for day pupils varied from £45 to £60 a year. I worked during the summer holidays to cover the school fees and the cost of my books.

The great visionary, Donogh O'Malley, changed all that. Not only did he provide free secondary education, he also provided free transport. The school buses became a familiar sight, morning and evening, on the roads of Ireland. It is almost impossible to overstate the significance of what O'Malley initiated. Just look at Ireland today: we have universal second-level education and almost 100 percent participation in third-level education.

O'Malley was lucky in having the enthusiastic support of our greatest Taoiseach, Sean Lemass. O'Malley and Lemass knew that the education plan would be met with opposition, even from within the Cabinet. Shrewd Lemass advised O'Malley to leak his proposed legislation to the press and get them on his side as a first step. The proposed legislation did meet with considerable opposition from many quarters, including some sections of the Catholic Church. Some school managers were content to let things carry on as they were and, of course, in my opinion, there were privileged parents who preferred secondary education to be the preserve of the few rather than the democratic right of all. The minister made this famous speech at a debate held in Seanad Éireann in February 1967:

> No one is going to stop me introducing my scheme next September. I know I
> am up against opposition, and serious organised opposition, but they are not
> going to defeat me on this. I shall tell you further that I shall expose them and
> I shall expose their tactics on every available occasion, whoever they are. I see

my responsibility very clearly to the Irish people and to the Irish children. No vested group or groups, whoever they be, at whatever level, will sabotage what every reasonable-minded man considers to be a just scheme. I had a deputation recently, and a reverend gentleman, as he went out the door, said jocosely, but there was malice in his joke, 'You will never catch us. We will always be ahead of you.' It was our Divine Lord who said 'Suffer little children to come unto me.' There will be a lot of suffering if that mentality prevails in Ireland. I am surprised and I am disillusioned because no Minister for Education came into this Department with more goodwill than I did, and I was very surprised. Maybe someday I shall tell the tale, and no better man to tell it. I shall pull no punches. Christian charity how are you . . . Can the schools continue with impunity to bounce up the fees and can the State continue to pay the capitation grant per pupil to those schools, irrespective of what increases they make?

With the media on his side, O'Malley got the necessary legislation through Cabinet, and free secondary education became the right of all children in September 1967.

Commenting on O'Malley's vision and achievement, John Healy wrote: 'If a Taoiseach made Donogh O'Malley Minister for Dustbins, he would make it the most exciting ministry in the Cabinet. O'Malley never worried about the paternity of any thought, or any project, any scheme: all that mattered was that, if it was right and he had the power to make it a reality or use it, he was away.'

O'Malley stands tall among the greats in twentieth-century Ireland. Too often we take for granted what is, and fail to appreciate who made it possible. O'Malley made possible Irish education as we know it today. He is up there with Seán Lemass and T. K. Whitaker.

I always enjoyed the company of Gordon Holmes, the Limerick solicitor, a great racing man. Gordon was a trustee to Eamon Walsh's estate. May they both rest in peace. Gordon once told me that Donogh O'Malley would not hide today's sun behind tomorrow's cloud. Donogh was in a hurry, and only Donogh had the character, drive and personality to announce and implement the free-education scheme. Donogh O'Malley's untimely death at forty-seven was a huge loss to his family and country.

Writing about Monsignor Horan and Donogh O'Malley has put me thinking that perhaps Ireland should have its own official honours system, as, for example, France and Britain have. Giving recognition to men and women of vision and achievement would say a lot about the values that we, as a people, respect. It would also do something else: it would provide inspirational role-models for each young generation, and it would enhance their sense of national pride. It should not be beyond our ingenuity to devise an appropriate Irish way of acknowledging vision and achievement. I believe that this idea is worth considering.

Chapter Thirty

'My Glory Was I Had Such Friends'

This is the year 2018; I am seventy-four years of age, and it is eleven years since I was diagnosed with Parkinsons. I have learnt to live with it – no more skiing, though. I enjoy flying to work, especially the thirty-minute flight from Dublin to Manchester. It is only a forty-minute drive from Manchester Airport to Chester, where I share an office with my son, Joseph, together with Ernest O'Brien, accountant and financial director, and the secretary/director, Vicki Sparkes. Joseph is hoping to build more units each year with his new foreman, myself. Philip Young, architectural designer, has the ability to improve the value of awkward sites by increasing the density. I know the house-building business backwards, and if I may say so, I am one of the best at identifying and acquiring building land.

I am often asked why I don't build in Ireland. Here are the reasons: the lack of bank lending to build houses, the outrageous financial contributions to the local authorities, the cost of getting services from the ESB, the gas company and the water company. The builder or developer pays 13.5 percent VAT to the Exchequer on the sale price of any new residential home. Rather than reducing or abolishing the 13.5 percent VAT rate, the Exchequer should return the VAT paid by the builder to the purchaser over four years to help with their mortgage. This would only apply to first- and second-time buyers. There is no VAT on the sale of residential buildings in England, and they have introduced measures to make sure that the small builder survives.

Joan Burton was the Labour leader in 2009, when the National Asset Management Agency was set up. Joan wanted the government at that time to start a new bank similar to the Agricultural Credit Corporation Bank of 1927. The ACC provided working capital for farmers. In 1974, Bobby Molloy, the then Minister for Local Government, introduced the Certificate of Reasonable Value to control the rapid increase in house prices. The Kenny Report of 1973 recommended that building land should be compulsorily acquired by local authorities for 25 percent more than its agricultural value, and then sold on to genuine builders. The Kenny Report was shouldered to one side and it has never been acted upon since. What we need now is a sensible man, like the late Bobby Molloy. He would listen to the views of people involved in the industry and would then introduce the necessary measures within twelve months to get house building moving, and get us out of our current mess. It is time to forget the one-time boom Taoiseach and his government, who encouraged the last house-price bubble, which brought the Irish economy to its knees.

As I conclude this story of my life, and reflect on its ups and downs, I become absolutely convinced that the great thing life should teach us is humility – humility to recognise how dependent we are on other people. Whatever success we have – whether in sport, business or academic life – it is achieved with the help of others. This has certainly been my experience. We sometimes hear of an individual being celebrated as a 'self-made' man. There is no such person. The man who believes that his achievements are due solely to his own efforts is a delusional egotist. I remember an old Irish saying from my school days in Mayo long ago: '*Ar scáth a chéile a mhaireann na daoine.*' (This can be translated as 'We all depend on each other.') This snippet of wisdom sums up our dependence on others. I owe a huge debt to many, many people – so many, in fact, that it would take pages and pages to list them all. Instead, I will just quote Yeats: 'My glory was I had such friends.'

I would like to thank the following people and organisations for granting permission to reproduce photographs that appear in this book: Peter Marlow of Magnum Ireland, Ed Byrnes, Peter Bills, *Horse & Hound, Harpers & Queen, Eventing* magazine, the *Irish Field*, the *Evening Telegraph*, Ricki Stephens, Liam Healy, Ruth Rogers, the *Stamford Mercury*, Wallis Photographs, Bernard Parkhill, Gerry Barry (for his drawing of Hartstown House), the *Irish Times*, the *Irish Independent*, Parks Photography and Robert Miller. In particular, I would like to thank Roger Kenny of Roger Kenny Photography for designing and correcting the photograph sections.